THE COMPLETE BOOK OF
DINOSAURS

Grades 1–3

McGraw Hill **Children's Publishing**

Columbus, Ohio

Credits:
McGraw-Hill Children's Publishing Editorial/Art & Design Team

Vincent F. Douglas	*President*
Tracey E. Dils	*Publisher*
Tracy R. Paulus	*Production Editor*
Nathan J. Hemmelgarn	*Project Editor*
Lindsay Mizer	*Project Editor*
Robert A. Sanford	*Director of Art & Design*
Christopher Fowler	*Art Director*
Joseph Giddings	*Cover Design, Interior Design, and Production*

Note: The illustrations in this book are artist's renditions only.

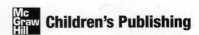

Published by American Education Publishing, an imprint of
McGraw-Hill Children's Publishing
Copyright © 2003 McGraw-Hill Children's Publishing.

Send all inquiries to:
McGraw-Hill Children's Publishing
8787 Orion Place
Columbus, OH 43240-4027

ISBN 1-57768-606-3

1 2 3 4 5 6 7 8 9 10 CJK 08 07 06 05 04 03

The Complete Book of Dinosaurs
Table of Contents

Table of Contents—Continued

Introduction

Since the discovery of the first dinosaur fossils, scientists have been searching for answers about these mysterious creatures. Even today, bones are being discovered all over the world that help us learn about dinosaurs and the world in which they lived.

Although dinosaur bones had been found for centuries, it was not until the early 1800s that scientists began to understand what they had discovered. In 1818, a scientist described a piece of jawbone as having come from an animal that was extinct. Before this statement, no one believed that a species of animal could become extinct.

The Complete Book of Dinosaurs helps explain the world of dinosaurs, the habitats in which they lived, and theories about why they became extinct. At the same time the book reinforces basic skills. You will read lively passages about dinosaurs, strengthen math, reading, spelling, and language arts skills, practice test-taking skills, and play games that reinforce learning.

A pronunciation key is located in the front of this book for your convenience. You will also find a dictionary of dinosaur terms at the back of this book.

Pronunciation Key

Acrocanthosaurus
(ACK-roh-KAN-thuh-SAW-rus)

Allosaurus
(AL-uh-SAW-rus)

Amphibian
(am-FI-be-an)

Anatosaurus
(uh-NAT-uh-SAW-rus)

Ankylosaurs
(ang-KYE-luh-SAWRS)

Ankylosaurus
(ang-KYE-luh-SAW-rus)

Apatosaurus
(uh-PAT-uh-SAW-rus)

Archaeoceratops
(AR-kee-oh-ser-uh-tops)

Archaeopteryx
(AR-kee-OP-ter-iks)

Argentinosaurus
(ahr-gen-TEEN-uh-SAW-rus)

Barosaurus
(BAYR-uh-SAW-rus)

Baryonyx
(BAYR-ee-ON-icks)

Brachiosaurus
(BRACK-ee-uh-SAW-rus)

Camarasaurus
(KAM-uh-ruh-SAW-rus)

Camptosaurus
(KAMP-tuh-SAW-rus)

Carnivore
(KAHR-ni-vore)

Carnotaurus
(KAHR-nuh-TOR-us)

Caudipteryx
(kaw-DIP-ter-iks)

Cenozoic
(SEE-nuh-ZOH-ik)

Centrosaurus
(sen-truh-SAW-rus)

Ceratosaurus
(si-RAT-uh-SAW-rus)

Coelophysis
(SEE-luh-FYE-sis)

Coelurus
(see-LURE-us)

Compsognathus
(KOMP-sog-NAY-thus)

Corythosaurus
(kor-ITH-uh-SAW-rus)

Cretaceous
(kri-TAY-shus)

Dacentrurus
(DAY-sen-TROO-rus)

Daspletosaurus
(das-PLEE-tuh-SAW-rus)

Deinonychus
(dye-NON-i-kus)

Dilophosaurus
(dye-LOH-fuh-SAW-rus)

Pronunciation Key

Dimetrodon
(dye-MET-ruh-don)

Dinosaur
(DYE-nuh-sawr)

Dinosaurus
(DYE-nuh-SAW-rus)

Diplodocus
(di-PLOH-duh-kus)

Dromaeosaurs
(DROH-mee-uh-SAWRS)

Edmontosaurus
(ed-MON-tuh-SAW-rus)

Enchodus
(EN-cho-dus)

Eoraptor
(EE-oh-RAP-tor)

Euoplocephalus
(YOO-oh-pluh-SEF-uh-lus)

Gallimimus
(GAL-i-MYE-mus)

Gastrolith
(GAS-troh-lith)

Giganotosaurus
(jye-GAN-uh-tuh-SAW-rus)

Hadrosaurs
(HAD-ruh-SAWRS)

Hadrosaurus
(HAD-ruh-SAW-rus)

Herbivore
(URB-uh-vor)

Herrerasaurus
(huh-RAYR-uh-SAW-rus)

Heterodontosaurus
(HET-ur-uh-DON-tuh-SAW-rus)

Hylaeosaurus
(HI-lee-uh-SAW-rus)

Hypsilophodon
(HIP-suh-LOH-fuh-don)

Ichthyosaurs
(IK-thee-uh-SAWRS)

Ichthyosaurus
(IK-thee-uh-SAW-rus)

Iguanodon
(i-GWAN-uh-don)

Ingenia
(in-JEE-nee-uh)

Jurassic
(joo-RAS-ik)

Kentrosaurus
(KEN-truh-SAW-rus)

Kuehneosaurus
(CUNE-ee-uh-SAW-rus)

Lambeosaurus
(LAM-bee-uh-SAW-rus)

Leaellynasaura
(lay-EL-i-nuh-SAW-ruh)

Lesothosaurus
(li-SOH-thuh-SAW-rus)

Maiasaura
(MYE-uh-SAW-ruh)

Pronunciation Key

Massospondylus
(MAS-uh-SPON-di-lus)

Megalosaurus
(MEG-uh-luh-SAW-rus)

Mesozoic
(mez-uh-ZO-ik)

Monoclonius
(MON-uh-KLOH-nee-us)

Ornithischia
(or-ni-THISS-key-uh)

Ornithomimosaurs
(or-NITH-uh-MIEM-uh-SAWRS)

Ornithomimus
(or-NITH-uh-MIEM-us)

Oviraptor
(OH-vi-RAP-tor)

Pachycephalosaurus
(PACK-i-SEF-uh-luh-SAW-rus)

Pachyrhinosaurus
(PACK-i-RYE-nuh-SAW-rus)

Paleontologist
(pay-le-un-TOL-uh-gist)

Pangaea
(pan-JE-uh)

Panoplosaurus
(PAN-uh-pluh-SAW-rus)

Parasaurolophus
(PAR-uh-SAW-ruh-LOH-fus)

Parksosaurus
(PAHRK-suh-SAW-rus)

Pentaceratops
(PEN-tuh-SER-uh-tops)

Plateosaurus
(PLAY-tee-uh-SAW-rus)

Plesiosaurs
(PLE-zio-SAWRS)

Plesiosaurus
(PLE-zio-SAW-rus)

Pliosaurs
(PLY-uh-SAWRS)

Podokesaurus
(POH-doh-kuh-SAW-rus)

Polacanthus
(POH-la-CAN-thus)

Procompsognathus
(proh-KOMP-soh-guh-NAY-thus)

Protoceratops
(PROH-tuh-SER-uh-tops)

Psittacosaurs
(si-TACK-uh-SAWRS)

Psittacosaurus
(si-TACK-uh-SAW-rus)

Pteranodon
(ter-AN-oh-DON)

Pterosaurs
(ter-uh-SAWRS)

Riojasaurus
(ree-OH-jah-SAW-rus)

Rutiodon
(ROO-tee-uh-don)

Pronunciation Key

Saltasaurus
(SAWL-tuh-SAW-rus)

Saltopus
(SAWL-tuh-puss)

Saurischia
(sawr-IS-key-ah)

Saurolophus
(SAW-ruh-LOH-fus)

Sauropods
(SAW-ruh-pods)

Scelidosaurus
(SKEL-eye-duh-SAW-rus)

Segnosaurus
(SEG-nuh-SAW-rus)

Seismosaurus
(SYEZ-muh-SAW-rus)

Shonisaurus
(SHOO-nuh-SAW-rus)

Spinosaurus
(SPYE-nuh-SAW-rus)

Staurikosaurus
(STOR-ee-kuh-SAW-rus)

Stegosaurus
(STEG-uh-SAW-rus)

Stenonychosaurus
(ste-NON-i-kuh-SAW-rus)

Struthiomimus
(STROO-thee-uh-MYE-mus)

Stygimoloch
(STIG-i-MOL-uck)

Styracosaurus
(stye-RACK-uh-SAW-rus)

Supersaurus
(soo-pur-SAW-rus)

Syntarsus
(sin-TAR-sus)

Tarbosaurus
(TAR-bow-SAW-rus)

Thecodontosaurus
(THE-co-dont-uh-SAW-rus)

Thecodonts
(THE-co-donts)

Thescelosaurus
(THES-ke-luh-SAW-rus)

Triassic
(tri-AS-ik)

Triceratops
(try-SER-uh-tops)

Troödon
(TROH-uh-don)

Tsintaosaurus
(sin-TOU-SAW-rus)

Tyrannosaurus
(tie-RAN-uh-SAW-rus)

Utahraptor
(Yoo-tah-RAP-tor)

Velociraptor
(ve-LOS-i-RAP-tor)

Zuniceratops christopheri
(ZOO-nee-SER-uh-tops
kris-TUHF-er-eye)

What Species of Animal Were Dinosaurs?

Dinosaurs were reptiles that lived millions of years ago. Like today's reptiles, dinosaurs laid eggs, and had backbones, lungs, and scaly skin.

Two key features that help scientists to identify dinosaurs are: (1) their skulls that have two holes behind the eye sockets, and (2) their hip bones that resemble those of lizards or birds.

Most scientists think that dinosaurs lived on land and walked with their legs under their bodies—not out to the sides like alligators. Many different kinds of dinosaurs lived all over the world.

1. Why are dinosaurs considered reptiles?

_____

_____

_____

2. How do dinosaurs differ from alligators?

_____

_____

_____

3. What two features help scientists identify dinosaurs?

_____

_____

_____

4. Name some reptiles that are living today.

_____

_____

_____

5. Which living reptile do you think looks most like a dinosaur? Why?

_____

_____

_____

6. Name some other animals that walk with their legs under their bodies.

_____

_____

_____

Where Did Dinosaurs Come From?

Scientists believe the ancestors, or early relatives, of dinosaurs developed from amphibians. Amphibians, such as frogs and salamanders, can live on land, but they must keep their skin wet and return to water to lay eggs.

Amphibians that lived long ago looked like big salamanders. Over millions of years, some of them developed into animals with stronger skeletons, tougher skins, and hard eggs. These new animals were the first reptiles. One ancient group of reptiles, called thecodonts, were slim and fast. In time, they developed into dinosaurs.

Answer the questions below by filling in the correct answers. The first one has been done for you.

1. Which animal is an amphibian?

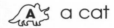 **A** a cat

 **B** an elephant

 **C** a thecodont

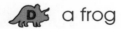 **D** a frog

2. What does ancient mean?

 **A** wet skin

B five years old

C very old

D young

3. How did some ancient amphibians develop into reptiles?

 They walked more on the ground.

 They developed stronger skeletons, tougher skins, and harder eggs.

 They laid their eggs in the water.

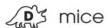 They became slim and fast.

4. Which animals lived first?

 amphibians

B dinosaurs

C alligators

D mice

5. What was one of the first groups of reptiles called?

A rats

B thecodonts

C salamanders

D frogs

6. Over time, thecodonts developed into _____.

A frogs

B amphibians

C dinosaurs

D salamanders

How Long Ago Did Dinosaurs Live?

The history of the earth is divided into eras, or time periods. Dinosaurs lived during the Mesozoic Era, which is also called the **Age of Reptiles**.

The Mesozoic Era began 245 million years ago and ended 65 million years ago. It is divided into three periods—the Triassic, the Jurassic, and the Cretaceous Periods. The landscape and vegetation of the earth changed from one period to another, as did life for the dinosaurs.

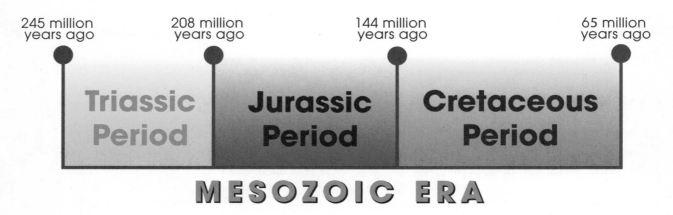

245 million years ago   208 million years ago   144 million years ago   65 million years ago

Triassic Period   **Jurassic Period**   **Cretaceous Period**

MESOZOIC ERA

1. What is an era?

_____

_____

_____

2. What era is known as the Age of Reptiles?

_____

_____

_____ .

3. Name the three periods in the Age of Reptiles.

_____

_____

_____

4. When did that era begin and end?

_____

_____

_____

5. If you had a time machine that could take you back to that era, would you go? Why or why not?

_____

_____

_____

6. Dinosaurs are prehistoric animals. What does prehistoric mean?

_____

_____

_____

What Was the World Like When Dinosaurs Lived?

The world's **climate**, or long-term weather, was generally warm during the Mesozoic Era. In the early part of the era, there were many evergreen trees and shrubs, and ferns. Later, gingko trees with fan-shaped leaves appeared. These were followed by flowering plants, which added flecks of color to the earth.

Just like today's earth, some places in the Mesozoic world had tropical rain forests, while others had sandy deserts or great plains. Different kinds of dinosaurs lived in each of these habitats, or areas.

1. What does climate mean?

  A a period of time

  B lived long ago

  C long-term weather

  D favored over another

2. What was the climate like when dinosaurs lived?

  A hot and humid

  B warm

  C rainy

  D overcast

3. During the early Mesozoic Era, the main types of plants were _____.

 oak and willow trees

 evergreen trees and shrubs, and ferns

 little shrubs

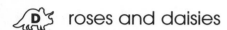 roses and daisies

4. In what order did these plants appear in the Mesozoic Era?

 evergreen trees and shrubs, flowering plants, ginkgo trees

 ginkgo trees, flowering plants, ferns

 flowering plants, ferns, ginkgo trees

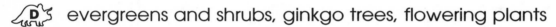 evergreens and shrubs, ginkgo trees, flowering plants

5. What is a habitat?

 a manner of behavior

an area where something lives

a sandy desert

a great plain

6. What type of habitat was not typical during the Mesozoic Era?

sandy deserts

tropical rain forests

great plains

icy mountains

Where Did Dinosaurs Live?

Most scientists think that when dinosaurs first appeared, the earth's continents were all joined together as one supercontinent called **Pangaea**, which means "all the land." Dinosaurs roamed all over the giant **landmass**, or large area of land. About 150 million years ago, Pangaea began to split into separate landmasses that looked like our modern-day continents. Dinosaurs traveled with the moving landmasses. As a result, dinosaurs lived on every continent on the earth.

Pangaea

(about 250 million years ago)

Pangaea splitting

(about 150 million years ago)

I. What was Pangaea?

_____

_____

_____

2. Why was Pangaea called a supercontinent?

_____

_____

_____

3. When did Pangaea begin to break apart?

_____

_____

_____

4. Why did dinosaurs live on every continent on the earth?

_____

_____

_____

5. What do you think surrounded Pangaea?

_____

_____

_____

6. How many continents are there on modern-day earth? Name them.

_____

_____

_____

Did Dinosaurs Migrate?

Scientists believe some dinosaurs **migrated,** or traveled from place to place, in search of food. One reason they believe this is because the fossils of the large, horned, plant-eater, Pachyrhinosaurus have been found in the Arctic, Alaska, and Canada. Just like today, Arctic winters were long and dark in the Mesozoic Era. Plants would not have lived due to the lack of sunshine. Scientists think Arctic dinosaurs may have migrated south in winter and north in spring to have a steady supply of food.

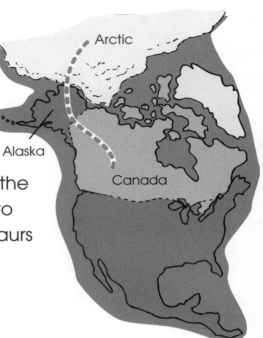

1. What does migrate mean?

   A travel to space

   B search for food

   C travel from place to place

   D long, dark winter

--------- : migration route of Pachyrhinosaurus

2. Why did some dinosaurs migrate?

   A They were looking for a house.

   B They were looking for food.

   C They were looking for other dinosaurs.

   D They were outgrowing their habitats.

Pachyrhinosaurus

3. Where have the bones of Pachyrhinosaurus not been found?

 **A** the Arctic

 **B** Alaska

 **C** Africa

D Canada

4. Arctic winters in the Mesozoic Era were _____.

A warm, short, and sunny

B rainy and windy

 **C** hot and humid

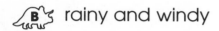 **D** cold, long, and dark

5. Why were plants not able to live in the Mesozoic Era Arctic?

 **A** There was not enough light.

 **B** There were not enough dinosaurs.

C There was no wind.

D There was not enough water.

6. Which modern-day animals migrate south in the winter and north in the spring?

A lions

 **B** birds

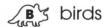 **C** ants

 D dogs

Word Search Activity

Use the word list to help you find the words about dinosaurs that are hidden in the block below. Some of the words are hidden backward or diagonally.

```
T C L I M A T E G N E J U R A S
O I A V E G H R R B D X P Z O R
Z S N W S R X A A M I G R A T E
O S U P E R C O N T I N E N T P
T A E I A E T A T I B A H K R T
H R P L B N C Z X V N A I D I I
E U G J I L G K H F S Q S E A L
C J L T U T O A P I Y R T W S E
O D A N C A P M E B C X O L S S
D E N J G D A E K A H F R S I P
O V D I Y R W O R U T E I Q C Z
N L M C B V Z M X F N A C L S K
T O A C R E T A C E O U S F J F
S V S H G Q P W O T N E I C N A
M E S O Z O I C E R A E G I R U
T Y M Z N X A M P H I B I A N S
```

WORD LIST

AGE OF REPTILES
AMPHIBIANS
ANCIENT
CLIMATE
CRETACEOUS
ERA

EVOLVED
HABITAT
JURASSIC
LANDMASS
MESOZOIC ERA
MIGRATE

PANGAEA
PREHISTORIC
REPTILES
SUPERCONTINENT
THECODONTS
TRIASSIC

Get a Clue!

Unscramble the words below. Then, use the words as clues to fill in the answers to the questions.

geA fo ptsReile _____

hpminasbia _____

ecmlait _____

sariscuJ _____

digmrtae _____

tscoineupnnter _____

1. Dinosaurs are believed to have _____, much like birds do today.

2. The Mesozoic Era is also known as the _____.

3. Pangaea was a _____ that split apart into separate continents during the Mesozoic Era.

4. _____ are animals that must keep their skin wet and return to the water to lay their eggs.

5. The _____ Period lasted from 208 million years ago to 144 million years ago.

6. Plants were able to flourish during the Mesozoic Era because the world's _____ was generally warm.

What Was the Biggest Dinosaur?

The largest known meat-eating dinosaur was Giganotosaurus, from what is now Argentina. Giganotosaurus measured 45 feet in length—as long as three cars—and weighed 8 tons, or slightly more than an African elephant. It walked on two legs and had long, sharp teeth.

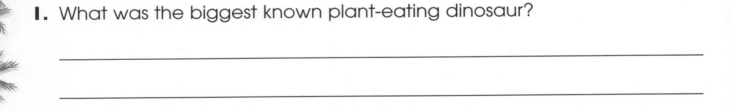

Argentinosaurus

The largest known plant-eating dinosaur was the four-legged long-neck Argentinosaurus, also from what is now Argentina. It measured 115 feet in length—almost as long as eight cars—and weighed 100 tons, or as much as fourteen African elephants.

1. What was the biggest known plant-eating dinosaur?

_____

_____

_____

2. What was the biggest known meat-eating dinosaur?

_____

_____

_____

3. Was the largest known dinosaur a meat-eater or a plant-eater?

_____

_____

_____

4. Which of these two biggest dinosaurs do you think moved faster? Why?

_____

_____

_____

5. Why do you think Argentinosaurus walked on four legs instead of two?

_____

_____

_____

6. How many Giganotosauruses would need to be lined up to equal the length of one Argentinosaurus?

_____

_____

_____

What Was the Smallest Dinosaur?

Compsognathus was one of the smallest known dinosaurs. This meat-eater was about as big as a turkey and weighed about as much as a newborn human baby. Scientists think Compsognathus was a fast runner that chased down small lizards and other prey.

Compsognathus

Heterodontosaurus, also about as big as a turkey, was among the smallest known plant-eaters. It had several kinds of teeth, which it may have used to bite, tear, and grind plants.

1. What was the smallest known plant-eating dinosaur?

   A Compsognathus

   B Giganotosaurus

   C Heterodontosaurus

   D Argentinosaurus

2. What was the smallest known meat-eating dinosaur?

   A Argentinosaurus

   B Compsognathus

   C Giganotosaurus

   D Heterodontosaurus

3. Compsognathus and Heterodontosaurus were about the same size as _____.

    A   a mouse

    B   a horse

    C   a newborn baby

    D   a turkey

4. Scientists think that Compsognathus was a _____.

    A   fast runner

    B   quick eater

    C   newborn baby

    D   turkey

5. Heterodontosaurus had many different types of _____.

    A   feet

    B   scales

    C   teeth

    D   eyes

6. What was Compsognathus believed to have eaten?

    A   rats

    B   plants

    C   small lizards

    D   large birds

How Big Were Dinosaurs?

Some dinosaurs were incredibly big, while others were small. The pictures below, and on the next page, should give you an idea of how big, or how small, some dinosaurs were compared to a grown-up man and a cat.

Apatosaurus

Saltopus

Compsognathus

1. Which of the dinosaurs on these pages were smaller than you are?

_____

2. Can you think of something that is about the size of a Stegosaurus?

_____

3. Can you think of anything that is bigger than an Apatosaurus?

_____

Stegosaurus

Hadrosaurus

Crossword Activity

Read the clues about dinosaurs. Then, complete the puzzle using the word list below.

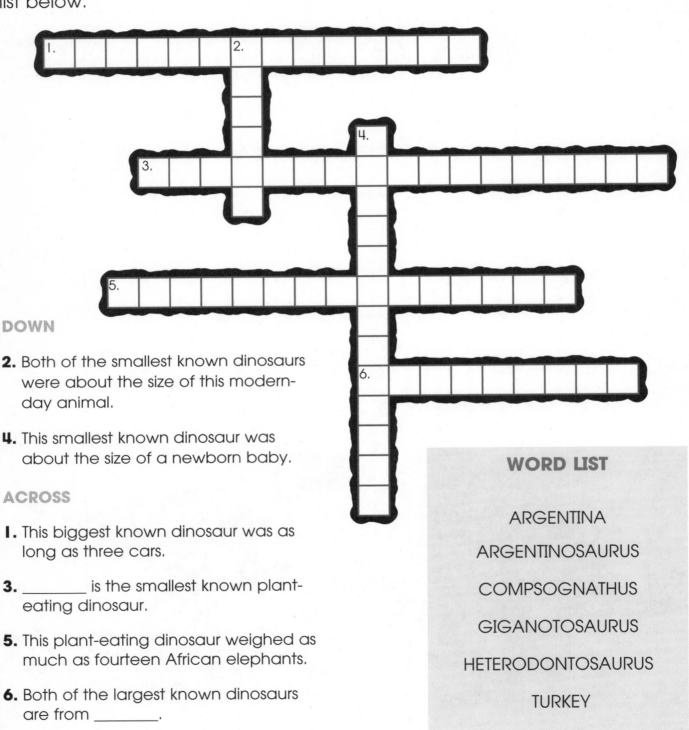

DOWN

2. Both of the smallest known dinosaurs were about the size of this modern-day animal.

4. This smallest known dinosaur was about the size of a newborn baby.

ACROSS

1. This biggest known dinosaur was as long as three cars.

3. _____ is the smallest known plant-eating dinosaur.

5. This plant-eating dinosaur weighed as much as fourteen African elephants.

6. Both of the largest known dinosaurs are from _____.

WORD LIST

ARGENTINA

ARGENTINOSAURUS

COMPSOGNATHUS

GIGANOTOSAURUS

HETERODONTOSAURUS

TURKEY

How Long Were Dinosaurs?

Dinosaurs varied greatly in size. Some were up to 90 feet long! Use the charts on pages 130, 140, and 154 to find the lengths of some dinosaurs. Write the names of the dinosaurs along the bottom of the line graph. Color in the lengths (in feet) with different colors.

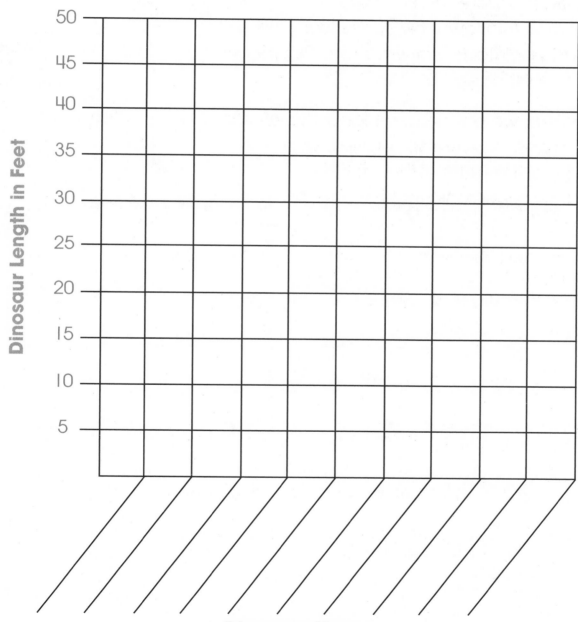

Dinosaur Names

What Were the Two Main Groups of Dinosaurs?

Dinosaurs are divided into two main groups, based on the arrangement of their hipbones.

The **Ornithischia** were the bird-hipped dinosaurs. Their two lower hipbones were close together and pointed backward. The Ornithischia included only plant-eaters.

bird-hipped (Ornithischia)

The **Saurischia** were the lizard-hipped dinosaurs. Their two lower hipbones were separated, with one pointed forward and the other pointed backward. The Saurischia included both plant-eaters and meat-eaters.

lizard-hipped (Saurischia)

I. What are the two main groups of dinosaurs?

_____

_____

_____

2. How are the two main groups of dinosaurs divided?

_____

_____

_____

3. Which group were bird-hipped dinosaurs? Explain what bird-hipped means.

_____

_____

_____

4. Which group were lizard-hipped dinosaurs? Explain what lizard-hipped means.

_____

_____

_____

5. Which group included only plant-eating dinosaurs?

_____

_____

_____

6. Which group would Tyrannosaurus, a meat-eater, be in?

_____

_____

_____

What Were Meat-eating Dinosaurs?

Meat-eating dinosaurs were **carnivores** that hunted other animals for food. The meat-eaters had long, strong legs so that they could run fast in order to catch their prey. They also had strong jaws, and sharp teeth and claws to kill and tear apart their catch.

Meat-eating dinosaurs had different ways of hunting. Some carnivores hunted alone while others hunted in groups, called packs. Some were scavengers. They ate the meat that was left over from another's kill.

All together, meat-eating dinosaurs made up only 35 percent of the entire dinosaur population. The smaller number of meat-eaters balanced out the food chain. If there were more meat-eaters than plant-eaters, there would not have been enough food and the meat-eaters would have most likely starved.

1. Meat-eating dinosaurs were _____.

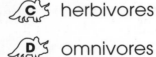 **A** vegetarians

B carnivores

C herbivores

D omnivores

2. Carnivores made up _____ of the entire dinosaur population.

A 75 percent

B 35 billion

C 35 million

D 35 percent

What Were Plant-eating Dinosaurs?

Plant-eating dinosaurs were **herbivores** that ate only plants. Plant-eaters had many features on their bodies that helped them eat. Some had blunt snouts, or beaks, for stripping leaves and twigs from plants. Others had blunt teeth for chewing and grinding their food. Many had pouches in their cheeks in which they stored food before eating it. Plus some plant-eaters swallowed rocks, called **gastroliths**, to help them digest their food. Some herbivores also had thumb spikes that they could have used for defense or for gathering food.

Plant-eating dinosaurs could have more than one of these features to help them eat. They probably spent most of their time eating to get enough food to survive.

1. Plant-eating dinosaurs are also called _____.

_____

_____

_____

2. What are the rocks called that some herbivores swallowed? Why did they swallow the rocks?

_____

_____

_____

3. Why did some plant-eaters have cheek pouches?

_____

_____

_____

What Were Nippers, Rippers, and Grinders?

1.

2.

3.

How do scientists know that some dinosaurs were meat-eaters and others were plant-eaters? By looking at the teeth of certain dinosaur fossils, scientists can tell what those dinosaurs ate. Meat-eaters had sharp, saw-edged teeth (figure 1) for cutting and ripping flesh. Plant-eating dinosaurs had either peg-like teeth (figure 2) for nipping plants or flat grinding teeth (figure 3) to munch tough twigs or leaves.

Look at the teeth of each dinosaur below.
Then, circle either "M" for meat-eater or "P" for plant-eater.

**Meat-eater
or
Plant-eater**

Tyrannosaurus			M P
Parasaurolophus			M P
Monoclonius			M P
Hypsilophodon			M P
Triceratops			M P

What Is the Difference?

1. Which of the two dinosaur skulls shown below do you think belongs to a meat-eater? Circle your answer.

2. How do you know?

_____

_____

3. How else can you tell the difference between a carnivore and an herbivore?

_____

_____

4. What do you think the dinosaur pictured below ate?

_____

_____

_____

_____

Velociraptor

Which Was Which?

Circle the dinosaurs pictured below and on the next page that you think were meat-eaters. Put a square around the plant-eaters.

Saltopus

Parksosaurus

Pentaceratops

Corythosaurus

Tarbosaurus

Podokesaurus

Parasaurolophus

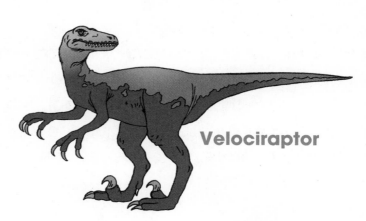

Velociraptor

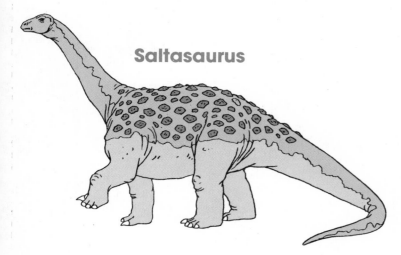

Saltasaurus

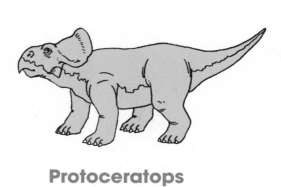

Protoceratops

Deinonychus

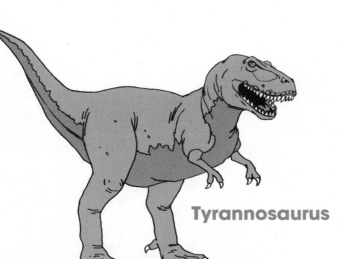

Tyrannosaurus

What Did Dinosaurs Use Their Claws For?

Hunters, or predators, such as Utahraptor, used the huge, knifelike claws on their hands and feet to kill prey. The crocodile-jawed Baryonyx may have used its enormous thumb claws to scoop fish out of the water for food. Most plant-eating dinosaurs, such as Iguanodon, used their broad, flat claws to dig up plants and to protect themselves from attackers.

Iguanodon   Tyrannosaurus   Baryonyx   Deinonychus

1. Carnivores used their claws for _____.

   - **A** digging up plants
   - **B** attacking prey
   - **C** climbing trees
   - **D** swimming

2. The claws of carnivores were _____.

   - **A** broad and flat
   - **B** large and round
   - **C** huge and knifelike
   - **D** flat and curved

3. Herbivores used their claws for _____.

    A swimming

    B climbing trees

    C attacking prey

    D digging up plants

4. The claws of herbivores were _____.

    A flat and curved

    B broad and flat

    C huge and knifelike

    D large and round

5. A predator is something that _____.

    A is hunted by another

    B eats a lot of food

    C hunts other animals

    D scoops fish out of the water

6. Prey is something that _____.

    A is hatched from eggs

    B uses its claws for defense

    C is hunted by another

    D eats its own kind

What Is Happening?

Tarbosaurus is looking for food. What is Psittacosaurus doing? What do you think will happen next? Color the picture below, then write a story about this picture on the next page.

The tarbosaurus is looking for a little dinosaur. Find the dinosaur and then try to guess the name of the dinosaur if he can't read.

Why Did Some Dinosaurs Have Armor Plates?

Daspletosaurus

Ankylosaurus

Some plant-eating dinosaurs, called **ankylosaurs**, had hard scales and bony plates all over their bodies—even their eyelids! This **armor** protected them from the bites and claws of meat-eaters. Only their underbellies were unprotected, so predators would have to flip them over to bite or claw them.

Ankylosaurus, for example, was covered with thick plates and bony spikes that a predator couldn't bite through. It also had a bony club on its tail that it used as a weapon.

I. What are the hard scales and bony plates on some dinosaurs called?

_____

_____

_____

2. What kind of dinosaurs had hard scales and bony plates?

_____

_____

_____

3. Why did these dinosaurs have armor?

_____

_____

_____

4. What was the only part of ankylosaurs that did not have armor?

_____

_____

_____

5. Some small plant-eaters had no horns or armor. How do you think they avoided being eaten by predators?

_____

_____

_____

6. Name some modern-day animals that have armor or horns.

_____

_____

_____

What Are Frills?

Besides armor plates, some plant-eating dinosaurs had other ways to defend themselves against meat-eaters. Some dinosaurs had sharp horns on their faces, spikes on their bodies, or a hard bony collar, called a **frill**, on their heads to protect their necks.

Color the frill on this dinosaur red.
Color the horns blue.

Triceratops

Color the spikes on this dinosaur green.

Ankylosaurus

Which type of body defense feature do you think was the most useful for the plant-eating dinosaurs? Explain. _____

_____

How Do I Defend Myself?

Look at the plant-eating dinosaurs below. Find the features of their bodies that gave them protection from their enemies. Explain in the space provided.

Stegosaurus

_____

_____

_____

_____

Ankylosaurus

_____

_____

_____

_____

Triceratops

_____

_____

_____

_____

What Did Dinosaurs Use Their Tails For?

Plant-eating dinosaurs used their tails to defend themselves. Long-necked dinosaurs, such as Diplodocus, had whiplike tails that they used to lash out at meat-eaters. They also used their tails for balance when they walked.

Diplodocus

Armored dinosaurs had dangerous tails. For example, Stegosaurus had spikes on its tail as long as baseball bats. When slammed into a predator, its tail would have caused serious wounds.

Some meat-eaters such as Deinonychus probably used their tails for balance when they ran.

1. What kind of dinosaurs had dangerous tails?

- Ⓐ long-necked dinosaurs
- Ⓑ meat-eating dinosaurs
- Ⓒ armored dinosaurs
- Ⓓ plant-eating dinosaurs

Stegosaurus

2. _____ had a long neck and a whiplike tail.

- Ⓐ Deinonychus
- Ⓑ Herbivore
- Ⓒ Stegosaurus
- Ⓓ Diplodocus

Deinonychus

3. Deinonychus used its tail for _____.

A balance when it ran

B clearing away trees from a path

C attracting a mate

D holding onto food

4. _____ is an armored dinosaur.

A Diplodocus

B Deinonychus

C Tyrannosaurus

D Stegosaurus

5. Long-necked dinosaurs used their tail for defense and for _____.

A swinging from vine to vine

B balance when they walked

C catching fish in the water

D holding up their heads

6. Stegosaurus had spikes on its tail as long as a _____.

A toothpick

B pencil

C baseball bat

D banana

Did Dinosaurs Live Alone or In Groups?

Scientists think that many plant-eating dinosaurs lived in groups to protect themselves from predators. Proof of this has been found in fossil beds containing many Maiasaura, both young and adult.

Clusters of fossil bones from some meat-eaters, such as Coelophysis, show that they formed groups as well. Other meat-eaters may have formed temporary packs for hunting, but many predatory dinosaurs hunted alone.

Coelophysis dinosaurs

1. Why do scientists think that many plant-eating dinosaurs lived in groups?

_____

_____

_____

2. How do scientists know that some dinosaurs lived in groups?

_____

_____

_____

3. Why do scientists theorize that some meat-eating dinosaurs formed groups?

_____

_____

_____

4. Why do scientists feel that some meat-eating dinosaurs hunted by themselves?

_____

_____

_____

5. What are some modern-day animals that live in groups?

_____

_____

_____

6. People sometimes form groups called *clubs.* If you formed a dinosaur fan club, what would you call it?

_____

_____

_____

What Is a Group of Dinosaurs Called?

The groups that some dinosaurs lived in are called herds. Fossil tracks show that when some herds migrated, or moved, they kept their young dinosaurs in the middle of the pack.

Why would this be a good way for some dinosaurs to protect their young?

_____

_____

_____

Color the picture below any way you like.

What Is the Secret Word?

Cross out the letters that spell the name of each of these items pictured below. Then, use the remaining letters to complete the sentence.

e   g   h   g

h   o   r   e   n

b   r   o   n   e

t   r   e   d   e

Some dinosaurs, such as this sauropod, travel in a

____ ____ ____ ____ for safety.

How Fast Did Dinosaurs Run?

Some dinosaurs protected themselves by running away from other dinosaurs. Running fast also helped some carnivores catch slow-moving dinosaurs. Scientists figured out the speed that a dinosaur ran by measuring the distance between its tracks and by studying the length of its legs. Scientists found that dinosaurs with long legs could probably run faster than dinosaurs with short legs.

The graph below shows how fast some dinosaurs may have been able to run. Use the graph to answer the questions below.

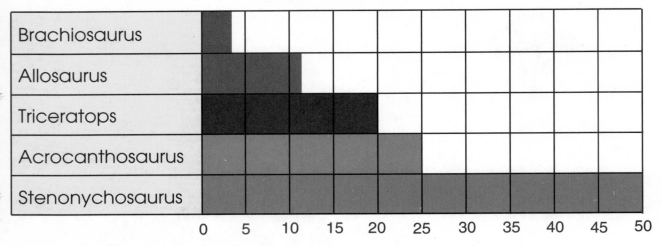

Miles Per Hour

1. Which dinosaurs on the graph could run faster than Allosaurus?

_____

2. Which dinosaur could run faster, Acrocanthosaurus or Triceratops?

_____

3. Which dinosaur could run faster than any other dinosaur on the graph?

_____

Word Search Activity

Use the word list to help you find the words about dinosaurs that are hidden in the block below. Some of the words are hidden backward or diagonally.

M	Z	N	X	B	B	E	R	O	V	I	N	R	A	C	S
L	A	K	S	J	O	H	D	H	F	S	G	P	Q	C	O
W	I	S	E	U	N	R	E	Y	T	Z	L	C	A	B	M
A	D	G	W	J	Y	L	Q	R	T	A	I	L	S	E	T
A	U	O	H	A	P	X	V	N	D	V	E	F	I	H	J
I	C	W	O	R	L	Y	S	I	P	S	M	B	C	R	Z
H	L	J	R	G	A	C	P	D	A	P	I	Y	E	R	F
C	O	R	N	I	T	H	I	S	C	H	I	A	S	W	N
S	V	X	S	K	E	H	K	F	S	O	U	R	N	T	E
I	Q	X	V	N	S	S	E	F	H	K	W	M	E	R	P
R	Y	I	K	A	L	S	S	K	D	J	F	O	F	G	A
U	P	Q	O	W	H	E	R	B	I	V	O	R	E	I	C
A	E	U	R	Y	T	Z	M	X	N	C	B	V	D	T	K
S	R	E	D	N	I	R	G	Y	R	U	E	I	W	O	S
Q	P	L	R	I	P	P	E	R	S	A	K	S	J	D	H
H	F	G	V	M	Z	N	S	R	E	P	P	I	N	X	V

WORD LIST

ARMOR	GRINDERS	PACKS
BONY PLATES	HERBIVORE	RIPPERS
CARNIVORE	HERDS	SAURISCHIA
CLAWS	HORNS	SCALES
DEFENSE	NIPPERS	SPIKES
FRILLS	ORNITHISCHIA	TAILS

How Did Dinosaurs Reproduce?

Dinosaurs laid eggs in nests on the ground. Scientists think that some dinosaurs stayed with their eggs until they hatched. Small dinosaurs, such as Oviraptor, may have sat on their eggs much like chickens do. Many dinosaurs, though, probably covered their eggs with sand and plants to keep them warm and left them behind.

Dinosaur eggs ranged in size. Some were the size of golf balls. Others were the size of footballs. Eggs could not have been too large or too thick. Air had to pass through the shells and young dinosaurs had to break out. That is why some scientists think giant dinosaurs may have given birth to live young as big as adult pigs.

Oviraptor

1. How did dinosaurs reproduce?

   A They laid eggs in the water.

   B They gave birth.

   C They laid eggs in caves.

   D They laid eggs in nests.

2. Why did some dinosaurs sit on their eggs?

   A to hide the color of their eggs

   B to keep their eggs warm until they hatched

   C to alert predators of the eggs

   D to keep them clean

3. Where did dinosaurs make their nests?

A in tree branches

B in the water

C on the ground

D in a cave

4. Why couldn't dinosaur eggs be too large or too thick?

A so air could get in the shells and babies could break out

B so the eggs could be hidden easily

C so the eggs would not roll around

D because no big, thick eggs have been found

5. Why did scientists think that giant dinosaurs gave birth to live babies?

A They thought the eggs would have been fossilized.

B They never found the remains of dinosaur eggs.

C The eggs would have been too large and too thick for the babies to hatch.

D They thought only birds laid eggs.

6. What modern-day animals lay eggs?

A tigers

B elephants

C turtles

D hamsters

Did Dinosaurs Take Care of Their Young?

Scientists think that some dinosaurs simply covered their eggs and walked away. They also think that other dinosaurs protected their eggs and cared for their young. Fossilized nests of Maiasaura, a plant-eater, have been found containing the fossils of many helpless baby dinosaurs. Scientists think that one or both parents protected these youngsters and brought them food.

Maiasaura

Other baby dinosaurs hatched with well-developed legs. Scientists believe these youngsters left the nest as soon as they hatched to find their own plants to eat.

I. What proof do scientist have that some dinosaurs took care of their young?

_____

_____

_____

2. Why do scientists believe that some babies left their nests as soon as they were born?

_____

_____

_____

3. Maiasaura means "good mother lizard." Why do you think scientists chose this name?

_____

_____

_____

4. Of the dinosaurs that did not care for their young, do you think there were more or less of them than the dinosaurs that protected their young? Why?

_____

_____

_____

5. Name some modern-day animals that take care of their young.

_____

_____

_____

6. How did your parents take care of you when you were a baby?

_____

_____

_____

Did Baby Dinosaurs Look Like Their Parents?

Most dinosaurs looked very much like their parents when they were born, but some features, such as horns and frills, took time to develop. This is how an adult Protoceratops looked.

Number the pictures in order to show how a baby Protoceratops grew.

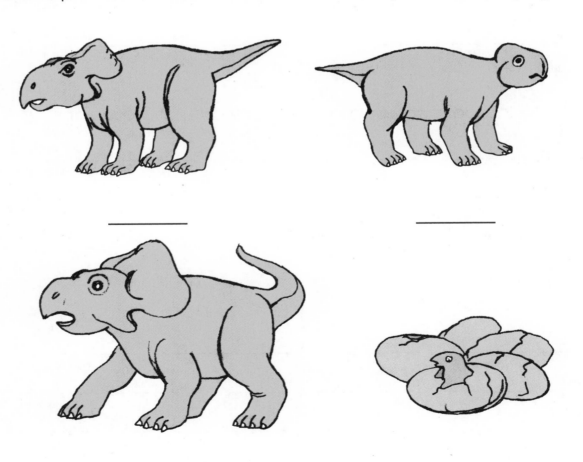

_____   _____

_____   _____

Crossword Activity

Read the clues about dinosaurs. Then, complete the puzzle using the word list below.

ACROSS

2. Dinosaurs laid their eggs in _____ on the ground.

3. This dinosaur name means "good mother lizard."

5. Some baby dinosaurs left the nest as soon as they _____.

DOWN

1. A dinosaur egg could be as big as a _____.

4. Dinosaurs _____ by laying eggs.

6. Some dinosaurs sat on their _____ until they hatched.

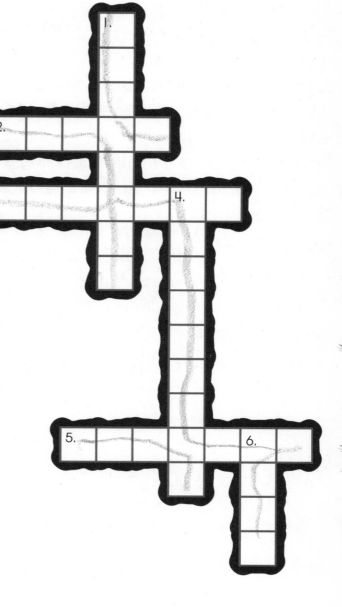

WORD LIST

EGGS

FOOTBALL

HATCHED

MAIASAURA

NESTS

REPRODUCE

When Were Dinosaurs First Discovered?

The first fossilized dinosaur teeth were discovered by rock quarry workers in England in the early 1820s. The workers brought the fossils to Dr. Gideon Mantell, a fossil collector, who thought the fossilized teeth came from a huge lizard that no longer existed. Because the teeth resembled iguana teeth, Dr. Mantell named the animal **Iguanodon**, which means "iguana tooth."

Iguanodon

Around the same time, Professor William Buckland described an animal called **Megalosaurus**, which means "big lizard." Scientists later discovered that Iguanodon was a plant-eating dinosaur and Megalosaurus was a meat-eating dinosaur.

1. Where were the first fossilized dinosaur teeth found?

   A in a nest in Argentina

   B in a rock quarry in England

   C in an aquarium in Australia

   D in a museum in the United States

2. Who named the dinosaur whose teeth were the first found?

   A Professor William Buckland

   B Dr. Dino Saur

   C Dr. Gideon Mantell

   D Professor Pal E. Ontologist

3. Why was the first named dinosaur called Iguanodon?

A Because it looked like an iguana.

B Because it looked like a lizard.

C Because its teeth looked like those of an iguana.

D Because it was found next to an Iguanodon nest.

4. What dinosaur did Professor William Buckland first describe?

A Iguanodon

B Tyrannosaurus

C Megalosaurus

D Troödon

5. Why were dinosaurs originally called lizards?

A They had scales like lizards.

B Their bones were fossilized.

C They were green.

D Their teeth and bones resembled those of lizards.

6. Which animal's name means "big lizard"?

A Troödon

B Iguanodon

C Tyrannosaurus

D Megalosaurus

How Are Dinosaurs Named?

Names for new animals are usually created from Latin or Greek words. Giganotosaurus, for example, was a huge dinosaur found in South America. Its name comes from the Greek words *gigas* (giant), *notos* (south), and *sauros* (lizard).

Dinosaurs can also be named for people. Zuniceratops christopheri, found in New Mexico, was named for the Zuni Indians and for nine-year-old Christopher Wolfe who helped discover the fossils.

I. What languages are usually used to name new animals?

_____

_____

_____

2. What does the name Giganotosaurus mean?

_____

_____

_____

3. Has a dinosaur ever been named after a person? If so, name the dinosaur and the person, or persons, it was named for.

_____

_____

_____

4. Are dinosaurs found all over the world? If so, why?

_____

_____

_____

5. Do you think dinosaurs have different names in different countries? Explain.

_____

_____

_____

6. If a dinosaur was named after you, what would you want it to be called?

_____

_____

_____

What Is In a Name?

Did you know that most dinosaur names tell us something about the animal? Look at the list of name meanings and the pictures on this page and the next. Match the correct meaning to the dinosaur names. Write the letters in the boxes next to the dinosaur names.

Name Meanings

A. Plated or Roofed Creature

B. Fish Creature

C. Three-horned Face Creature

D. Terrible Creature

E. Duck Creature

F. Helmet Creature

G. Armored Creature

H. Pretty Jaw

I. Spiked Creature

J. Single-horned Creature

☐ **Deinonychus**

☐ **Stegosaurus**

☐ **Corythosaurus**

☐ **Styracosaurus**

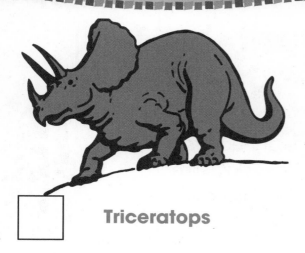

☐ **Triceratops**

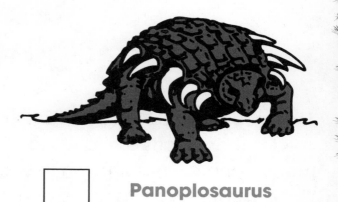

☐ **Panoplosaurus**

☐ **Ichthyosaurus**

☐ **Monoclonius**

☐ **Anatosaurus**

☐ **Compsognathus**

What Were Duck-billed Dinosaurs?

Hadrosaurs, or duck-billed dinosaurs, were plant-eaters that lived in many parts of the world. They had wide, duck-like mouths and rows of teeth in their cheeks. Scientists believe duckbills were able to make honking or bellowing noises.

Corythosaurus

Different kinds of duckbills had different head ornaments. Some had tall spines, while others had crests or bony lumps. Some had no ornaments at all. Scientists think that duckbills cared for their young and traveled in herds.

Lambeosaurus

I. The group of duck-billed dinosaurs is called _____.

 Parasaurolophus

 hadrosaurs

 Corythosaurus

 Tsinataosaurus

Parasaurolophus

2. What kind of noises did duck-billed dinosaurs make?

 honking or bellowing

 barking or quacking

 howling or singing

 chirping or whistling

Saurolophus

Tsintaosaurus

3. Hadrosaurs were _____.

- **A** herbivores
- **B** carnivores
- **C** siblings
- **D** friends

4. Why were hadrosaurs called duckbills?

- **A** They had webbed feet.
- **B** They had feathers.
- **C** They had duck-like mouths.
- **D** They liked to be around water.

5. Duckbills had these types of head ornaments.

- **A** horns or spikes
- **B** frills, armor plates, or curled horns
- **C** crests, bony lumps, or spines
- **D** crests or egg-shaped bumps

6. Duckbills traveled _____.

- **A** with a buddy
- **B** by themselves
- **C** as a herd
- **D** when the wind changed

What Were Parrot-beaked Dinosaurs?

Psittacosaurs, or parrot-beaked dinosaurs, had a long beak at the front of their mouths. Psittacosaurs were plant-eaters and used their beak and teeth to snip off vegetation. They could not chew well, so they used **gastroliths**, or stomach stones, to crush food. All known parrot-beaked dinosaurs lived in what is now Asia, and none were longer than about 6 feet. Psittacosaurs are related to dinosaurs that have horns and bony frills around their necks, such as Triceratops.

Psittacosaurus

1. What are parrot-beaked dinosaurs called?

_____

_____

_____

2. What did parrot-beaked dinosaurs use their beaks for?

_____

_____

_____

3. How did psittacosaurs use gastroliths?

_____

_____

_____

4. Do you think that parrot-beaked dinosaurs would have problems eating if they were carnivores? Why?

_____

_____

_____

5. Where did parrot-beaked dinosaurs live?

_____

_____

_____

6. What other kinds of dinosaurs are psittacosaurs related to?

_____

_____

_____

What Were Long-Necks?

Sauropods, or long-necks, were plant-eating dinosaurs with long necks and tails. Found all over the world, long-necks were the largest known dinosaurs.

The longest sauropod may have been Seismosaurus, from what is now Mexico. Seismosaurus was about 150 feet in length—as long as 10 cars—and weighed around 30 tons, or more than four African elephants. Sauropods walked on four legs and usually had no armor. Scientists think that their enormous size and herding habits kept them safe from meat-eaters.

Seismosaurus

1. Long-necked dinosaurs are also known as _____.

 **A** Seismosaurus

B African elephants

C hadrosaurs

 **D** sauropods

2. Long-necks were _____.

A carnivores with short tails

 **B** herbivores with long necks and tails

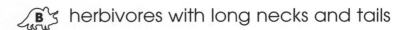 **C** carnivores with long necks and tails

D herbivores with short tails

3. How long was Seismosaurus?

  A about 70 feet

  B as long as 15 cars

  C about 150 feet

  D about 110 feet

4. How much did Seismosaurus weigh?

  A 100 tons

  B 100 pounds

  C 30 tons

  D 300 pounds

5. What kept sauropods safe from predators?

  A their size and herding habits

  B their clubbed tails

  C their speed

  D their long necks

6. What modern-day animals have long necks?

  A African elephants

  B giraffes

  C snakes

  D zebras

What Were Ostrich Dinosaurs?

Ornithomimosaurs were meat-eating dinosaurs with beaks, small heads, long necks, and long legs. Scientists think that ornithomimosaurs looked and ran like ostriches and sometimes call them **ostrich dinosaurs**. Struthiomimus, an ornithomimosaur from what is now North America, was probably one of the smartest and fastest dinosaurs. It was about 12 feet long and as tall as a human adult.

Struthiomimus

1. Why are ornithomimosaurs called ostrich dinosaurs?

_____

_____

_____

2. Describe how ornithomimosaurs looked.

_____

_____

_____

3. What features helped ornithomimosaurs catch its prey?

_____

_____

_____

4. Were ornithomimosaurs herbivores or carnivores?

_____

_____

_____

5. Where was Struthiomimus from?

_____

_____

_____

6. How long and tall was Struthiomimus?

_____

_____

_____

What Were Curved-claw Dinosaurs?

Velociraptors belonged to a group of meat-eating dinosaurs called **dromaeosaurs**. Dromaeosaurs had an enormous curved claw on the second toe of each foot for attacking prey. They also had birdlike skeletons, and scientists think they were closely related to birds. Found in what is now Asia, Velociraptor was about 6 feet in length. It was probably intelligent, fast, had good eyesight, and may have hunted in packs.

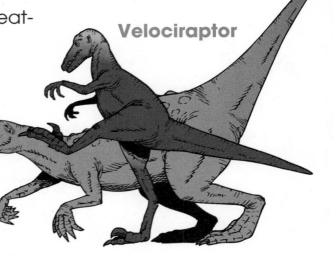

Velociraptor

Thescelosaurus

1. Curved-claw dinosaurs are called _____.

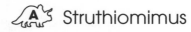 Struthiomimus

 dromaeosaurs

 ornithomimosaurs

 Triceratops

2. They had a curved claw on _____.

A the second finger of each hand

B their right hands only

C the second toe of each foot

D the end of their tails

3. Their curved claw was used for _____.

    A digging up plants

    B breaking open fruit

    C attacking prey

    D building shelter

4. Scientists think that the dromaeosaurs were closely related to _____.

    A tigers

    B birds

    C crocodiles

    D elephants

5. Dromaeosaurs had birdlike _____.

    A wings

    B skeletons

    C hips

    D beaks

6. Velociraptor is a dromaeosaur that was from _____.

    A Australia

    B England

    C Asia

    D South Africa

Get a Clue!

Unscramble the words below. Then, use the words to fill in the answers to the questions.

sHroadursa _____

undIgaoon _____

ekerG _____

tsgtilohsar _____

psarousdo _____

rmustthSiomui _____

vrudec wcla _____

ssgaleauMrou _____

1. The first dinosaur teeth found were from _____.

2. Dinosaur names are created from Latin or _____ words.

3. _____ had wide, duck-like mouths and rows of teeth in their cheeks.

4. Psittacosaurs used _____ to crush food in their stomachs.

5. Long-necked dinosaurs are called _____.

6. _____, an ostrich dinosaur, was one of the smartest and fastest dinosaurs.

7. Velociraptors had an enormous _____ _____ on the second toe of each of their feet.

8. Professor William Buckland described a dinosaur called _____.

Word Search Activity

Use the word list to help you find the words about dinosaurs that are hidden in the block below. Some of the words are hidden backward or diagonally.

```
S  U  R  U  A  S  O  M  S  I  E  S  M  W  Z  G
R  R  N  L  O  N  G  N  E  C  K  S  X  I  B  I
U  O  U  C  B  V  L  A  S  K  D  T  V  L  D  G
A  C  J  A  G  H  P  Q  O  W  N  E  H  L  E  A
S  K  I  R  S  T  U  Y  V  E  L  Z  O  I  K  N
O  Q  C  X  M  O  B  N  M  O  P  Q  N  A  A  O
E  U  O  W  I  E  M  A  C  U  R  U  K  M  E  T
A  A  T  Y  L  A  N  I  K  S  J  D  I  B  B  O
M  R  H  F  G  R  R  M  M  Z  N  X  N  U  T  S
O  R  B  C  O  A  V  Y  T  O  U  R  G  C  O  A
R  Y  I  D  P  E  O  W  P  Q  H  H  G  K  R  U
D  J  A  T  H  C  I  R  T  S  O  T  F  L  R  R
K  E  O  S  J  S  A  L  V  B  C  N  I  A  A  U
H  R  X  D  U  C  K  B  I  L  L  E  D  N  P  S
S  R  U  A  S  O  C  A  T  T  I  S  P  D  R  M
Z  Y  G  I  D  E  O  N  M  A  N  T  E  L  L  O
```

WORD LIST

DROMAEOSAURS

DUCK-BILLED

GIDEON MANTELL

GIGANOTOSAURUS

HEAD ORNAMENT

HONKING

LONG-NECKS

ORNITHOMIMOSAURS

OSTRICH

PARROT-BEAKED

PSITTACOSAURS

ROCK QUARRY

SEISMOSAURUS

VELOCIRAPTORS

WILLIAM BUCKLAND

79

What Are Fossils?

Fossils are the remains—or pieces left behind—of plants and animals that have been preserved in the earth. There are different types of fossils, including **true form fossils** and **trace fossils**. True form fossils are formed from hard animal parts such as shells, bones, or teeth. Trace fossils are formed from impressions left behind from an animal such as skin, footprints, burrows, nests, or droppings. Trace fossils do not include hard parts but are evidence that a living thing existed. They provide a record of an animal's behavior or movement.

One of the ways fossils are formed is when the hard parts of animals are buried for millions of years. Mineral-rich water soaks into the remains and the minerals replace the original hard parts. The remains turn to stone. Most fossils form deep underground. They are exposed when the overlying rock wears away or are pushed up to form mountains.

1. What are fossils?

   A pieces of rock

   B remains of plants or animals

   C muscle tissues

   D parts of a bicycle

2. What does the word evidence mean?

   A trace fossils

   B behavior

   C proof

   D true from fossils

3. Where do most fossils form?

 on hills

 in trees

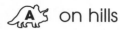 deep underground

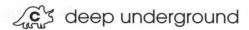 in water

4. What are true from fossils?

 hard animal parts

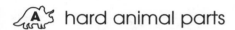 soft animal parts

 plants

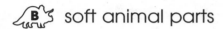 footprint impressions

5. What are trace fossils?

 hard animal parts

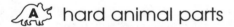 impressions

 bones

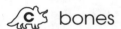 teeth

6. Trace fossils are evidence that a living thing _____.

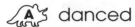 danced

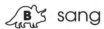 sang

ate

existed

What Do Trace Fossils Look Like?

The pictures below are examples of different kinds of trace fossils. Draw a line from the description of the kind of trace fossil to its picture.

A dinosaur makes footprints in the soft mud. The mud hardens and turns into rock.

The eggs of some dinosaurs have been changed into fossil eggs.

Sometimes the skin of a dinosaur is changed into a fossil.

Carefully study these footprint impressions. Draw a line from the dinosaur to its correct footprints.

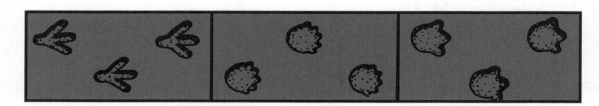

Triceratops   **Megalosaurus**   **Parasaurolophus**

What Do Fossils Tell Us?

It's exciting when a scientist finds a dinosaur fossil. The fossil might be from a dinosaur no one has ever discovered before.

It might take years for scientists to put together most of a dinosaur's bones. The lumps, bumps, and scars on the bones give them clues as to what the dinosaur might have looked like. These marks on the bones show where muscles were attached. By looking at the whole skeleton and the lumps, bumps, and scars on each bone, scientists can come up with a theory about the shape of the dinosaur's body.

The two skeletons below are make-believe dinosaurs that nobody has ever found. Study the skeletons. Use colored pencils, crayons, or markers to draw right over the skeleton to show what these dinosaurs might have looked like. Then, name your dinosaurs.

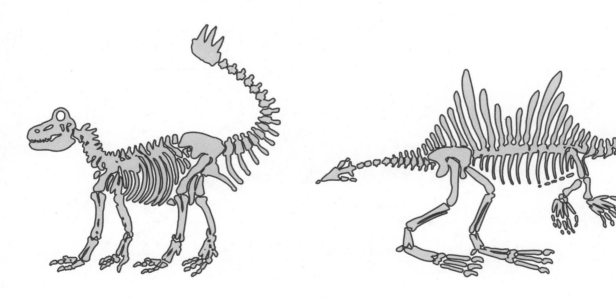

_____   _____

What Are Scientists Who Study Dinosaurs Called?

Scientists who study **fossils** are called **paleontologists**. Dinosaur paleontologists search for dinosaur remains all over the world. When they discover dinosaur fossils, paleontologists make notes about their find and map the area where they made their find. Then they carefully remove the fossils, pack them in plaster jackets, and take them to laboratories for study.

1. Where do paleontologists search for dinosaur fossils?

_____

_____

_____

2. What do paleontologists do when they discover a fossil?

_____

_____

_____

3. Do paleontologists only study dinosaur fossils? If not, what else do they study?

_____

_____

_____

4. Why do you think fossils are wrapped in plaster jackets before they are sent to laboratories?

_____

_____

_____

5. Why do you think it is important for scientists to take notes about their finds?

_____

_____

_____

6. What kind of tools do you think paleontologists use while hunting for fossils?

_____

_____

_____

Where Do Paleontologists Look for Dinosaur Fossils?

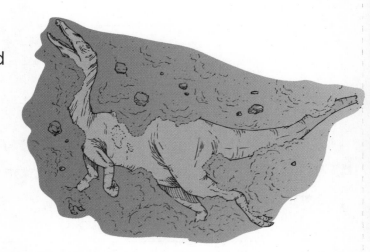

Paleontologists look for dinosaur fossils all over the world. Most fossils are found in **sedimentary rocks**. Sedimentary rocks are made from layers of **sediments**—mud, sand, and gravel—that harden into stone. When dinosaurs died, their remains were sometimes covered with windblown sand or washed into rivers or lakes. If the remains were quickly covered with sediments, the bones were preserved. As the sediments hardened into rock, the bones became fossils.

1. Most fossils are found in _____.

 **A** water

B trees

C leaves

D sedimentary rocks

2. Sedimentary rocks can be made up of any of these sediments except _____.

A mud

B tree bark

C sand

D gravel

3. To have a chance of becoming fossils, dinosaur bodies had to be _____ after they died.

   A cleaned

   B left out in the sun

   C kept warm

   D covered quickly

4. As sediments hardened into rocks, the bones became _____.

   A sedimentary rocks

   B fossils

   C rocks

   D sandstone

5. Some dinosaur remains were washed into _____.

   A rivers or lakes

   B mountains

   C rocks

   D sand

6. Why did bones need to be covered by sediments to become fossils?

   A to keep them out of the way

   B to preserve them

   C to slow the fossil process down

   D so that scientists could find them

To What Group Do Dinosaurs Belong?

Before the 1800s, people who found dinosaur bones and teeth did not know what they were. Little by little, scientists realized that these fossils were different from those of any other group of animals. These animals were somewhat like lizards, a type of reptile, but were generally much bigger. They decided to call this group **Dinosauria**. The name **dinosaur** comes from this word, which means "terrible lizards."

Why do you think "terrible lizards" was chosen for the name of dinosaurs? What do you think paleontologists knew about dinosaurs at this time?

_____

_____

_____

Over the years, paleontologists have been able to learn a lot about dinosaurs and other animals that lived a long time ago.

Why do you think paleontologists and other people continue to look for fossils today?

_____

_____

_____

What Do Paleontoligists Do When They Find a Fossil?

When paleontoligists find fossils they want to study, they make notes about their find, map the area, and carefully dig the fossils out of the ground. The bones are wrapped in plaster so they won't break. Then they are sent to a laboratory. Once there, they are carefully unwrapped. Paleontologists study the fossils to find out what type of animal they belonged to and when it lived.

Sometimes paleontologists find a number of parts to a dinosaur's **skeleton**. The skeleton can be reconstructed, or put together, and shown in a museum.

These pictures show some of the jobs paleontologists do. Number the pictures to show the order of when each job would be completed.

How Do Paleontologists Know How Dinosaurs Moved?

Paleontologists figure out how dinosaurs moved by studying their bones.
Muscle scars on dinosaur bones show where muscles were attached to the bones, and how big they were. Strong bones and larger muscles were needed for running and fighting. Studying **joints**, the places where bones come together, gives scientists an idea of how an animal's body could bend and turn.

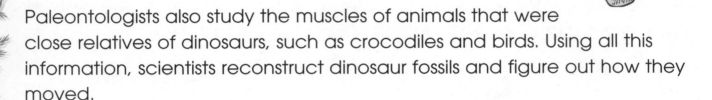

muscle scars

Paleontologists also study the muscles of animals that were close relatives of dinosaurs, such as crocodiles and birds. Using all this information, scientists reconstruct dinosaur fossils and figure out how they moved.

1. Why do scientists study dinosaur bones?

_____

_____

_____

2. What do muscle scars tell paleontologists?

_____

_____

_____

3. Why did dinosaurs need strong bones and larger muscles?

_____

_____

_____

4. Why do scientists study the joints of bone fossils?

_____

_____

_____

5. What kind of modern-day animal muscles do paleontologists study?

_____

_____

_____

6. What do scientists do with all the information they get from studying dinosaur bones and modern-day animals?

_____

_____

_____

What Was Dinosaur Skin Like?

Impressions of dinosaur skin are sometimes preserved in rocks. They show that most dinosaurs probably had tough, scaly, waterproof skin, like other reptiles.

Polacanthus was an armored plant-eater. It had bumpy skin with bony spikes and plates for extra protection. Meat-eaters such as Carnotaurus had smooth scales, like that of a lizard. Some small meat-eaters may have had feathers like birds.

Scientists cannot determine the color of a dinosaur's skin from its fossils. They theorize though, that dinosaurs had various patterns and colors, just like today's reptiles.

1. Impressions of dinosaur skin can be preserved in _____.

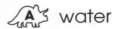 **A** water

B rocks

C trees

D sand

2. The impressions show that most dinosaur scales were like _____.

A bird feathers

B those of other reptiles

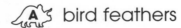 **C** lion fur

D seal skin

3. What kind of dinosaur was Polacanthus?

A an unarmored herbivore

B a carnivore with armor

C a carnivore

D an armored herbivore

4. The skin of a Carnotaurus was _____.

A bumpy

B smooth and scaly

C rough and dry

D orange

5. Scientists think that some small meat-eaters may have had _____.

A armor plates

B spikes

C fur

D feathers

6. Paleontologists theorize that dinosaur skin _____.

A could have been different colors

B was brown

C was green and brown

D was green

What Color Were Dinosaurs?

Some people think that dinosaurs were green and brown. These colors would have allowed the dinosaurs to blend in with the plants and trees around them. Other people think the dinosaurs were very colorful, like some birds and lizards are today. Bright colors sometimes help an animal attract a mate.

Here is a picture of two dinosaurs. What colors do you think these dinosaurs were? Color the picture below how you think the dinosaurs would have looked.

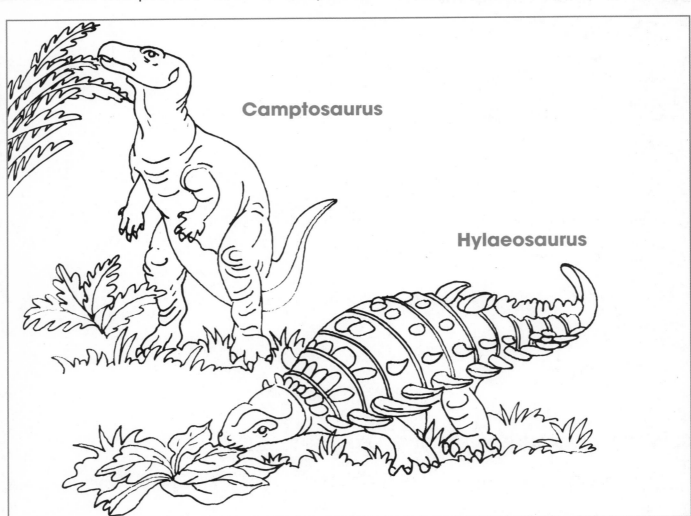

Camptosaurus

Hylaeosaurus

Explain the colors you chose. _____

_____

Word Search Activity

Use the word list to help you find the words about dinosaurs that are hidden in the block below. Some of the words are hidden backward or diagonally.

```
T  S  P  A  L  E  O  E  V  R  E  S  E  R  P  M
R  E  R  M  U  S  C  L  E  S  C  A  R  S  A  U
A  D  R  E  C  O  N  S  T  R  U  C  T  E  L  S
Q  I  S  R  N  I  L  T  E  P  R  B  O  M  E  C
Z  M  C  E  I  M  P  R  E  S  S  I  O  N  O  E
A  E  O  K  V  B  J  A  O  Y  E  R  D  B  N  K
R  N  N  S  K  E  L  E  T  O  N  U  I  Z  T  E
D  T  S  D  P  J  G  E  P  J  W  K  N  A  O  G
I  A  F  I  A  O  D  K  L  O  C  A  O  I  L  A
T  R  A  C  E  F  O  S  S  I  L  S  S  R  O  L
R  Y  I  U  T  K  S  K  F  N  Z  D  A  U  G  F
U  R  S  E  D  I  M  E  N  T  S  A  U  A  I  U
M  O  J  R  S  T  W  L  C  S  M  E  R  S  S  O
R  C  O  E  C  N  E  D  I  V  E  S  I  D  T  M
L  K  M  L  S  R  R  H  Q  T  F  L  A  O  S  A
T  R  U  E  F  O  R  M  F  O  S  S  I  L  S  C
```

WORD LIST

CAMOUFLAGE

DINOSAURIA

EVIDENCE

IMPRESSION

JOINTS

MUSCLE SCARS

PALEONTOLOGISTS

PRESERVE

RECONSTRUCT

SEDIMENTARY ROCK

SEDIMENTS

SKELETON

TERRIBLE LIZARDS

TRACE FOSSILS

TRUE FORM FOSSILS

Were Dinosaurs Warm-blooded or Cold-blooded?

Warm-blooded animals, such as mammals and birds, make enough heat from their body processes to keep their body temperature high. They can be active all the time.

Cold-blooded animals, such as crocodiles and frogs, do not make enough heat from their body processes to keep a high body temperature. They ***absorb***, or draw in, heat from their surroundings to help them become active.

Paleontologists do not agree about whether dinosaurs were warm-blooded or cold-blooded. Some think fast-moving animals like dinosaurs must have been warm-blooded. Others think certain features of dinosaur bones prove they were cold-blooded. Many other scientists say dinosaurs were cold-blooded, but the active lifestyle of small dinosaurs and the huge size of big dinosaurs kept them warm.

I. Describe what makes an animal warm-blooded.

_____

_____

_____

2. Describe what makes an animal cold-blooded.

_____

_____

_____

3. Name some modern-day animals that are warm-blooded.

_____

_____

_____

4. Name some modern-day animals that are cold-blooded.

_____

_____

_____

5. Why do some paleontologists think that dinosaurs were warm-blooded?

_____

_____

_____

6. Why do some paleontologists think that dinosaurs were cold-blooded?

_____

_____

_____

Did Dinosaurs Have Good Eyesight?

Paleontologists study a dinosaur's skull to figure out how big different parts of its brain were. Large **sight areas** in the brain mean that a dinosaur had good eyesight. Leaellynasaura was a plant-eater that had sharp vision, perhaps to help it see in the dark. Velociraptor and Oviraptor also had good vision and may have hunted at night. It is likely that not all dinosaurs had good eyesight.

Some plant-eating dinosaurs probably had a better sense of smell than of sight.

1. What do paleontologists study to figure out how big different parts of a dinosaur's brain were?

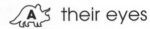 **A** their eyes

 **B** their size

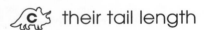 **C** their tail length

 **D** their skulls

2. What is a sight area?

A An area in which everything is viewed.

B A dinosaur's field of vision.

C An area where dinosaurs have been found.

D An area in the brain that controls the sense of sight.

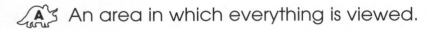

3. A large sight area in a dinosaur's skull meant _____.

A it had bad eyesight

B it had good eyesight

C it had more than two eyes

D it could not see color

4. Some paleontologists believe that Leaellynasaura could _____.

A not see at all

B see only during the day

C see in the dark

D see with only one eye

5. Scientists think that Oviraptor hunted _____.

A only during the day

B at night

C in the water

D from the branches of trees

6. Did all dinosaurs have good eyesight?

A Yes, all dinosaurs had large sight areas.

B No, only carnivores had large sight areas.

C No, only herbivores had good eyesight.

D No, some dinosaurs had a better sense of smell.

Did Dinosaurs Make Sounds?

Skull bones show that many dinosaurs probably made sounds. Young dinosaurs may have squeaked or squealed, and older dinosaurs may have croaked, barked, or roared. The skulls of some duck-billed dinosaurs have fan- or tube-shaped **crests**, or tops. Paleontologists think these crests may have been echo chambers that helped the dinosaurs make sounds. Duckbills may have bellowed to attract mates, like a modern moose would.

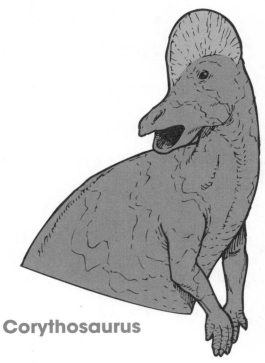

Corythosaurus

1. What part of a dinosaur's remains did scientists use to determine how dinosaurs made sounds?

_____

_____

_____

2. What kinds of sounds might some young dinosaurs have made?

_____

_____

_____

3. What kinds of sounds might some older dinosaurs have made?

_____

_____

_____

4. Paleontologists think that the crests on duck-billed dinosaurs may have been used as what?

_____

_____

_____

5. Why do scientists think that duckbills made sounds?

_____

_____

_____

6. Name some modern-day animals that make sounds to attract mates.

_____

_____

_____

How Smart Were Dinosaurs?

To figure out how smart a dinosaur was, paleontologists compare the size of its brain to the size of its body. Scientists think dinosaurs that had large brains compared to their bodies were smart. Small, nimble meat-eaters, such as Troödon and Oviraptor, had big brains. Both guarded their eggs, and paleontologists think they were among the smartest dinosaurs. Giant long-necks, such as Brachiosaurus, had rather small brains. They probably walked slowly and performed only simple activities.

Troödon

1. To figure out how smart a dinosaur was paleontologists compare the size of its brain to the size of its _____.

   Ⓐ head

   Ⓑ feet

   Ⓒ tail

   Ⓓ body

2. The larger the size of a dinosaur's brain compared to the size of its body meant that _____.

   Ⓐ the dinosaur was smarter than other dinosaurs

   Ⓑ the dinosaur could only walk slowly

   Ⓒ the dinosaur performed only simple activities

   Ⓓ the dinosaur could not slow down

3. Small, nimble carnivores had _____.

    A small brains

    B large brains

    C average-sized brains

    D no brains

4. Scientists think that Troödon and Oviraptor did all of these except _____.

    A guard their eggs

    B eat plants

    C run quickly and nimbly

    D hunt other dinosaurs

5. To what group of dinosaurs does Brachiosaurus belong?

    A long-necks

    B duckbills

    C curved-claws

    D parrot-beaked

6. Which sentence does not describe what paleontologists believe about long-necks?

    A They walked slowly.

    B They had big brains.

    C They had small brains.

    D They performed only simple tasks.

Am I Smart?

Which of the dinosaurs below do you think would have been "smart" dinosaurs? Circle the correct pictures.

Pentaceratops

Podokesaurus

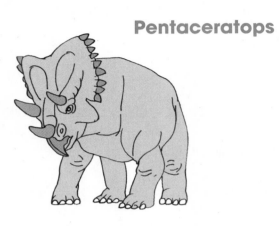

Corythosaurus

Tarbosaurus

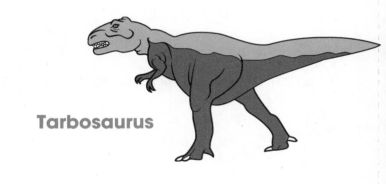

Parksosaurus

Saltopus

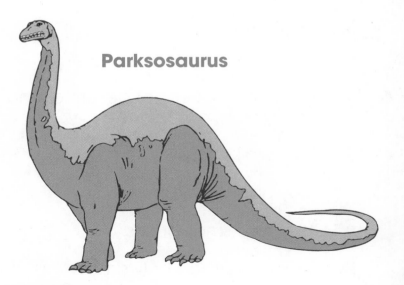

Crossword Activity

Read the clues about dinosaurs. Then, complete the puzzle using the word list below.

DOWN

1. Animals whose bodies do not produce enough heat to keep them warm are called _____.

3. Animals that make enough body heat to keep their body temperatures high are called _____.

5. If a dinosaur had large _____, then it was believe to have had excellent sight.

ACROSS

2. Cold-blooded animals _____ heat from their surroundings.

4. Scientists think that _____ may have bellowed to attract mates.

6. Some duck-billed dinosaurs had _____ on the tops of their heads.

WORD LIST

COLD-BLOODED

SIGHT AREAS

WARM-BLOODED

CRESTS

ABSORB

DUCKBILLS

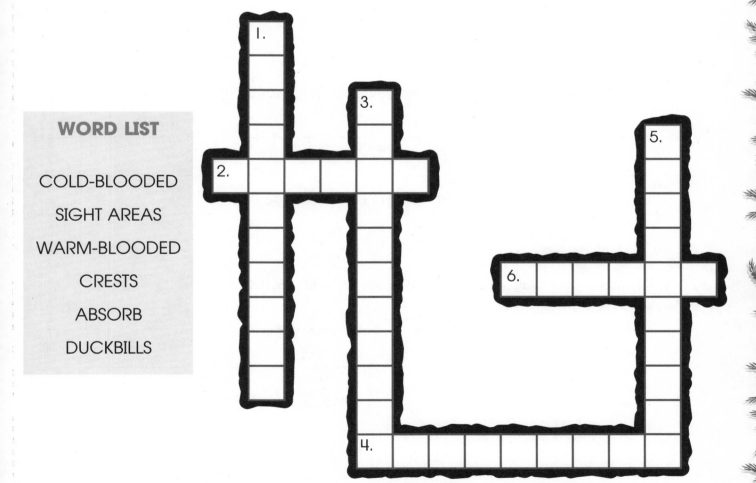

What Other Kinds of Animals Lived When Dinosaurs Lived?

Many kinds of animals were alive during the Age of Reptiles—the time when dinosaurs lived. The oceans were filled with sponges, jellyfish, crabs, shrimp, snails, oysters, corals, sea stars, sea urchins, squid, and fish. The seas also contained swimming reptiles, like **pliosaurs**, **plesiosaurs**, and **ichthyosaurs**. The land provided homes for insects, spiders, centipedes, salamander-like amphibians, crocodiles, and turtles. Flying reptiles, like **pterosaurs**, filled the air. Lizards, snakes, small mammals, and birds also appeared during this time.

Enchodus

Kuehneosaurus

I. What kinds of animals lived in the oceans and seas when dinosaurs lived?

_____

_____

_____

2. What kinds of animals lived on land when dinosaurs lived?

_____

_____

_____

3. What kinds of flying animals lived when dinosaurs lived?

_____

_____

_____

4. Do you think any of these different kinds of animals are alive today? If so, name them.

_____

_____

_____

5. What kinds of animals first appeared during the Mesozoic Era?

_____

_____

_____

6. What kind of defense did these animals have against the dinosaurs?

_____

_____

_____

What Were Plesiosaurs?

Plesiosaurs were ocean-dwelling reptiles that lived during the Age of Reptiles. They had flippers for swimming and sharp teeth for eating sea creatures. Plesiosaurs ranged in size from about 8 feet to 46 feet—about the length of three cars. Some plesiosaurs had long necks and tiny heads. Others had short necks and big heads. Scientists do not know if plesiosaurs laid eggs on the beach, like sea turtles, or gave birth to live young, like most sharks.

Plesiosaurus

1. What are plesiosaurs?

A. ocean-dwelling sea hags

B. land-dwelling reptiles

C. ocean-dwelling reptiles

D. mountain-dwelling bears

2. When did plesiosaurs live?

A. Mesozoic Era

B. Permian Era

C. Cenozoic Era

D. Dinosaur Era

3. How did plesiosaurs swim?

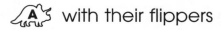 with their flippers

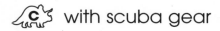 with a partner

 with scuba gear

 with a surf board

4. Plesiosaurs could be as long as _____.

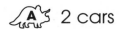 2 cars

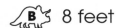 8 feet

 46 feet

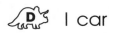 I car

5. How do scientists think plesiosaurs reproduced?

A They laid eggs.

B They gave birth.

C They cloned themselves.

D Scientists are unsure.

6. Which statement about plesiosaurs is correct?

A They all had long necks.

B They all laid their eggs on the beach.

C Some were short, and some were long.

D They gave birth to live young in the sea.

What Did Water-dwelling Creatures Look Like?

To find out what the three prehistoric sea creatures below looked like, follow the correct path. The correct path will also give you some interesting facts to help you answer the questions at the bottom of the page.

Plesiosaurs   **Ichthyosaurs**   **Pliosaurs**

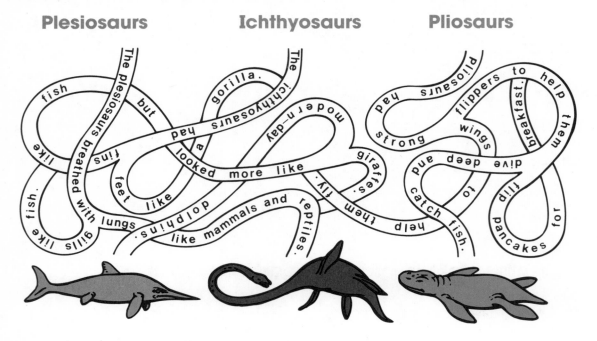

Circle true (T) or false (F).

T   F   Plesiosaurs breathed with gills.

T   F   Ichthyosaurs looked very much like giant dolphins.

T   F   Most prehistoric sea creatures laid eggs.

T   F   Reptiles breathe air with their lungs.

T   F   Pliosaurs were meat-eating sea creatures.

T   F   Ichthyosaurs were big fish.

What Do Scientists Know About Plesiosaurus?

Plesiosaurus was about 10 feet long. It was not a dinosaur, but it did live during the same time period. Plesiosaurus lived in the sea, and it had flippers to help it move through the water. Plesiosaurus used its long, snake-like neck to search for fish and other small animals in the sea.

Fill in the blanks. The first one is done for you.

1. Scientists learned about Plesiosaurus by studying __f__ __o__ __s__ __s__ __i__ __l__ remains.

2. Plesiosaurus was about _____ _____ _____ feet long.

3. Plesiosaurus was not a _____ _____ _____ _____ _____ _____ _____ _____.

4. It lived in the _____ _____ _____.

5. Plesiosaurus had _____ _____ _____ _____ _____ _____ _____ instead of legs.

6. It had a _____ _____ _____ _____ neck.

7. It ate _____ _____ _____ _____.

What Were Pterosaurs?

Pterosaurs were featherless, flying reptiles that lived during the Age of Reptiles. Though distantly related to dinosaurs, pterosaurs were not dinosaurs. Pterosaurs ranged from robin-sized creatures to large animals with wingspans of 35 feet. The leathery wings of pterosaurs extended back from rods made of arm and finger bones. Scientists believed that pterosaurs used all four limbs to walk. Pterosaurs probably ate fish and small animals.

Pteranodon

I. Describe the features of pterosaurs.

_____

_____

_____

2. What are some of the differences between pterosaurs and dinosaurs?

_____

_____

_____

3. How did pterosaurs move when they were on the ground?

_____

_____

_____

4. What did pterosaurs eat?

_____

_____

_____

5. How do you think pterosaurs were able to catch their prey?

_____

_____

_____

6. What modern-day animals are similar to pterosaurs?

_____

_____

_____

What Was Archaeopteryx?

Archaeopteryx is the oldest known bird. It lived about 150 million years ago, during the Age of Reptiles. Archaeopteryx was about the size of a modern-day crow and had both bird and dinosaur features. Like a bird, it had wings, feathers, and a beak. Like a dinosaur, it had teeth and a bony tail. Its skeleton was also similar to those of some small dinosaurs. Most paleontologists think Archaeopteryx and other birds developed from a dinosaur ancestor and that modern birds are living dinosaurs.

Archaeopteryx

1. Archaeopteryx is the oldest known _____.

 **A** dinosaur

B animal

C bird

D fish

2. It lived about _____ years ago.

A 75 million

B 256 million

C 14 million

D 150 million

3. How big was an Archaeopteryx?

A about the size of a modern-day crow

B about the size of a modern-day eagle

C about the size of a modern-day chicken

D about the size of a modern-day vulture

4. Archaeopteryx had all of these features in common with a bird except
_____.

A wings

B teeth

C feathers

D a beak

5. Archaeopteryx had all of these features in common with a dinosaur
except _____.

A teeth

B wings

C a bony tail

D a similar skeleton to some small dinosaurs

6. Most paleontologists believe that _____.

A modern birds are ancestors of dinosaurs

B dinosaurs developed from ancient birds

C reptiles and birds are the same

D Archaeopteryx is a living bird

Were There Any People When Dinosaurs Lived?

Dinosaurs lived long before people appeared on earth. However, the theory of evolution suggests that distant ancestors of human beings, the first **primates**, a kind of mammal, appeared at the end of the dinosaur age. The first primates were probably similar to tree shrews—squirrel-sized animals with pointed noses, long tails, and sharp claws.

Most scientists think that over many millions of years, these early primates **evolved**, or developed, into advanced primates— monkeys, then apes, then humans. Scientists theorize that the first human beings appeared about 5 million years ago.

evolution of primates

I. Did human beings live during the time of the dinosaurs?

_____

_____

_____

2. What is a primate?

_____

_____

_____

3. Describe the first primates.

_____

_____

_____

4. How did the first primates evolve into human beings?

_____

_____

_____

5. Did the early primates evolve quickly or slowly? How do you know?

_____

_____

_____

6. When did the first human beings appear on earth?

_____

_____

_____

Why Did Dinosaurs Disappear?

Nobody knows exactly why dinosaurs became **extinct**, or died out. Below are a few theories that scientists have suggested. One or more of these events may have caused the extinction of the dinosaurs.

Asteroid Crash Theory: An asteroid, a large rocky object from space, smashed into the earth. The collision created a cloud of dust that surrounded the planet and blocked the sun. The earth grew cold, and most plants died. The dinosaurs froze or died from starvation.

Volcano Theory: Volcanic eruptions over millions of years produced clouds of dust that surrounded the earth. The dust blocked the sun. The planet grew cold, and most plants died. The dinosaurs froze and died from starvation.

Climate Theory: Continental movements and shrinking oceans broke up the areas where dinosaurs lived and made the climate cooler. The dinosaurs froze to death.

1. What does extinct mean?

 **A** to die out

B to reappear

C to think of a theory

D to freeze

2. What caused the dinosaurs to become extinct?

A An asteroid crashed into the earth.

B Volcanic eruptions all over the world occurred over millions of years.

C No one knows exactly what happened.

D The earth's climate changed.

3. The Asteroid Crash Theory suggests that _____.

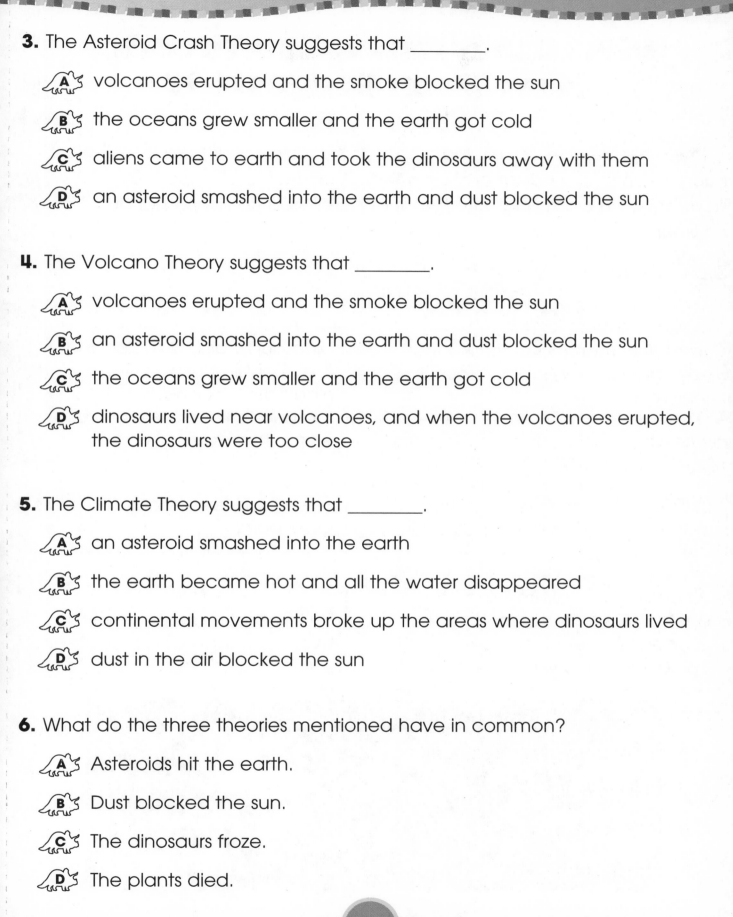

A volcanoes erupted and the smoke blocked the sun

B the oceans grew smaller and the earth got cold

C aliens came to earth and took the dinosaurs away with them

D an asteroid smashed into the earth and dust blocked the sun

4. The Volcano Theory suggests that _____.

A volcanoes erupted and the smoke blocked the sun

B an asteroid smashed into the earth and dust blocked the sun

C the oceans grew smaller and the earth got cold

D dinosaurs lived near volcanoes, and when the volcanoes erupted, the dinosaurs were too close

5. The Climate Theory suggests that _____.

A an asteroid smashed into the earth

B the earth became hot and all the water disappeared

C continental movements broke up the areas where dinosaurs lived

D dust in the air blocked the sun

6. What do the three theories mentioned have in common?

A Asteroids hit the earth.

B Dust blocked the sun.

C The dinosaurs froze.

D The plants died.

What Other Extinction Theories Have Been Suggested?

A few other theories of why the dinosaurs became extinct are listed below. Each theory has a **cause** and an **effect**. A cause is a change that happened on earth and an effect is what resulted from the change on earth.

Draw a line from each cause to its effect.

Cause

Small, fast mammals that liked to eat eggs quickly spread around the world.

New kinds of flowering plants started to grow on the earth. These plants had poison in them that the dinosaurs could not taste.

When dinosaurs were living, the earth was warm all year long. Suddenly the earth became cooler with cold winter months.

Effect

Dinosaurs were cold-blooded. They couldn't find places to hibernate. They had no fur or feathers to keep themselves warm. They froze to death.

Fewer and fewer baby dinosaurs were born.

The dinosaurs ate poison without even knowing it and they died.

What Do You Think Happened to the Dinosaurs?

No one knows for sure why the dinosaurs died out, but after surviving for 150 million years or more, the dinosaurs were gone. Can you think of some reasons that the dinosaurs disappeared? Write your own theory on the lines below.

_____

_____

_____

_____

_____

_____

_____

_____

_____

_____

_____

_____

Are New Kinds of Dinosaurs Still Being Found?

Paleontologists are finding new kinds of dinosaurs all the time. Every year, they go on **dinosaur digs**, or fossil hunts, in areas that contain sedimentary rocks. Dinosaur digs have been done in Africa, Antarctica, Argentina, Canada, China, Madagascar, Mongolia, and the United States. Scientists think there are hundreds of kinds of dinosaurs still to be discovered.

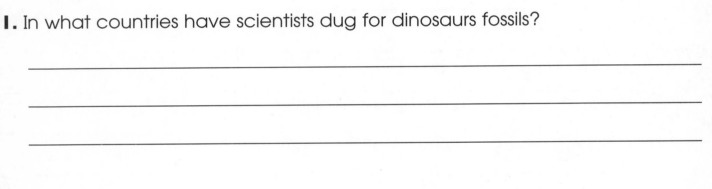

1. In what countries have scientists dug for dinosaurs fossils?

_____

_____

_____

2. What areas do paleontologists look for fossils? Why do they look there?

_____

_____

_____

3. Why do scientists think that there are still more kinds of dinosaurs to be found?

_____

_____

_____

4. Why is a fossil hunt called a dinosaur dig?

_____

_____

_____

5. Besides fossils, what do you think scientists find during a dinosaur dig?

_____

_____

_____

6. If you could go on a fossil hunt in one of the countries mentioned above, which one would you go to? Why?

_____

_____

_____

What Are Some Living Relatives of Dinosaurs?

All living reptiles, such as turtles, crocodiles, snakes, and lizards, are distantly related to dinosaurs. The closest relatives of dinosaurs, though, are birds. In fact, most paleontologists believe that birds are living dinosaurs.

In China, paleontologists discovered the fossils of dinosaurs that had feathers but could not fly, such as Caudipteryx. Scientists also discovered the fossils of an ancient bird that looked like a small dinosaur. They think some small dinosaurs developed wings and the ability to fly and then became birds.

Caudipteryx

1. What are the closest living relatives to dinosaurs?

 **A** reptiles

B humans

C ants

D birds

2. Name the dinosaur that had feathers but could not fly.

A Caudipteryx

B Plesiosaurus

C primates

D Archaeopteryx

3. Where was the dinosaur that had feathers but could not fly found?

    A North America

    B China

    C Africa

    D Japan

4. Paleontologists believe that birds are _____.

    A flying cats

    B living dolls

    C swimming sharks

    D living dinosaurs

5. Some small dinosaurs may have developed _____ and then became birds.

    A wings

    B beaks

    C feathers

    D eggs

6. How do scientists figure out which animals are closely related to each other and which are not?

    A by comparing weight

    B by comparing leg length

    C by comparing appearance

    D by comparing eye color

Keeping Up With the Dinosaurs

Read the dinosaur facts below. Then, write true (T) or false (F) in the blanks before the sentences at the bottom of the page.

Paleontologists believe that the first dinosaurs evolved on earth about 245 million years ago and became extinct about 65 million years ago. All dinosaurs were land-living creatures. The gigantic prehistoric sea creatures, such as ichthyosaurs and plesiosaurs, were not really dinosaurs. Pterosaurs were not really dinosaurs either. They were flying reptiles that looked like lizards with wings.

The word dinosaur means "terrible lizard," but dinosaurs were not lizards. Modern science now links dinosaurs to birds. Today's birds are thought to be the closest relatives to the dinosaurs. Crocodiles are also thought to be more distant relatives of the dinosaurs. Scientists believe all animals and plants living on earth today are descendants of creatures that lived when dinosaurs roamed the earth.

True (T) or false (F)?

1. _____ The first dinosaurs evolved on earth about 65 million years ago.

2. _____ Ichthyosaurs were dinosaurs.

3. _____ Dinosaurs were not lizards.

4. _____ Scientists believe birds are related to dinosaurs.

5. _____ Some dinosaurs were flying reptiles.

A Dinosaur Tale

Study the prehistoric animals pictured below. Then, complete each category with words that you associate with these animals. A few examples are already written under each category. Use the words to compose a poem or short story about these animals.

Nouns	Verbs	Adjectives
tail	walk	huge
teeth	run	spiked
head	eat	sharp

Title: _____

_____

_____

_____

_____

_____

_____

THE MESOZOIC ERA
245–65 Million Years Ago

The **Mesozoic Era** is known as the Age of the Reptiles. This time period occurred 245 million to 65 million years ago when dinosaurs and other prehistoric creatures lived. At the beginning of this period, scientists think that the earth had only one continent, a super-continent called Pangaea. Toward the middle of this era, Pangaea began to break apart. It eventually formed the seven continents of our world.

The Mesozoic Era is divided into three periods—the Triassic, the Jurassic, and the Cretaceous Periods. The Triassic Period began 245 million years ago and ended 208 million years ago. It was hot and dry. During this time, small, fast dinosaurs and nocturnal mammals evolved, and ichthyosaurs swam in the seas. Ferns and plants grew by lakes and rivers, and palm-like trees grew in the drier regions.

The Jurassic Period was next, lasting from 208 million years ago to 144 million years ago. Pangaea began to split up during this time. The Atlantic Ocean formed between the two plates. The climate became more humid and plants flourished. Dinosaurs were now the dominant animals, but small mammals and the first birds were alive at this time.

The Cretaceous Period lasted from 144 million years ago to 65 million years ago. Pangaea had split up, and the earth looked similar to what it looks like today. The climate had begun to cool. Many different types of animals and plants had developed during this time as well. At the end of this period, all of the dinosaurs and many other kinds of animals died out.

THE TRIASSIC PERIOD

245–208 Million Years Ago

At the beginning of this time period, the earth contained one landmass called Pangaea. The climate was warm and dry. Ferns and other plants grew along the banks of lakes and rivers. Frogs, early crocodiles, and tortoises inhabited these bodies of water. In the drier regions, palm-like trees and tall evergreens like Norfolk pines grew.

The first small mammals appeared in the Triassic Period. They were shrew-like animals.

Dinosaurs first appeared during the Triassic Period. Two examples of Triassic dinosaurs are Coelophysis, a small, lightweight insect- and meat-eater that was about ten feet long, and Thecodontosaurus, a seven-foot long plant-eater. Reptiles of the time include the first flying pterosaurs and swimming ichthyosaurs.

Triassic Dinosaurs

The chart below includes facts about a few dinosaurs that lived during the Triassic Period.

Dinosaur	Name Means	Description	Length	Interesting Fact
Coelophysis	Hollow Form	two-legged carnivore	about 10 feet	had hollow bones
Dinosaurus	Terrifying Lizard	two-legged herbivore	about 20 feet	may be the same as Plateosaurus
Eoraptor	Dawn Thief	two-legged carnivore	about 3 feet	one of the earliest known dinosaurs
Massospondylus	Massive Vertibra	four-legged herbivore	about 13 feet	also lived during the early Jurassic Period
Plateosaurus	Flat Lizard	four-legged herbivore	about 20-26 feet	may have been able to use its hands for grasping
Riojasaurus	La Rioja Lizard	four-legged herbivore	about 30-36 feet	probably could not run
Saltopus	Leaping Foot	two-legged carnivore	about 2 feet	probably ate mainly insects
Thecodontosaurus	Socket-toothed Lizard	two-legged herbivore	about 7 feet	had unusual teeth in distinct sockets

Use the information from the previous page to answer the following questions.

1. The name Coelophysis means "hollow form" because it had

_____ bones.

2. A two-legged herbivore that may have been able to use its hands for

grasping was named _____.

3. "Socket-toothed Lizard" had _____ teeth in distinct sockets.

4. Eoraptor was one of the _____ known dinosaurs.

5. _____ probably could not run.

6. Saltopus was only about two feet long and probably ate mainly

_____.

7. Dinosaurus's name means _____.

8. _____, whose name means "Massive Vertibra," also lived during the early Jurassic Period.

Coelophysis

Coelophysis was a small, slender dinosaur that weighed only about 60 or 70 pounds. This little dinosaur was a meat-eater, and it had sharp teeth and a long jaw. It was also a fast runner. Coelophysis lived in **herds**, or family groups.

Connect the letters in alphabetical order to find a picture of Coelophysis. Then, color the picture any way you like.

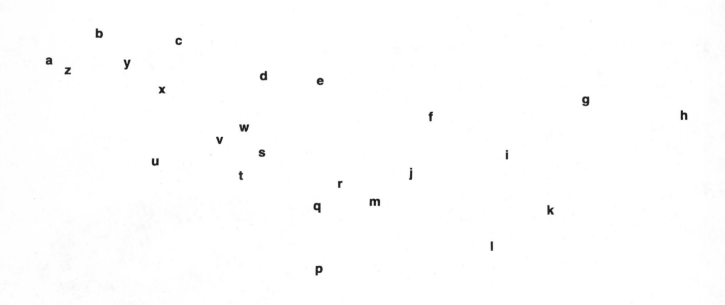

Plateosaurus

Plateosaurus was a large herbivore that lived during the late Triassic Period. It weighed about 1,500 pounds and was 20–26 feet long. It was one of the early long-necked dinosaurs and probably stood up on its back legs to reach leaves in the trees. It probably ate small stones as well to help grind food in its stomach. Plateosaurus had short claws on its front legs that did not provide much defense from meat-eaters, so it probably ran away from predators rather than trying to attack them. Plateosaurus fossils have been found in Europe.

Use the passage above to answer the questions below.

1. Plateosaurus lived during the _____ Period.

2. It probably stood on its _____ legs to reach leaves in the trees.

3. The _____ in its stomach helped grind up its food.

4. Plateosaurus only had small _____ on its front legs to use for defense.

5. Its fossils have been found in

_____ .

Saltopus

Very little is known about Saltopus, one of the earliest dinosaurs that lived during the late Triassic Period. It was a small carnivore, weighing about 2 pounds and was only about 2 feet long. It probably ate insects. Like Coelophysis, Saltopus had hollow bones, which allowed it to be a fast runner. Its jaw was lined with many sharp teeth. Saltopus had small claws on its hands. Saltopus's fossils have been found in Scotland.

Use the passage above to answer the questions below.

1. Saltopus was a small _____, and probably ate insects.

2. It only weighted about _____ pounds.

3. Like Coelophysis, Saltopus also had _____ bones.

4. It was also a _____ runner.

5. Saltopus's jaw was lined with _____ teeth.

Name That Dinosaur!

Complete the puzzle below by writing a dinosaur's name across each letter. Remember that the name you choose must contain that letter. The first one has been done for you. If you need help, use the Word Bank at the bottom of the page.

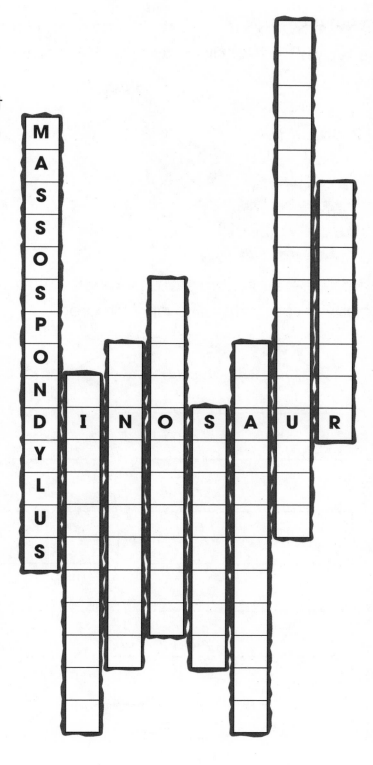

Word Bank

Coelophysis

Dinosaurus

Eoraptor

Plateosaurus

Riojasaurus

Saltopus

Thecodontosaurus

Dinosaur Diagram

A Venn diagram can be used to compare things. First, look at the picture to notice ways the two dinosaurs are the same. Then, look for how they are different.

Plateosaurus

Coelophysis

Complete the Venn diagram below by writing more ways Plateosaurus and Coelophysis are both alike and different.

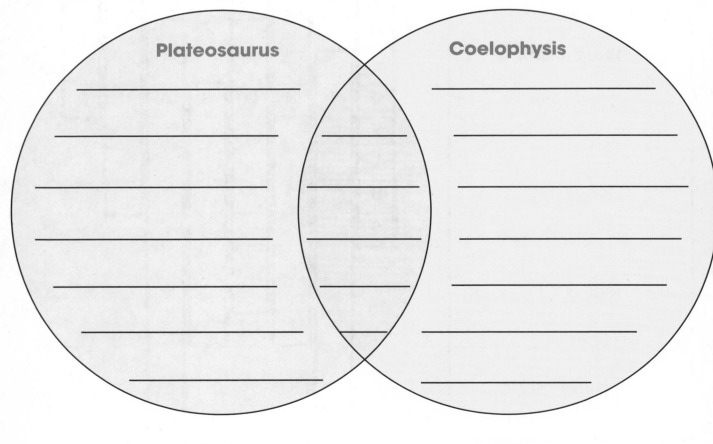

Different   **Same**   **Different**

Who Am I?

Read the 16 clues below about a certain dinosaur. Use a science book or other resource materials and your own logical thinking to guess the name of the dinosaur. When you are finished, write your own clues about another dinosaur. Give it to someone else to see if he or she can guess the answer.

I am a dinosaur.

1. My name means "La Rioja Lizard."
2. I had a small head.
3. I had spoon-shaped teeth.
4. I ate plants.
5. I walked on all four legs.
6. I was 30–36 feet long.
7. I had a bulky body.
8. I lived during the Triassic Period.
9. I had claws on my feet.
10. My fossils were found in Argentina.
11. I was a Saurischian.
12. I had a long neck.
13. I probably could not run.
14. My backbone was hollow.
15. I had a long tail.
16. I was named by José F. Bonaparte in 1969.

I am _____

I am a dinosaur.

_____   _____

_____   _____

_____   _____

_____   _____

_____   _____

_____   _____

_____   _____

I am _____

The Triassic World

Draw a picture of your favorite dinosaur from the Triassic Period in the picture below. Then, color the picture.

THE JURASSIC PERIOD

208–146 Million Years Ago

During the Jurassic Period, Pangea began to break apart. The Atlantic Ocean was beginning to form between the two landmasses as they separated. Molten rock from volcanic eruptions formed mountains. The climate, although still warm, was becoming more humid, and plants flourished. Small, palm-like plants grew thickly along lakes and rivers. A variety of dinosaurs—such as Apatosaurus, Brachiosaurus, and Stegosaurus—lived on the plentiful plant life. Carnivorous dinosaurs of the Jurassic period included Allosaurus, Compsognathus, and Megalosaurus.

Other animals lived with the dominant dinosaurs. The only mammals were very small animals that could climb or burrow or nocturnal animals that could escape the dinosaur predators. Early crocodiles lived in the lakes. The first bird, known as Archaeopteryx, appeared in the sky along with insects. Plesiosaurs joined ichthyosaurs in the seas.

Jurassic Dinosaurs

The chart below includes facts about a few dinosaurs that lived during the Jurassic Period.

Dinosaur	Name Means	Description	Length	Interesting Fact
Apatosaurus	Deceptive Lizard	four-legged herbivore	about 70-90 feet	used to be called Brontosaurus
Barosaurus	Heavy Lizard	four-legged herbivore	about 66-88 feet	thigh bone was 8 feet long
Camarasaurus	Chambered Lizard	four-legged herbivore	about 25-65 feet	had holes in its vertebrae that helped decrease its weight
Compsognathus	Pretty Jaw	two-legged carnivore	about 2-4 feet	the smallest dinosaur ever found
Dacentrurus	Very Sharp Point Tail	four-legged herbivore	about 15 feet	had two rows of spikes running along its back and tail
Diplodocus	Double-beamed	four-legged herbivore	about 90 feet	tail was about 45 feet long
Stegosaurus	Roofed Lizard	four-legged herbivore	about 26-30 feet	brain was the size of a walnut
Supersaurus	Super Lizard	four-legged herbivore	about 138 feet	one of the longest land animals that ever lived

Use the information from the previous page to answer the following questions.

1. _____ had two rows of spikes running along its back and tail.

2. Camarasaurus was named because it had holes in its vertebrae, and its name means _____.

3. Supersaurus was one of the longest _____ animals that ever lived.

4. _____ had a thigh bone that was eight feet long, taller than a human being.

5. Compsognathus was one of the _____ dinosaurs ever found.

6. _____ was another name for Apatosaurus.

7. Stegosaurus had a brain the size of a _____.

8. Diplodocus's name means _____.

Apatosaurus

Apatosaurus was a very large dinosaur that walked on four feet. It was about 70 feet long! It had a long neck, which allowed it to munch on leaves from tall trees. It also had a long tail. This dinosaur had very strong bones to support its weight. Apatosaurus was covered with tough, leathery skin.

Create a rhyme about Apatosaurus. Fill in each blank below using the information given above.

Its neck was long.

Its bones were ___ ___ ___ ___ ___ ___.

It reached with ease

To the tops of ___ ___ ___ ___ ___.

Its skin was ___ ___ ___ ___ ___.

And that's enough!

Barosaurus

Barosaurus was a huge four-legged herbivore from the Jurassic time period. Barosaurus had a small head at the end of its long neck. A long tail kept the dinosaur balanced. Though it had no claws to defend itself, its enormous size provided protection from carnivores.

Camarasaurus

Camarasaurus was a fairly large four-legged plant-eater. It had a long neck and a very strong but short tail.

Carefully copy the lines in each numbered box into the square on the grid that has the same number. Then, color the finished drawing any way you like.

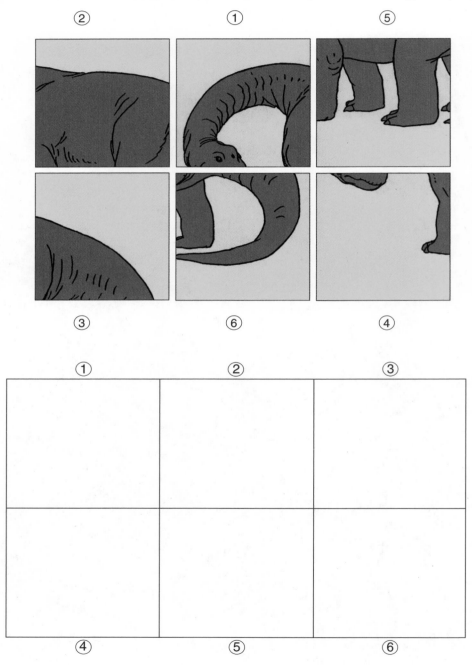

Compsognathus

Compsognathus was a tiny dinosaur that was no bigger than a chicken. Because it weighed about 5 pounds, Compsognathus was probably quick and light on its feet. It could chase down insects and other small animals, then use its sharp teeth and claws.

There are six of these tiny dinosaurs hiding in the picture below. Can you find them all? Circle each one.

Dacentrurus

Dacentrurus was a fairly small dinosaur. It was only 15 feet long, and it weighed about 1 ton. It had two rows of spikes on its back and tail. Dacentrurus walked on all four feet. It was a plant-eater.

How many different words can you make using the letters in the name Dacentrurus?

DACENTRURUS

_____   _____

_____   _____

_____   _____

Now use each of these words in a sentence. _____

_____

Diplodocus

Diplodocus was one of the longest dinosaurs. It was 85 to 100 feet long. Diplodocus had a very long neck and a small head. Its tail was about 45 feet long! Diplodocus probably swayed its tail back and forth to keep other dinosaurs away.

Connect the letters in alphabetical order to make a picture of Diplodocus. Then, color the picture any way you like.

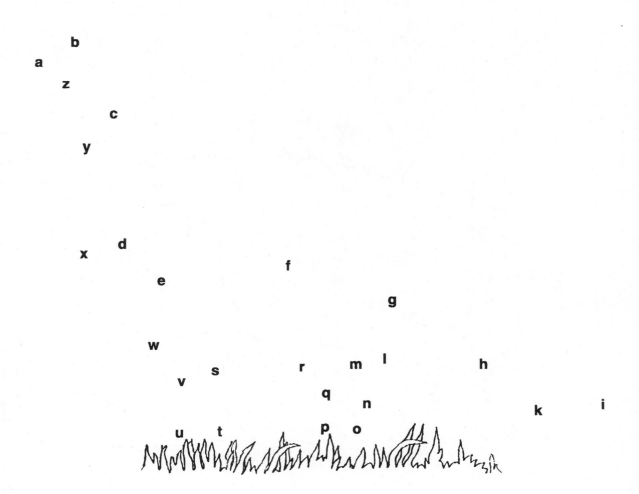

Stegosaurus

Stegosaurus had large bony plates on its neck, back, and tail. Scientists are not sure why the dinosaur had these plates. Perhaps the plates protected Stegosaurus, or maybe they helped it warm up and cool down.

Stegosaurus was about 25 feet long and weighed over 3 tons. It had a very small head and brain. Stegosaurus walked with its head close to the ground because its front legs were shorter than its back legs. Stegosaurus had sharp spikes on the end of its tail.

Color the Stegosaurus plates purple. Color the spikes red. Color the rest of the dinosaur any way you like.

Use the information from the previous page to complete each sentence below.

Stegosaurus had a small ___ ___ ◯ ___ .

Stegosaurus had sharp ___ ◯ ___ ___ ___ ___ on the end of its tail.

Stegosaurus was about 25 ___ ___ ___ ◯ long.

Stegosaurus weighed over 3 ___ ___ ___ ◯ .

Stegosaurus had bony ___ ◯ ___ ___ ___ ___ on its back.

Its head was close to the ___ ___ ___ ___ ◯ ___ .

Unscramble the letters in the circles to find out what Stegosaurus liked to eat.

Stegosaurus ate ___ ___ ___ ___ ___ ___ .

Supersaurus

Supersaurus was one of the longest animals ever discovered. It had a long tail and neck and ate plants. Due to its size—it could weight up to 54 tons—Supersaurus probably spent most of its time eating. It did not chew its food, but it would swallow whole leaves, and then the gastroliths in its stomach would grind up the leaves. Supersaurus probably traveled in herds when an area of its food source was cleared. Supersaurus did not have claws for protection, but its size and the fact that it traveled in herds protected it from predators. Supersaurus fossils have been found in North America.

Use the passage above to answer the questions below.

1. Supersaurus had a long _____ and

_____.

2. They did not _____ their food but swallowed it whole.

3. _____ in their stomachs would break down the food.

4. Supersaurus most likely traveled in _____.

5. Supersaurus fossils have been found in _____.

Dinosaur Diagram

A Venn diagram can be used to compare things. First, look at the pictures to notice ways the two dinosaurs are the same. Then, look for how they are different.

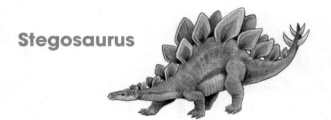

Stegosaurus

Compsognathus

Complete the Venn diagram below by writing ways Compsognathus and Stegosaurus are both alike and different.

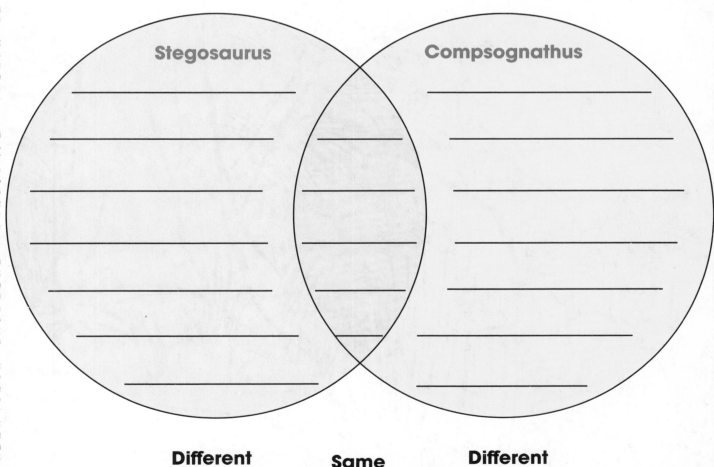

Stegosaurus   **Compsognathus**

Different   **Same**   **Different**

The Jurassic World

Draw a picture of your favorite dinosaur from the Jurassic Period in the picture below. Then, color the picture.

THE CRETACEOUS PERIOD

146 – 65 Million Years Ago

This final period of the Age of Reptiles lasted the longest. The shape and position of the continents more closely resembled those of the continents today. The earth was changing through the formation of mountains, and erupting volcanoes under the Atlantic Ocean formed the spreading sea floor.

The cooling climate changed the nature of the plant life. Heartier plant species with tough leaves were able to survive cool winters. Flowering plants also became plentiful. There were almost as many oak, maple, and walnut trees as there were conifers.

Dinosaurs capable of chewing the new plant life, such as Iguanodon and Triceratops, became more abundant. This was also the age of the powerful, meat-eating Tyrannosaurus. Other animals included early ancestors of bees, frogs, gulls, possums, salamanders, snakes, and turtles.

At the end of the Cretaceous Period, all of the dinosaurs and many of the other animal species had died out. Scientists are still making hypotheses on what happened to cause such a mass extinction.

Cretaceous Dinosaurs

The chart below includes facts about a few dinosaurs that lived during the Cretaceous Period.

Dinosaur	Name Means	Description	Length	Interesting Fact
Ankylosaurus	Fused Lizard	four-legged herbivore	25 – 35 feet	It had an armored and spiked back, club-like tail, and huge horns behind its head.
Corythosaurus	Helmet Lizard	two-legged herbivore	30 – 35 feet	It had a flat, bony crest on its head that looked like a helmet.
Gallimimus	Rooster Mimic	two-legged omnivore (ate both meat and plants)	13 – 20 feet	It used its tail for balance when running.
Ingenia	She-camel	two-legged carnivore	about 4 feet	It protected its eggs while in the nest.
Maiasaura	Good Mother Lizard	four-legged herbivore	about 30 feet	The first dinosaur fossils to be found alongside its fossilized eggs and nest.
Pachycephalosaurus	Thick-headed Lizard	two-legged herbivore	about 15 feet	It probably ran away from danger before using its head for defense.
Parasaurolophus	Beside Saurolophus	two-legged herbivore	about 40 feet	Its long crest was probably used to make a loud sound.
Pentaceratops	Five-horned Face	four-legged herbivore	about 30 feet	It had the largest known skull of a land animal.
Saltasaurus	Salta Lizard	four-legged herbivore	about 40 feet	It had armored plates that may have had spikes for protection.
Troödon	Wounding Tooth	two-legged carnivore	about 6 – 12 feet	It may have been the smartest dinosaur.
Tyrannosaurus rex	Tyrant Lizard King	two-legged carnivore	about 40 feet	Its teeth could be as long as 13 inches.
Velociraptor	Speedy Thief	two-legged carnivore	5 – 6 feet long	It could run 40 miles an hour for short distances.

Use the information from the previous page to answer the following questions.

1. _____ was a two-legged carnivore that protected its eggs.

2. Parasaurolophus had a long _____ on its head that it probably was used to make a loud noise.

3. An armored dinosaur, Ankylosaurus ate _____.

4. _____ fossils were found in the Salta Province in Argentina.

5. Scientists believe that Troödon may have been the _____ dinosaur.

6. The fossils of the four-legged herbivore _____ were the first to be found alongside its fossilized eggs and nest.

7. _____ could run up to 40 miles an hour for short distances.

8. Corythosaurus had a flat, bony crest on its head that looked like a _____.

9. Pachycephalosaurus, whose name means _____, probably ran away from danger before fighting.

10. Scientists believed that _____ used its tail for balance as it ran.

11. _____ had the largest known skull of any land animal.

12. Tyrannosaurus rex could have teeth up to _____ inches long.

Ankylosaurus

Ankylosaurus was about 35 feet long and weighed about 5 tons. It had a short neck and stubby legs. The body of Ankylosaurus was covered with thick, leathery skin and bony plates. It also had rows of knobs and spikes on its body. Ankylosaurus had a tail that ended in a big bony club, which could be used to fight off other dinosaurs. The dinosaur used its small teeth and jaws to eat plants near the ground.

Ankylosaurus weighed ___ ___ ___ ___   ___ ___ ___ ___.
                                        1   2   3   4   5   6   7   8

Ankylosaurus had a ___ ___ ___ ___ ___ neck.
                                 8   9   6   10   5

Ankylosaurus had bony plates, ___ ___ ___ ___ ___ ___, and knobs for armor.
                                           8   11   2   12   4   8

Ankylosaurus ate ___ ___ ___ ___ ___ ___.
                          11 13 14   7   5   8

Use the answers above to find the letter that goes with each number. Fill in the blanks to find a nickname for Ankylosaurus.

___ ___ ___ ___ ___ ___ ___ ___ ___   ___ ___ ___ ___
10 4 11 5 2 13 2 14 7   5 14 7 12

Why is this a good nickname for Ankylosaurus?_____

_____

Corythosaurus

Corythosaurus was fairly large in size. It was about 30 feet long and weighed more than 2 tons. It had bumpy skin and a hollow, rounded crest covering its head. Corythosaurus was a plant-eater, and it had many rows of teeth for grinding food. Scientists think it ate pine needles and leaves. Corythosaurus probably ran on two feet with its tail out for balance.

Corythosaurus was fairly large in $\underset{1}{\rule{1cm}{0.4pt}}$ $\underset{2}{\rule{1cm}{0.4pt}}$ $\underset{3}{\rule{1cm}{0.4pt}}$ $\underset{4}{\rule{1cm}{0.4pt}}$.

In fact, it was about $\underset{5}{\rule{1cm}{0.4pt}}$ $\underset{6}{\rule{1cm}{0.4pt}}$ $\underset{2}{\rule{1cm}{0.4pt}}$ $\underset{7}{\rule{1cm}{0.4pt}}$ $\underset{5}{\rule{1cm}{0.4pt}}$ $\underset{8}{\rule{1cm}{0.4pt}}$ $\underset{9}{\rule{1cm}{0.4pt}}$ $\underset{4}{\rule{1cm}{0.4pt}}$ $\underset{4}{\rule{1cm}{0.4pt}}$ $\underset{5}{\rule{1cm}{0.4pt}}$ long.

Corythosaurus had a large crest on its $\underset{6}{\rule{1cm}{0.4pt}}$ $\underset{4}{\rule{1cm}{0.4pt}}$ $\underset{10}{\rule{1cm}{0.4pt}}$ $\underset{11}{\rule{1cm}{0.4pt}}$.

Its skin was $\underset{12}{\rule{1cm}{0.4pt}}$ $\underset{13}{\rule{1cm}{0.4pt}}$ $\underset{14}{\rule{1cm}{0.4pt}}$ $\underset{15}{\rule{1cm}{0.4pt}}$ $\underset{8}{\rule{1cm}{0.4pt}}$.

It probably ate $\underset{16}{\rule{1cm}{0.4pt}}$ $\underset{4}{\rule{1cm}{0.4pt}}$ $\underset{10}{\rule{1cm}{0.4pt}}$ $\underset{17}{\rule{1cm}{0.4pt}}$ $\underset{4}{\rule{1cm}{0.4pt}}$ $\underset{1}{\rule{1cm}{0.4pt}}$.

Use the answers above to find the letter that goes with each number. Fill in the blanks to find the meaning of this dinosaur's name.

$\underset{6}{\rule{1cm}{0.4pt}}$ $\underset{4}{\rule{1cm}{0.4pt}}$ $\underset{16}{\rule{1cm}{0.4pt}}$ $\underset{14}{\rule{1cm}{0.4pt}}$ $\underset{4}{\rule{1cm}{0.4pt}}$ $\underset{5}{\rule{1cm}{0.4pt}}$ $\underset{16}{\rule{1cm}{0.4pt}}$ $\underset{2}{\rule{1cm}{0.4pt}}$ $\underset{3}{\rule{1cm}{0.4pt}}$ $\underset{10}{\rule{1cm}{0.4pt}}$ $\underset{7}{\rule{1cm}{0.4pt}}$ $\underset{11}{\rule{1cm}{0.4pt}}$

Do you think this is a good name for Corythosaurus? Why?_____

_____

Gallimimus

Gallimimus looked sort of like a giant ostrich. It had long, thin legs and could run fast. Its hands were probably not very strong. Gallimimus had a long neck and a small head. Scientists think that it had jaws that looked like a beak. Gallimimus did not have teeth. It probably ate eggs, plants, and fruit.

Fill in the blanks.

1. Gallimimus probably ate plants and ___ ___ ___ ___.

2. It did not have ___ ___ ___ ___ ___.

3. Its ___ ___ ___ ___ ___ were weak.

4. Gallimimus had jaws that looked like a ___ ___ ___ ___.

5. Gallimimus looked somewhat like a giant
   ___ ___ ___ ___ ___ ___ ___.

6. It could ___ ___ ___ fast.

7. It had a ___ ___ ___ ___ ___ head.

Ingenia

Ingenia was a small dinosaur. It weighed about 60 pounds and was less than 5 feet long. It probably ate insects and the eggs of other dinosaurs.

Color the path that Ingenia must take to get to its food.

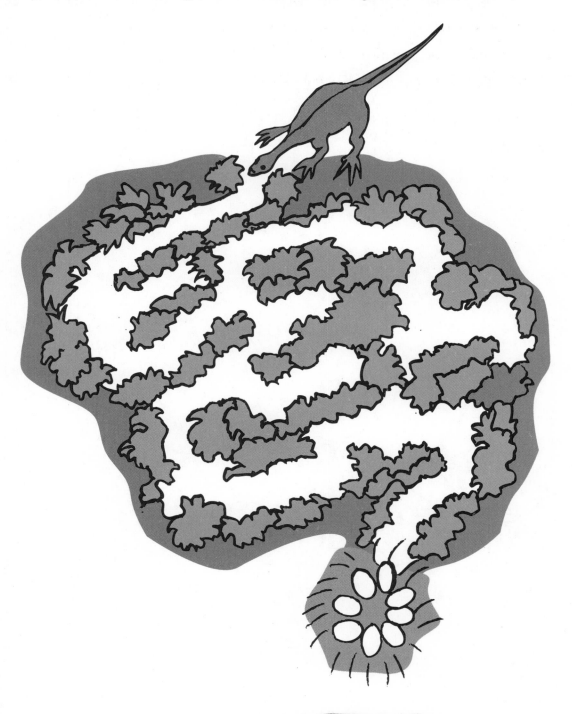

Maiasaura

Paleontologists believe that some dinosaurs took very good care of their babies after they hatched, unlike many reptiles today. In Montana, the bones of more than a dozen baby dinosaurs were found in and around a large round nest. It was 7 feet across. The remains of an adult dinosaur were also found near the nest. This dinosaur was named Maiasaura. The teeth of the baby dinosaurs were worn, showing that they had been eating plants. Perhaps the mother Maiasaura brought the plants to the nest for the babies to eat.

Color the picture any way you like.

Use the information on the previous page to complete each sentence below.

1. This Maiasaura nest was found in ◯◯ ___ ___ ___ ___ ___.

2. The remains of the adult were near a large ___◯___ ___.

3. The nest was ◯___ ___ ___ ___ in shape.

4. The ___ ___ ___ ___◯ of the baby dinosaurs were worn because

they had been eating ___ ___ ___ ___◯___.

Unscramble the letters in the circles above to find the meaning of the name Maiasaura.

"Good ___ ___ ___ ___ ___ ___ lizard"

Think of some animals living today that care for their young until they are grown. What are some of the things these animals do to care for the baby animals? _____

_____

_____

Pachycephalosaurus

Pachycephalosaurus had a thick bone on the top of its head. Knobs and spikes stuck out from this dome and the dinosaur's nose. Pachycephalosaurus may have crashed heads with rival dinosaurs to become the leader of the herd or to win mates.

Circle the two pictures below that are exactly alike.

Parasaurolophus

Parasaurolophus had a long crest on the top of its head. This crest was about 5 feet long! Some paleontologists think that the tube helped the dinosaur smell. Others believe that the tube gave Parasaurolophus a loud voice.

Look at each Parasaurolophus shown below. Circle the two pictures that are exactly alike.

What is different about each of the other pictures?_____

_____

_____

Pentaceratops

Pentaceratops was one of the dinosaurs that had a lot of armor. It had a horn above each eye and one on its nose. It also had something that looked like a horn on each cheek. Pentaceratops had a very large frill. Its body was about 30 feet long. Pentaceratops was a plant-eater.

Complete the picture by drawing the missing half of this Pentaceratops. Then, color the picture any way you like.

Saltasaurus

Saltasaurus was a large dinosaur that walked on four feet. It had a fairly long neck and a long, thick tail. Saltasaurus was almost 40 feet long from nose to tail. Saltasaurus had tough plates, studs, and tiny spikes covering its back.

Cut a piece of string that is 40 feet long. Take the string outside and lay it out in a straight line on the sidewalk.

1. Was Saltasaurus bigger than a car? _____

2. Can you think of something that is as big as Saltasaurus was?

_____

3. Can you name an animal living today that has hard plates covering part

of its body?_____

_____

Troödon

Troödon was a very fast and smart dinosaur. In fact, some scientists think it was the most intelligent of all the dinosaurs. It had sharp claws and could see well, so it was probably a good hunter.

Copy the lines in each numbered box into the square on the grid below that has the same number. Then, color the finished drawing any way you like.

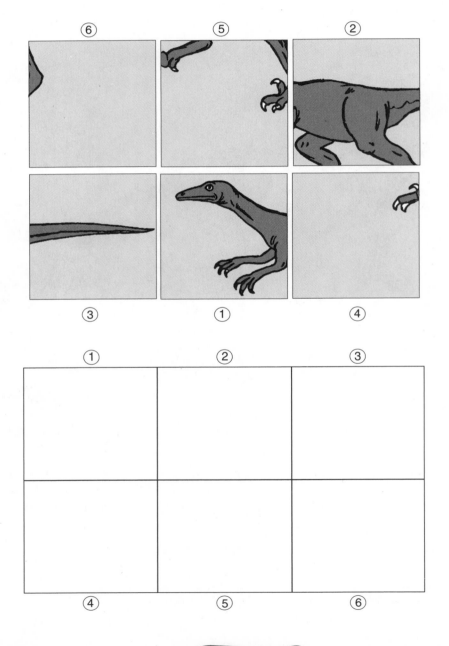

Heads or Tails?

Listed below are dinosaurs from the Cretaceous Period and important physical features about them. Draw a line to match the name of each dinosaur on the right to the interesting fact about its head or tail on the left.

Ankylosaurus •

Corythosaurus •

Gallimimus •

Pachycephalosaurus •

Parasaurolophus •

Pentaceratops •

Saltasaurus •

• This dinosaur had a long crest on top of its head that was about 5 feet long!

• This dinosaur had a very small head and a long neck.

• This dinosaur's tail ended in a big, bony club.

• This dinosaur had a hollow, rounded crest covering its head.

• This dinosaur had a long, thick tail, which added to its length of over 40 feet!

• This dinosaur had a horn above each eye and one on its nose.

• This dinosaur had a thick bone on top of its head with knobs and spikes sticking out of it.

Tyrannosaurus rex

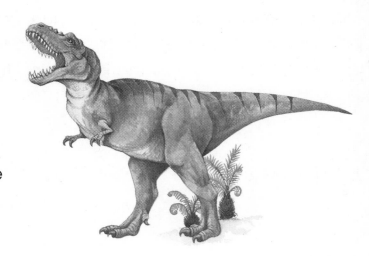

Tyrannosaurus rex was a large carnivore that lived during the Cretaceous Period. It walked on two strong hind legs and had a massive head with large teeth that could easily tear apart food. Tyrannosaurus also had two tiny arms that may have been used to grab its prey. Studies of its skull revealed large sight and smell areas in its brain, which meant that Tyrannosaurus had an excellent sense of sight and smell. Tyrannosaurus's tail was straight, giving Tyrannosaurus the ability to keep its balance while running and turning fast. This dinosaur was about 40 feet long and weighed about 7 tons. Some paleontologists believe that Tyrannosaurus was a scavenger, eating animals that were already dead. Others believe that Tyrannosaurus was a predator that killed its own prey.

Answer the questions below in the blanks provided.

1. Tyrannosaurus lived during the _____ Period.

2. It had _____ sight and smell areas in its brain.

3. Tyrannosaurus was about _____ feet long.

4. Do you think that Tyrannosaurus was a scavenger or a predator? Why?

_____

_____

_____

A Dinosaur Named Sue

The first Tyrannosaurus fossil was found in 1902 in Montana. There have only been about 30 different Tyrannosaurus finds since then, most of which were not even half complete. In August of 1990, Susan Hendrickson found an almost complete Tyrannosaurs rex fossil in South Dakota. The fossil was named Sue, after the fossil hunter who found it. Sue is the most complete and best-preserved Tyrannosaurus rex fossil ever found. There was a debate about who owned the fossil. In 1997, it was bought at auction for $8.4 million by the Field Museum in Chicago. This allowed Sue to be studied by scientists and seen by the public.

Answer the questions below in the blanks provided.

1. When and where was the first Tyrannosaurus rex fossil found?

_____

_____

_____

2. _____ found the Tyrannosaurus, Sue.

3. Why is the fossil Sue so important?

_____

_____

_____

4. Do you think that it was important for the Field Museum (or another museum) to get Sue? Why or why not?

_____

_____

_____

Velociraptor

Velociraptor was a meat-eating dinosaur. It was only about 6 feet tall. Velociraptor had sharp claws on its hands and feet. One claw on each foot was like a long, slashing knife. Velociraptor could run fast. Its name means "speedy thief."

Why do you think this dinosaur was called "speedy thief"?

_____

How many different words can you make using the letters in the name Velociraptor?

VELOCIRAPTOR

_____   _____

_____   _____

_____   _____

_____   _____

Name That Dinosaur!

Complete the puzzle below by writing a dinosaur's name across each letter. Remember that the name you choose must contain that letter. The first one has been done for you. If you need help, use the Word Bank at the bottom of the page.

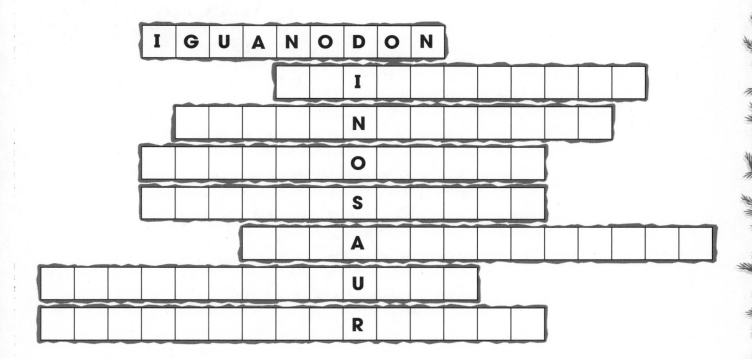

I G U A N O D O N

I

N

O

S

A

U

R

Word Bank

Archaeoceratops

Ankylosaurus

Giganotosaurus

Ornithomimus

Brachiosaurus

Triceratops

Tyrannosaurus

Dinosaur Diagram

A Venn diagram can be used to compare things. First, look at the picture to notice ways the two dinosaurs are the same. Then, look for how they are different.

Iguanodon   **Triceratops**

Complete the Venn diagram below by writing ways Iguanodon and Triceratops are both alike and different.

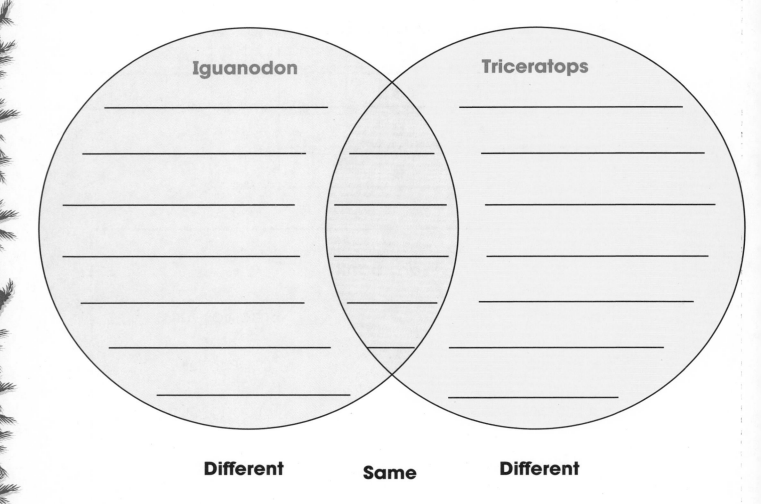

Different   **Same**   **Different**

Get a Clue!

Read the 16 clues below about a certain dinosaur. Use a science book or other resource materials and your own logical thinking to guess the name of the dinosaur. When you are finished, write your own clues about another dinosaur. Give it to someone else to see if he or she can guess the answer.

I am a dinosaur.

1. My name means "three-horned face."

2. My skull was 7 or 8 feet long.

3. I had a beaked mouth like a parrot.

4. I ate plants.

5. I walked on all four legs.

6. I was 30 feet long.

7. I weighed up to 10 tons.

8. I was one of the last dinosaurs to live.

9. I had 3 claws on my front feet.

10. I lived in Canada and the U.S.

11. I had a thick neck frill.

12. I had 3 horns on my skull.

13. I am the best-known horned dinosaur.

14. I used my horns for protection.

15. I had a small hoof on each toe.

16. I was named by O.C. Marsh in 1889.

I am _____

I am a dinosaur.

_____ _____

_____ _____

_____ _____

_____ _____

_____ _____

_____ _____

_____ _____

I am _____

Dino-Find

Find the hidden words in the puzzle below. The words may be written forward, backward, up, down, or diagonally. Circle the words. When you have located all the words, write the remaining letters at the bottom of the page to spell out a message.

ALLOSAURUS	BIRD HIP	FOSSIL	PLANT-EATER
APATOSAURUS	COELURUS	JURASSIC	PLATED
ARMORED	DINOSAUR	MEAT-EATER	SAUROPOD
ARCHAEOPTERYX	DIPLODOCUS	PALEONTOLOGIST	STEGOSAURUS

```
S D B U R L I S S O F I S M N
G U I T H I S P E R I O T E T
J D R U A S O N I D S H E A S
U A D U L D L O S E W S G T I
R E H A A S O U C R O V O E G
A S I R E S R P D O M U S A O
S R T H L A M T E R R I U E L
I C A E A N D E A A U U R R O
C R O O D E T A L P P A U E T
A C N D R A I N S C A A S M N
E X Y R E T P O E A H C R A O
T O T H D I P L O D O C U S E
R E T A E T N A L P E D E S L
E R A L L O S A U R U S T S P
```

One Mixed-Up Dinosaur!

Imagine that you have just discovered a new dinosaur! In the box below, draw a picture of what this dinosaur looks like. But be careful. You must use different physical features and body parts from dinosaurs you have already learned about. For example, your new dinosaur might look like it has the tail of Saltasaurus, the head of Pachycephalosaurus, and the teeth of Tyrannosaurus!

Now, name your new dinosaur! _____

_____

The Cretaceous World

Draw a picture of your favorite dinosaur from the Cretaceous Period in the picture below. Then, color the picture.

Activities

Math Practice

Dot-To-Dots

Hidden Pictures

Mazes

Brain Teasers

Where's the Egg?

Color the correct set of tracks to help the dinosaur find the egg.

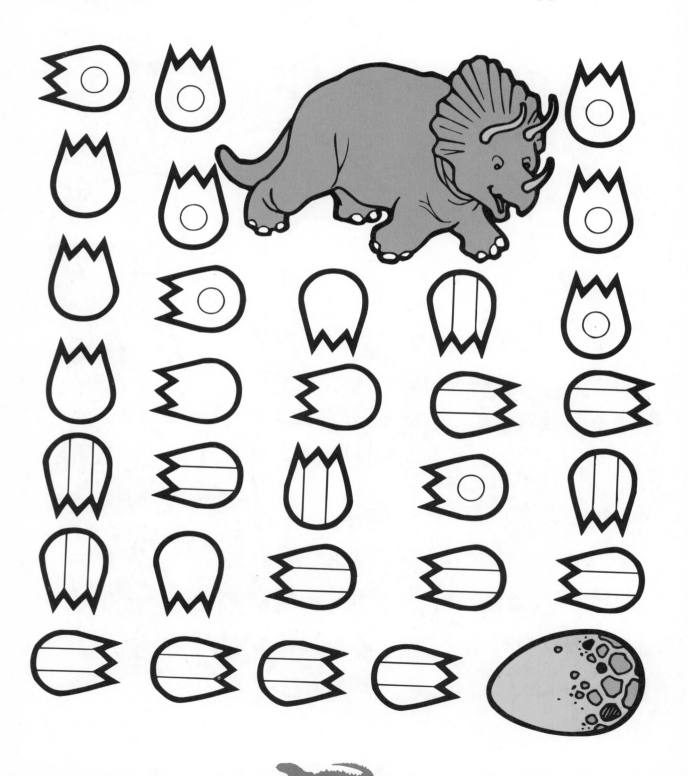

The Lost Dinosaur

Help the baby dinosaur find its mother. Color the path in order from **A** to **M**.

A Very Worried Dinosaur

Help the mother dinosaur find its baby.

Start

Finish

Parasaurolophus

Draw a line through the maze from the dinosaur's nose to its tail.

Volcano!

Follow the maze to help the dinosaur get away from the volcano!

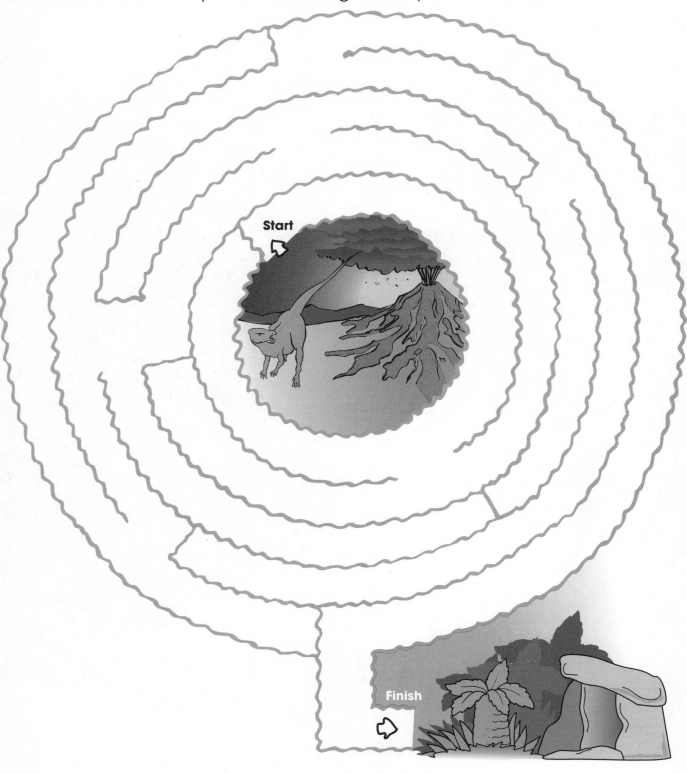

Start

Finish

Down at the Dig

Color to find the shapes in the picture. Use the key to help you.

△ = **green**   ○ = **yellow**   ▢ = **red**

More Dinosaur Dig

Find 7 shovels below and color them purple. Then, color the rest of the picture.

Claudia's Dinosaur!

Look at the Tyrannasaurus and Triceratops pictures below. One of them belongs to Claudia. Read the clues to find out which one. *Hint:* Columns go up and down. Rows go across.

The dinosaur is in a column that has two Tyrannasaurus.

The dinosaur is in a row that has two Triceratops.

There is no Triceratops to the right of the dinosaur.

Which dinosaur belongs to Claudia? Circle the correct dinosaur.

From Shortest to Tallest

Look at the five different dinosaurs below. The dinosaurs are lined up from shortest to tallest. Read the clues to figure out the name of each dinosaur in the picture. Then, write their names in the blanks.

Apatosaurus is taller than Hadrosaurus.

Stegosaurus is taller than Saltopus.

Saltopus is taller than Compsognathus.

Hadrosaurus is taller than Stegosaurus.

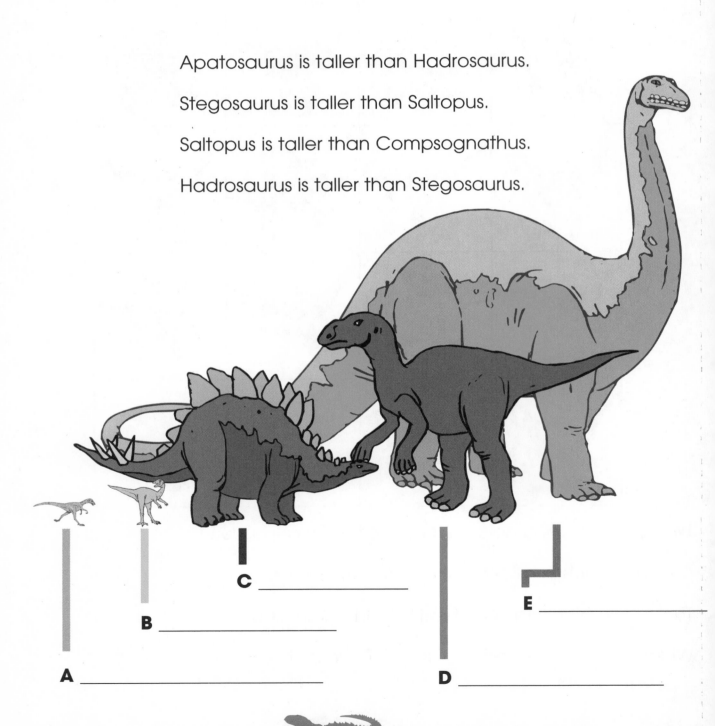

A _____

B _____

C _____

D _____

E _____

Making Moves

Can you change these two rows of dinosaurs into a circle? Try it and see! Cut out the six dinosaurs. Put the dinosaurs on a table so that they look like this:

Now change the rows into a circle by moving only two dinosaurs!

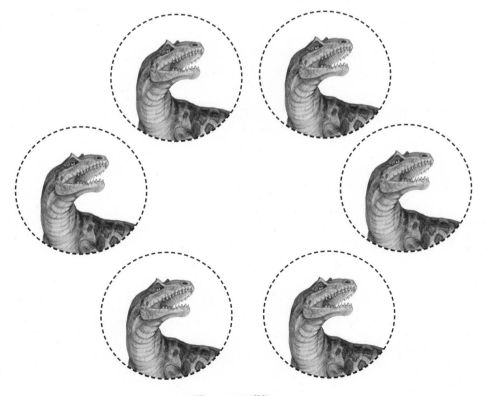

This page is intentionally left blank.

Flip, Flop

Cut out the ten dinosaurs below. Lay them out in rows to make a triangle that points up like as shown.

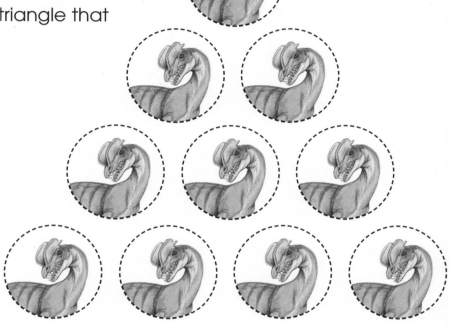

Now move one dinosaur at a time. In three moves, change the triangle so that it points down as shown.

This page is intentionally left blank.

Centrosaurus

Connect the dots from 1 to 100. Then color the dinosaur.

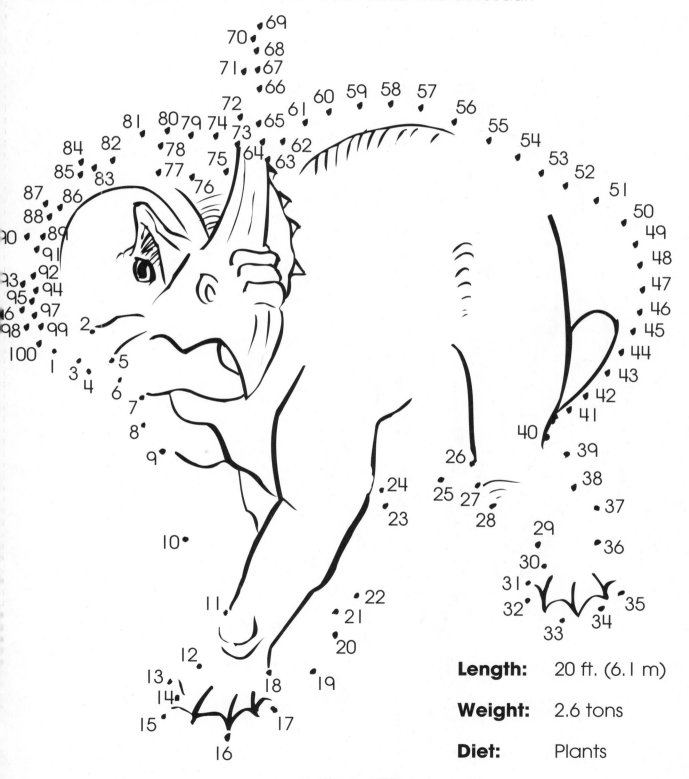

Length: 20 ft. (6.1 m)

Weight: 2.6 tons

Diet: Plants

Struthiomimus

Count by 2s to connect the dots. Then, color the dinosaur.

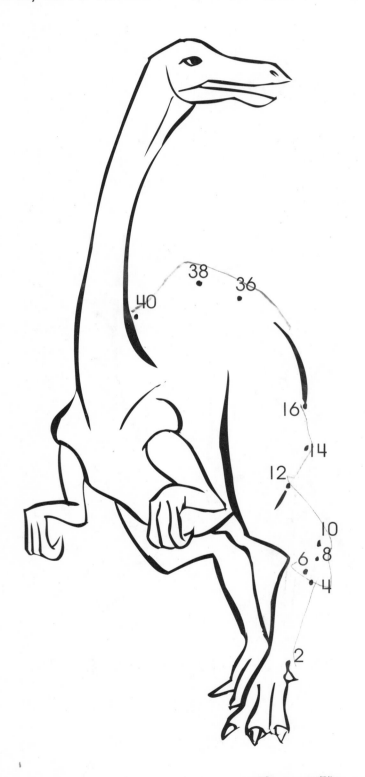

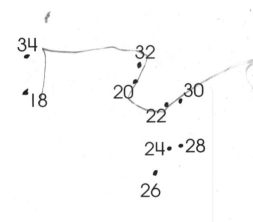

Length: 13 ft. (4 m)

Weight: 440 lb. (150 kg)

Diet: Small animals, plants

Tyrannosaurus

Count by 5s to connect the dots. Then, color the dinosaur.

Length: 39 ft. (12 m)

Weight: 6.3 tons

Diet: Large plant-eating dinosaurs

Apatosaurus

Count by 3s to connect the dots. Then, color the dinosaur.

Length: 69 ft. (21 m)

Weight: 24.6 tons

Diet: Tree leaves, ferns

Paleontologist Tools

Connect the dots from A to Z. Then, color the picture.

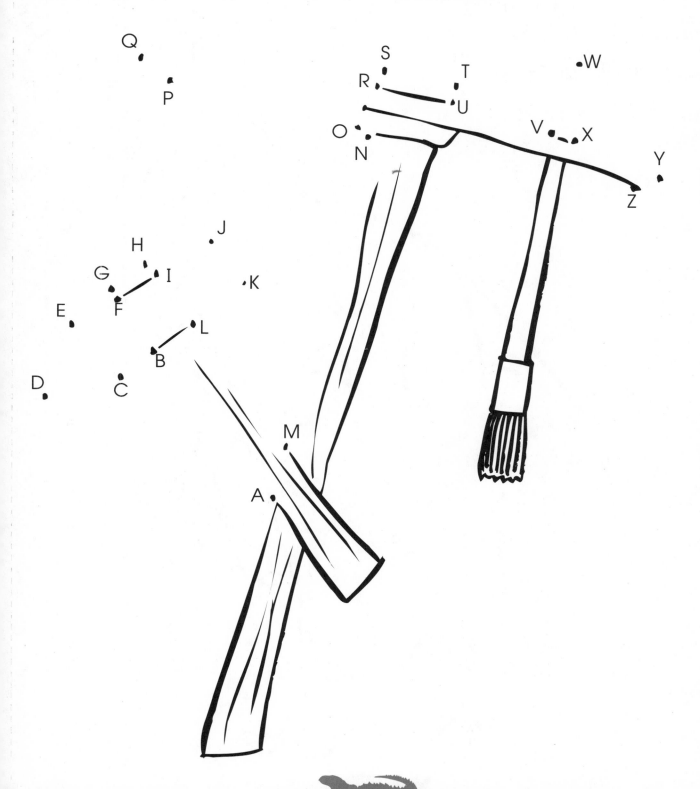

Deinonychus

Connect the dots to spell the dinosaur's name. Then, color it.

Length: 10 ft. (3 m)

Weight: 130 lb. (60 kg)

Diet: Plant-eating dinosaurs

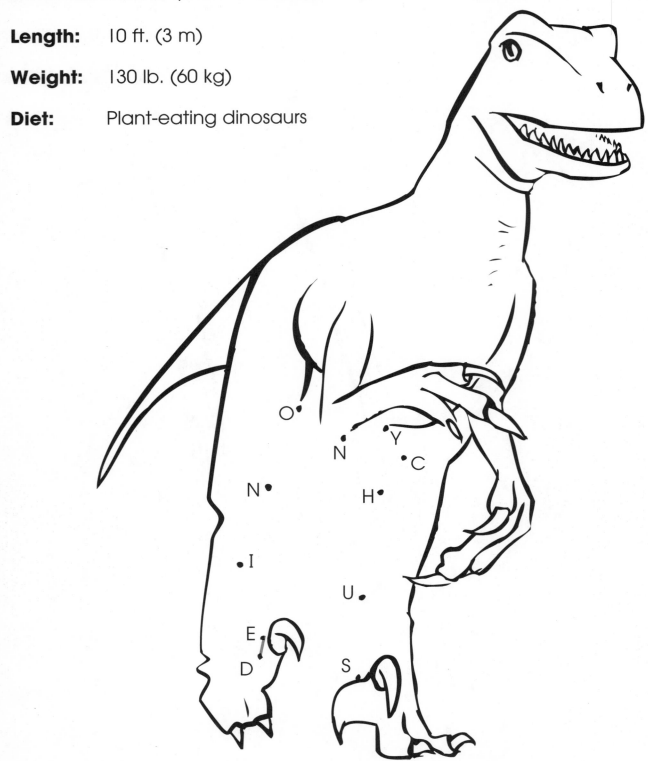

Troödon

Connect the dots to spell the dinosaur's name. Then, color it.

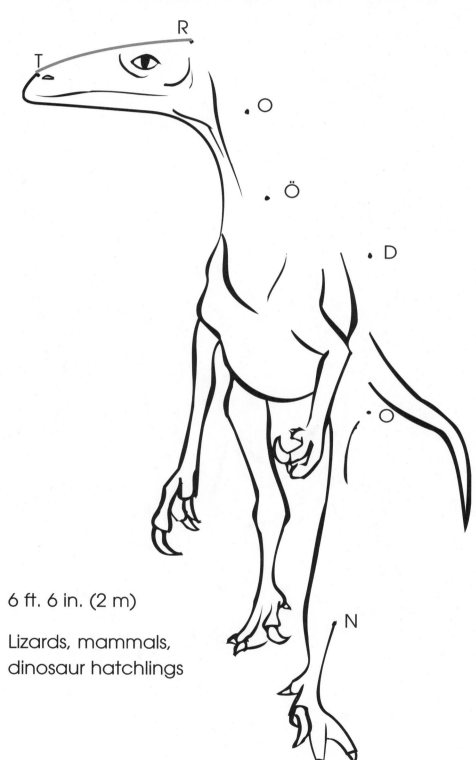

Length: 6 ft. 6 in. (2 m)

Diet: Lizards, mammals,
dinosaur hatchlings

Segnosaurus

Connect the dots to spell the dinosaur's name. Then, color it.

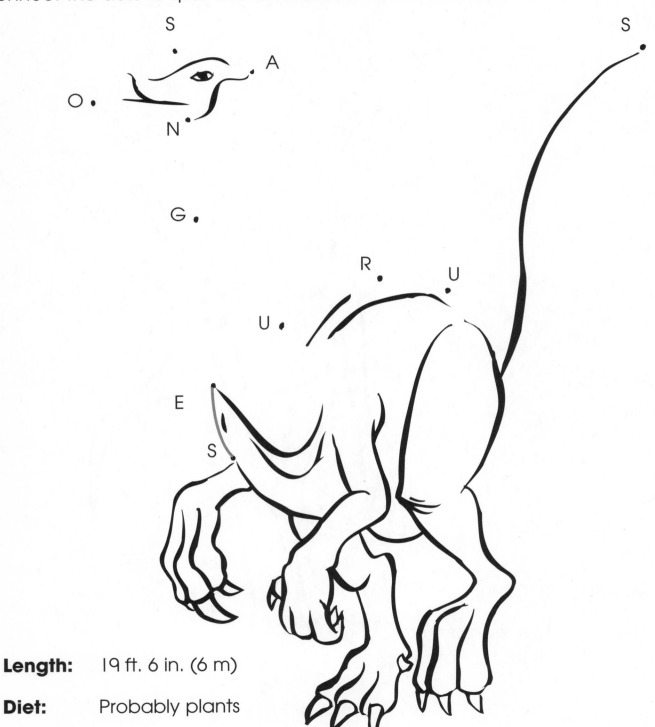

Length: 19 ft. 6 in. (6 m)

Diet: Probably plants

A Nest of Dinosaur Eggs!

Count the dinosaurs eggs in each nest. Write the number of eggs on the lines.

_____

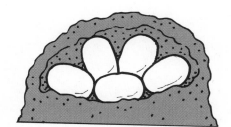

_____

_____

_____

_____

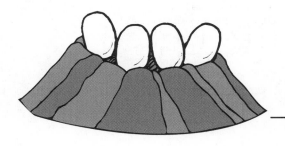

_____

One Long Dinosaur!

Diplodocus was one of the longest dinosaurs. It was 90 feet long! Color the picture of Diplodocus below.

A school bus is 30 feet long. Color the number of school buses it would take to equal the length of one Diplodocus.

Dinosaur Tracks

An inch is a unit of length. Cut out the inch ruler at the bottom of the page. Use it to measure the impressions of dinosaur tracks below to the nearest inch.

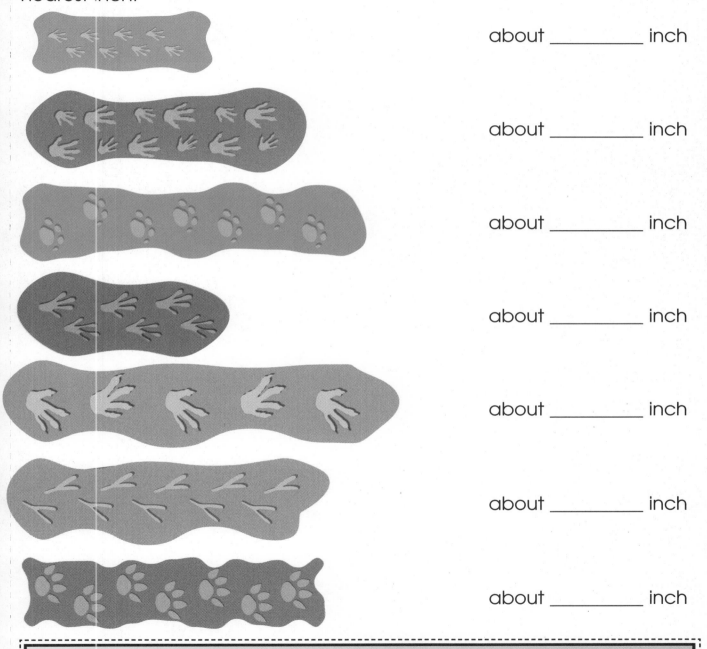

about _____ inch

about _____ inch

about _____ inch

about _____ inch

about _____ inch

about _____ inch

about _____ inch

This page is intentionally left blank.

Sea Friends

Color the picture. Count the Shonisaurus. Then, answer the question below.

How many Shonisaurus are there?_____

What's the Difference?

Circle the pairs that have a difference of 2.

$$
\begin{array}{ccccccc}
3 & 1 & 10 & 9 & 7 & 3 & 5 \\
4 & 6 & 8 & 5 & 1 & 2 & 6 \\
8 & 0 & 2 & 3 & 4 & 0 & 4 \\
2 & 4 & 10 & 1 & 10 & 6 & 9 \\
6 & 2 & 8 & 10 & 8 & 6 & 7 \\
1 & 9 & 3 & 5 & 4 & 4 & 3 \\
5 & 7 & 1 & 0 & 2 & 7 & 9 \\
\end{array}
$$

Building the Nest

Help the Maiasaura count the twigs needed to build its nest. Count by 5s.
Write the numbers in the boxes.

A Dino Discovery

Add together all the numbers shown in each space. Then, color to find the hidden picture using the number key to help you.

even answers = **blue**   odd answers = **green**

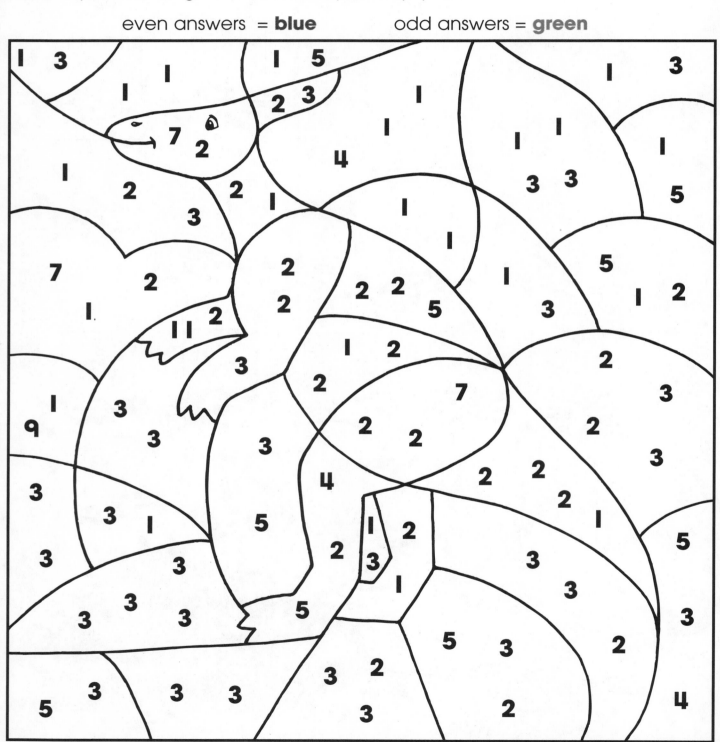

Adding Fun

Find a pair of dice. Roll one die and write the number of dots from the die in the top box. Repeat until all the top boxes are filled in. Then, complete the addition sentences.

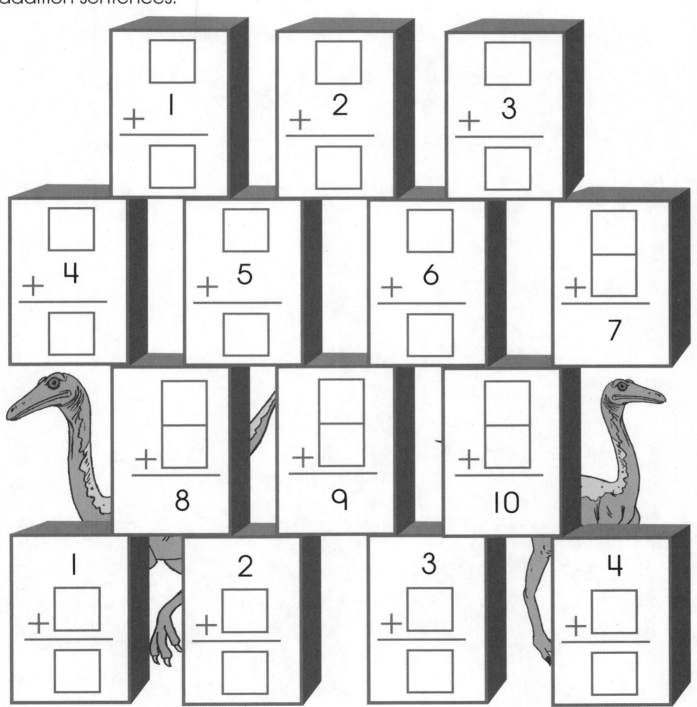

Add-a-saurus

Write the missing addend in each blank to help Add-a-saurus complete the addition sentences.

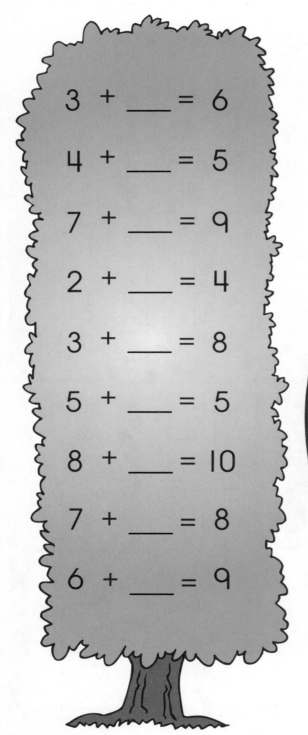

$3 + \underline{\quad} = 6$

$4 + \underline{\quad} = 5$

$7 + \underline{\quad} = 9$

$2 + \underline{\quad} = 4$

$3 + \underline{\quad} = 8$

$5 + \underline{\quad} = 5$

$8 + \underline{\quad} = 10$

$7 + \underline{\quad} = 8$

$6 + \underline{\quad} = 9$

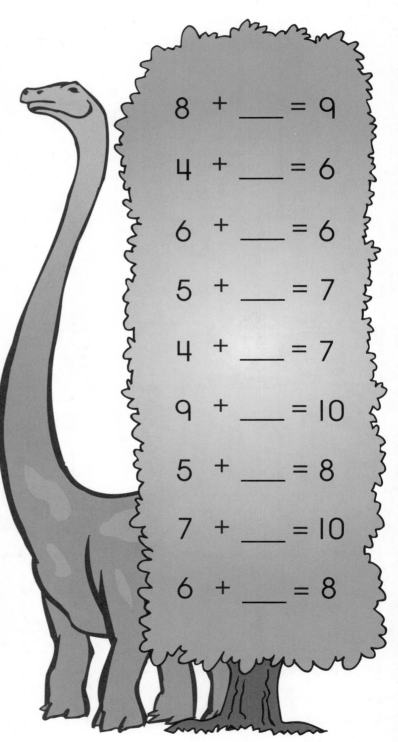

$8 + \underline{\quad} = 9$

$4 + \underline{\quad} = 6$

$6 + \underline{\quad} = 6$

$5 + \underline{\quad} = 7$

$4 + \underline{\quad} = 7$

$9 + \underline{\quad} = 10$

$5 + \underline{\quad} = 8$

$7 + \underline{\quad} = 10$

$6 + \underline{\quad} = 8$

A Gentle Giant

Solve the equations in each space below. Then, color the spaces using the color key to help you find the hidden picture.

14 = **blue**　　　　15 = **green**　　　　16 = **yellow**

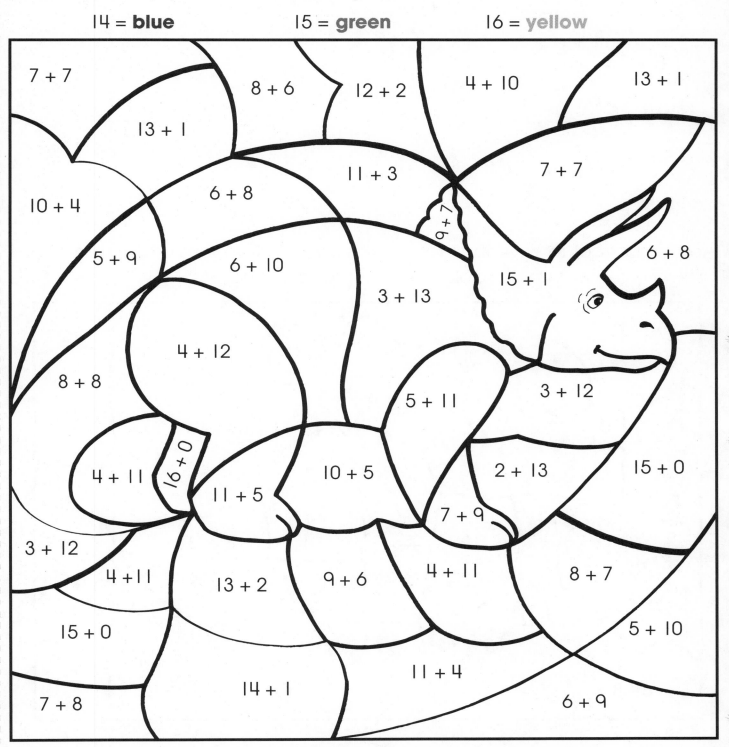

7 + 7
8 + 6
12 + 2
4 + 10
13 + 1
13 + 1
11 + 3
7 + 7
10 + 4
6 + 8
9 + 7
5 + 9
6 + 10
3 + 13
15 + 1
6 + 8
4 + 12
8 + 8
5 + 11
3 + 12
16 + 0
4 + 11
10 + 5
2 + 13
15 + 0
11 + 5
7 + 9
3 + 12
4 + 11
4 + 11
8 + 7
13 + 2
9 + 6
15 + 0
5 + 10
11 + 4
7 + 8
14 + 1
6 + 9

Dino-mite!

Add or subtract. Match the related facts.

5 + 9 = <u>14</u> •

8 + 7 = ____ •

15 − 9 = ____ •

17 − 8 = ____ •

7 + 7 = ____ •

• 6 + 9 = ____

• 14 − 9 = <u>5</u>

• 15 − 7 = ____

• 14 − 7 = ____

• 9 + 8 = ____

Add or subtract to solve the problems below. Color spaces brown with answers greater than 12. Color the other spaces green.

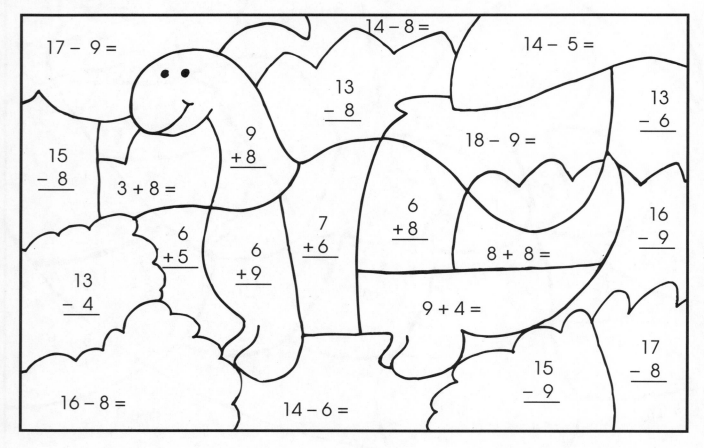

Dan's Footprints

Why did Dan the Dinosaur go outside with just one boot on? The answer is started for you at the bottom of the page. To finish the answer, work through these footprints. Start at the top with the letter T. Then do the math problem on that footprint (7+7) and look for its answer (14) on another footprint. Then write the letter that appears on that footprint in the next blank below. Continue from footprint to footprint until you've covered all your tracks!

Why did Dan the Dinosaur go outside with just one boot on? Because he

heard ___ ___ ___   ___ ___ ___ ___ ___   ___ ___ ___

___ ___ ___ ___ ___   ___ ___ ___   ___ ___ ___

___ ___ ___ ___ !

Prehistoric Problems

Solve the subtraction problems. Then use the code to color the picture.

Code: 25 — **blue**   57 — **green**

   31 — yellow   14 — orange

   21 — **brown**   11 — **red**

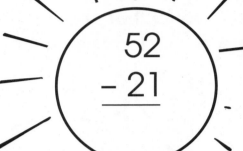

$$\begin{array}{r} 52 \\ -\ 21 \\ \hline \end{array}$$

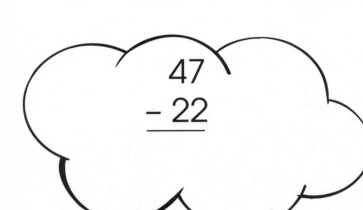

$$\begin{array}{r} 47 \\ -\ 22 \\ \hline \end{array}$$

$$\begin{array}{r} 25 \\ -\ 11 \\ \hline \end{array}$$

$$\begin{array}{r} 62 \\ -\ 31 \\ \hline \end{array}$$

$$\begin{array}{r} 77 \\ -\ 20 \\ \hline \end{array}$$

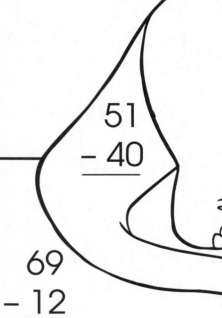

$$\begin{array}{r} 51 \\ -\ 40 \\ \hline \end{array}$$

$$\begin{array}{r} 69 \\ -\ 12 \\ \hline \end{array}$$

$$\begin{array}{r} 98 \\ -\ 41 \\ \hline \end{array}$$

$$\begin{array}{r} 55 \\ -\ 34 \\ \hline \end{array}$$

Dino Code

How is a T-Rex like an explosion? To find out, solve the following problems and write the matching letter above each answer on the blanks.

He's $\overline{\hspace{0.5cm}}_{195}$ $\overline{\hspace{0.5cm}}_{185}$ $\overline{\hspace{0.5cm}}_{92}$ $\overline{\hspace{0.5cm}}_{92}$ $\overline{\hspace{0.5cm}}_{171}$ $\overline{\hspace{0.5cm}}_{195}$

$\overline{\hspace{0.5cm}}_{265}$ $\overline{\hspace{0.5cm}}_{74}$ $\overline{\hspace{0.5cm}}_{183}$ $\overline{\hspace{0.5cm}}_{171}$ — $\overline{\hspace{0.5cm}}_{93}$ $\overline{\hspace{0.5cm}}_{74}$ $\overline{\hspace{0.5cm}}_{45}$ $\overline{\hspace{0.5cm}}_{181}$ $\overline{\hspace{0.5cm}}_{191}$!

Remember to regroup when the bottom number is larger than the top number in a column.

$$F = \begin{array}{r} 348 \\ -153 \\ \hline \end{array}$$

$$L = \begin{array}{r} 765 \\ -673 \\ \hline \end{array}$$

$$G = \begin{array}{r} 427 \\ -382 \\ \hline \end{array}$$

$$T = \begin{array}{r} 637 \\ -446 \\ \hline \end{array}$$

$$H = \begin{array}{r} 878 \\ -697 \\ \hline \end{array}$$

$$U = \begin{array}{r} 548 \\ -363 \\ \hline \end{array}$$

$$O = \begin{array}{r} 824 \\ -653 \\ \hline \end{array}$$

$$N = \begin{array}{r} 439 \\ -256 \\ \hline \end{array}$$

$$I = \begin{array}{r} 447 \\ -373 \\ \hline \end{array}$$

$$M = \begin{array}{r} 568 \\ -475 \\ \hline \end{array}$$

$$D = \begin{array}{r} 748 \\ -483 \\ \hline \end{array}$$

Racing to the Finish

Solve the multiplication problems.

5 x 3	2 x 8	4 x 6	9 x 3	7 x 5	3 x 9
4 x 2	6 x 2	4 x 4	0 x 6	3 x 2	7 x 2
6 x 5	3 x 4	8 x 3	4 x 5	5 x 2	7 x 4
6 x 3	4 x 8	2 x 2	8 x 5	3 x 7	5 x 5
5 x 9	9 x 2	4 x 6	9 x 4		

Hunt For The Answer

Solve the division problems.

3⟌63	3⟌84	4⟌97	6⟌74
4⟌74	2⟌46	2⟌48	3⟌75

6⟌96

5⟌92	3⟌41	3⟌57	4⟌84	4⟌76	7⟌86	5⟌72
5⟌57	3⟌65	2⟌87	5⟌55	7⟌84	3⟌87	7⟌93
3⟌96	6⟌94	5⟌93	9⟌36	2⟌97	6⟌84	3⟌68

Dino Divide!

Solve the division problems.

6⟌888   2⟌956   2⟌712   4⟌860      5⟌845

6⟌750   9⟌999   8⟌968   3⟌774   5⟌735   8⟌920

   8⟌984   4⟌500   2⟌846   4⟌712

Mr. Dinosaur Means Business

Solve the division problems below. Write the quotient and the remainder.

Use a remainder when a problem doesn't come out even.

No Remainder	Remainder
6	5 R 2
4⟌22	4⟌22
−24	−20
	2

```
   5 R 3
5⟌28
  −25
    3
```

```
   4 R
4⟌19
```

```
   3 R
8⟌26
```

```
   6 R
7⟌45
```

```
   R
3⟌26
```

```
   R
2⟌19
```

```
   R
6⟌51
```

```
   R
9⟌65
```

```
   R
8⟌43
```

```
   R
9⟌59
```

```
   R
7⟌33
```

```
   R
4⟌27
```

Dino Tic-Tac-Toe

Solve the problems. Draw a **T** (for Tyrannosaurus) on the odd (3, 5, 7, 9) answers. Draw an **S** (for Stegosaurus) on the even (2, 4, 6, 8) answers. Which dinosaur wins the most?

4⟌36	4⟌24	10 ÷ 5		4⟌32	12 ÷ 4	5⟌30		24 ÷ 4	5⟌45	28 ÷ 4
5⟌40	32 ÷ 4	25 ÷ 5		4⟌28	4⟌20	20 ÷ 4		5⟌45	5⟌20	8 ÷ 4
35 ÷ 5	20 ÷ 4	12 ÷ 4		20 ÷ 5	10 ÷ 5	15 ÷ 5		4⟌16	5⟌15	30 ÷ 5

25 ÷ 5	4⟌8	16 ÷ 4		5⟌10	4⟌8	24 ÷ 4		8 ÷ 4	45 ÷ 5	4⟌16
32 ÷ 4	5⟌20	5⟌35		4⟌36	5⟌35	4⟌32		5⟌25	36 ÷ 4	4⟌24
40 ÷ 5	4⟌12	15 ÷ 5		45 ÷ 5	5⟌30	4⟌12		5⟌10	25 ÷ 5	4⟌36

4⟌12	5⟌10	5⟌45		36 ÷ 4	4⟌28	16 ÷ 4		28 ÷ 4	5⟌30	45 ÷ 5
30 ÷ 5	5⟌25	35 ÷ 5		24 ÷ 4	5⟌35	5⟌40		16 ÷ 4	32 ÷ 4	15 ÷ 5
4⟌32	8 ÷ 4	5⟌20		5⟌25	8 ÷ 4	36 ÷ 4		4⟌20	4⟌12	4⟌8

Reduce It!

Reduce each sum to a whole number or a mixed number in the lowest terms.

$$\frac{6}{9}$$ $$+\frac{6}{9}$$

$$\frac{4}{5}$$ $$+\frac{6}{5}$$

$$\frac{3}{4}$$ $$+\frac{2}{4}$$

$$\frac{8}{11}$$ $$+\frac{8}{11}$$

$$\frac{2}{5}$$ $$+\frac{3}{5}$$

$$\frac{8}{9}$$ $$+\frac{3}{9}$$

$$\frac{4}{8}$$ $$+\frac{6}{8}$$

$$\frac{5}{4}$$ $$+\frac{2}{4}$$

$$\frac{4}{3}$$ $$+\frac{2}{3}$$

$$\frac{5}{7}$$ $$+\frac{6}{7}$$

$$\frac{8}{11}$$ $$+\frac{3}{11}$$

$$\frac{3}{12}$$ $$+\frac{10}{12}$$

$$\frac{3}{6}$$ $$+\frac{3}{6}$$

$$\frac{6}{12}$$ $$+\frac{8}{12}$$

$$\frac{4}{8}$$ $$+\frac{4}{8}$$

$$\frac{5}{12}$$ $$+\frac{8}{12}$$

$$\frac{5}{12}$$ $$+\frac{10}{12}$$

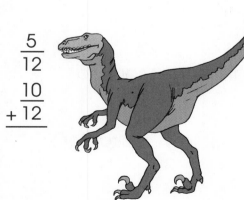

$$\frac{7}{13}$$ $$+\frac{6}{13}$$

$$\frac{8}{15}$$ $$+\frac{14}{15}$$

$$\frac{5}{7}$$ $$+\frac{6}{7}$$

Spinosaurus's Trip

Spinosaurus took a trip to Velociraptor's den. Read the map and answer the questions. Be sure to stay on the path.

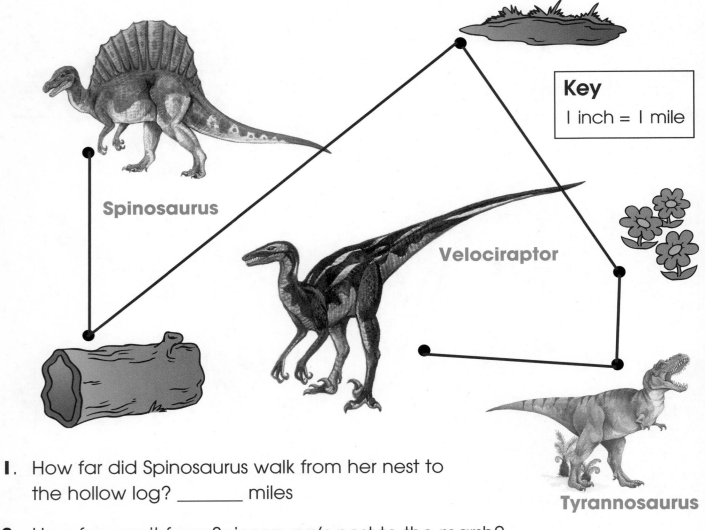

Key
1 inch = 1 mile

Spinosaurus

Velociraptor

Tyrannosaurus

1. How far did Spinosaurus walk from her nest to the hollow log? _____ miles

2. How far was it from Spinosaurus's nest to the marsh? _____ miles

3. Spinosaurus rested at the marsh. How far was it from the marsh to Tyrannosaurus's nest? _____ miles

4. How many miles did Spinosaurus walk from her nest to Velociraptor's nest? _____ miles

Story Problems

Read each story problem. Write a number sentence to solve each problem.

1. Clyde the Coelophysis walked 7 miles
to reach the river to get a
drink of water. He walked
another 5 miles and found a
place to sleep. How many
miles did Clyde walk altogether?

_____ miles

2. Patty the Plateosaurus nibbled 9
leaves off the top of a tree and
2 more that had fallen to the
ground. How many did she eat
in all?

_____ leaves

3. Ron the Rutiodon dug a hole
that was 1 inch deep. His
friend, Ralph, dug a 9-inch
hole. How many more inches
did Ralph dig than Ron?

_____ inches

4. Peter the Procompsognathus tried
to eat 7 insects. He missed 2. How
many insects did he eat?

_____ insects

Sink Your Teeth Into This!

Solve the story problems.

1. Alvin Allosaurus had 94 teeth. He broke off 23 while eating. Alvin had _____ teeth left.

2. Bart Brachiosaurus had 20 leaves. in his mouth. He swallowed 17 leaves and then bit off 19 more leaves. Barry had _____ leaves left in his mouth.

3. David Dilophosaurus had 28 teeth. He ate too many plants, and 14 teeth fell out. David had _____ teeth left.

4. Ian Ichthyosaurus had 51 teeth. He grew 38 more teeth. Ian had _____ teeth all together.

Arts and Crafts

How Big Is a Dino?

You will need
a pen or a marker
a few plain paper plates
a hole punch
a tape measure
a pair of scissors
a skein of yarn

1. Write down the names of a few dinosaurs and their lengths (refer to pages 130, 140, and 154 for this information).

2. On a few paper plates, draw a simple picture of each dinosaur as shown in the illustration below. Write the name and length of each dinosaur on the back of its plate.

3. Have an adult help you punch a hole in the rim of each plate at the top.

4. Go with an adult to a nearby park, playground, or field—take with you the dinosaur plates, a tape measure, a pair of scissors, and a large skein of yarn.

5. Measure and cut pieces of yarn the same length as each dinosaur.

6. Tie each piece of yarn to the hole in the correct dinosaur plate.

7. Lay out the different plates on the ground and compare the lengths.

Prehistoric Pasta

You will need:

a book with pictures of
dinosaurs

various uncooked pasta shapes

some construction paper

a bottle of glue

1. Find a book with pictures of dinosaurs that you like.

2. Gather a variety of uncooked pasta shapes, such as elbows, wheels, shells, and tubes.

3. Choose a piece of construction paper, and get a bottle of glue.

4. Glue some pasta shapes onto the piece of paper to recreate each dinosaur picture you chose from the book.

5. Wait for the glue to dry and display your pasta art on your refrigerator or on a door.

Dinosaur Dig

You will need:
a large baking pan
a box of cornmeal
a few plastic dinosaurs
a plastic spoon
a pastry brush or an old toothbrush

1. Ask an adult to help you fill a large baking pan with cornmeal and set it on a table.

2. Bury several plastic dinosaurs in the cornmeal.

3. Gather a plastic spoon and a pastry brush (or an old toothbrush).

4. Go on a dinosaur dig to hunt for buried fossils! Using the spoon, carefully dig into the cornmeal until you find a "fossil." Then use the pastry brush to clean away the cornmeal.

5. Name each dinosaur you find by looking carefully at its features.

I Have a Dino!

You will need:
a small shoebox (without the lid)
some green construction paper
a pair of scissors
a roll of tape
a bottle of glue
a couple empty paper towel tubes
an empty toilet paper tube
an empty egg carton
a paper cup
a marker
a craft knife

1. Wrap a small shoebox with green construction paper securing the paper using tape.

2. To form legs, cut two paper towel tubes in half. With the open side of the box facing up, set the four legs into the corners and glue them in place. Allow the glue to dry and flip the shoebox over—you now have the main body section.

3. Ask an adult to help you remove the top from an empty egg carton and cut the bottom half down the middle using a craft knife. Glue one bottom section to the top of the main body section to form a lumpy spine and tail.

4. To the front of the main body section, glue a toilet paper tube to form the neck.

5. Cover the sides of a small paper cup with green construction paper. Draw eyes on the cup using a marker. Ask an adult to use a craft knife to help you cut big, jagged teeth out of the cup. Then cut two triangular sections out of the sides of the cup to form jaws.

6. Place some glue around the edge of the toilet paper roll and place the cup over the end of the neck to form a head. Remember to allow the glue to dry before moving the dinosaur.

Fishy Fossil

You will need:
a pair of scissors
a hole punch
some white and brown
construction paper
a bottle of glue
some flat toothpicks

1. Ask an adult to help you cut a simple fish head shape from white construction paper. Punch a whole in the shape to make an eye socket.

2. Lay out a piece of brown construction paper lengthwise in front of you. Glue the head shape on the right end of the paper.

3. Squeeze a line of glue from the head shape toward the other end of the brown paper.

4. Place flat toothpicks on the glue to form a spine.

5. Add more glue in a series of lines extending outward from the spine to form ribs. Make the lines longer toward the head, gradually becoming shorter toward the tail.

6. Place broken toothpick pieces on the glue for the ribs.

7. When dry, display the finished "fossil" on your refrigerator or wall!

Picture This!

You will need:

some construction paper

several nature items (twigs, leaves, grass clipping, or pieces of bark)

a bowl

a spoon

some water

a bottle of glue

a paintbrush

some dinosaur stickers

a pair of scissors

1. Find a long piece of construction paper, or tape together a few pieces of construction paper, on a table or on the floor.

2. Go with an adult to collect nature items (see list above).

3. Put some glue in a small bowl and ask an adult to help you add a small amount of water to thin the glue.

4. Brush the glue onto the paper and attach the nature items to make a swampland.

5. Find dinosaur stickers or cut simple dinosaur shapes from dark green or brown construction paper.

6. Place the stickers or shapes on the paper so it looks like the dinosaurs are grazing, walking, or standing in the swampland.

7. Share your swampland picture! Display it on a bulletin board.

My Dinosaur Book

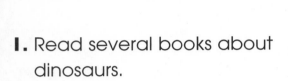

You will need:

some picture books

a pen

some decorating materials

a stapler

1. Read several books about dinosaurs.

2. Look at the illustrations on the next page.

3. Think of some interesting facts about dinosaurs that go along with the illustrations.

4. Write a story in the empty spaces below the pictures. Color the pages any way that you like.

5. Carefully cut on the lines to make the pages of your book. Put the pages together in order and staple them on the left edge.

6. Write your name on the front cover. Now you have your very own dinosaur book!

The Discovery of a Dinosaur!

Name: _____

1

2

3

4

5

6

7

This page is intentionally left blank.

Dinosaur Land

You will need:

a large piece of sturdy cardboard

some newspaper

a small bowl

a bottle of glue

some water

a paintbrush

some green or brown tissue paper

some plastic dinosaurs

1. Lay out a large, sturdy piece of cardboard for a base.

2. Have an adult help you tear newspaper into strips of various lengths.

3. In a small bowl, mix equal parts glue and water.

4. Dip the newspaper strips one at a time into the thinned glue and then layer them on the cardboard in various places to make a bumpy terrain.

5. If necessary, brush the layers with the glue mixture to make them stick.

6. Glue a large sheet of green or brown tissue paper over the newspaper for the final layer.

7. When the terrain is dry, use small plastic dinosaurs to roam about in Dinosaur Land.

Dinos in the Water

You will need:

some play sand

a tub or a bucket

some water

some nature items (rocks, blades of grass, etc.)

some sponges or corks

some small plastic dinosaurs

1. Have an adult help you pour sand into a shallow tub or bucket to a depth of 1 or 2 inches.

2. Add a few inches of water in the tub or bucket.

3. Create a dinosaur environment by adding sponges or corks for driftwood, and nature items, such as one or two large rocks for islands, and a few blades of grass for seaweed. Use whatever items you find, they do not have to be the items that are listed here.

4. Using small plastic dinosaurs, pretend they are swimming and climbing around in the water.

Tyrannosaurus Toss

You will need:
a pen or a marker
a large piece of sturdy
cardboard
a craft knife
a chair
some masking tape
some beanbags

1. Have an adult help you draw a picture of a large Tyrannosaurus head on a piece of sturdy cardboard.

2. Then, ask him or her to cut out the dinosaur's mouth, forming lots of teeth, using a craft knife.

3. Prop the cardboard Tyrannosaurus head against a chair or across a doorway and secure it with tape.

4. Attach a line of masking tape to the floor a few feet away from the cardboard.

5. With a friend or two, stand behind the line and take turns "feeding" the dinosaur by tossing beanbags into its mouth. The first person to toss ten beanbags in the Tyrannosaurus's mouth is the winner.

Mold Fossils

You will need:

some leaves
some clay
a jar of petroleum jelly
a small ink roller
some plaster of Paris
a rolling pin
a table knife

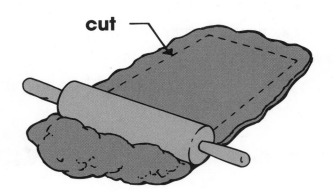

cut

1. Using the rolling pin, roll the clay until it is about $1/2$" thick. Cut around the edges to make an oval or rectangle. Remove the excess clay.

2. Roll out more clay. Cut it into strips. Put the strips around the oval and pinch them securely into place.

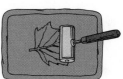

3. Rub petroleum jelly over the rectangle or oval and on the inside of the strips.

4. Press a leaf into the bottom of the clay tray. Use the ink roller to roll over the leaf and make an impression. Remove the leaf.

5. Pour plaster of Paris into the clay tray and let it set. When set, separate the clay and plaster.

A Dinosaur Mobile

You will need:

a piece of poster board
(any color)
a hole punch
some yarn or string

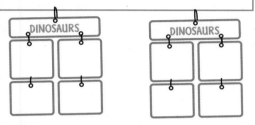

1. Locate the mobile pieces on pages 237 and 239. Tear the pages out of the book and color the pieces any way you like.

2. Glue the pages to a piece of poster board. After the glue has dried, cut out the mobile pieces following the border lines on each piece.

3. Punch out holes on each piece as indicated by the dots.

4. String the pieces together with yarn or string, and hang your mobile.

Tyrannosaurus

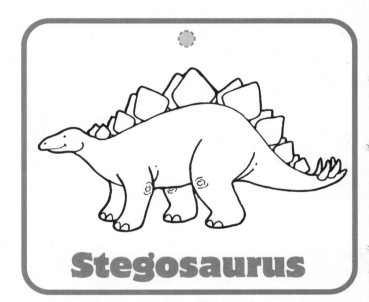

Stegosaurus

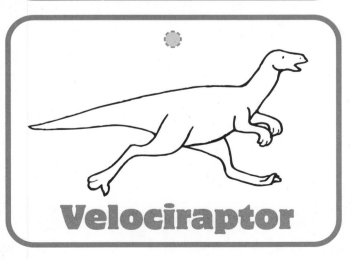

Velociraptor

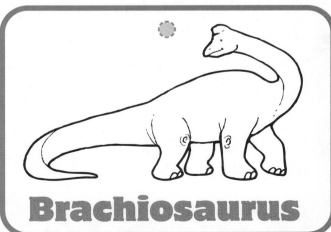

Brachiosaurus

This page is intentionally left blank.

A Dinosaur Mobile

DINOSAURS

DINOSAURS

Apatosaurus

Psittacosaurus

Triceratops

Allosaurus

This page is intentionally left blank.

Games

Game Directions

The games on pages 243–251 are designed to provide important practice for learning math facts. Locate some items that can be used as game markers, such as small plastic dinosaurs, buttons, paper clips, or dried beans. Cut out the game card sets on pages 253–265 and store each set of cards in a separate plastic bag—be sure to label the bags with the card set name. Game play requires two or more players.

To Play:

- Choose a game and read the object of the game below. Tear out the corresponding gameboard. Mix up the game card set(s) required to play the game and place them facedown in a pile.
- For games 1–6, player 1 takes a card, reads it aloud, calls out the answer, and marks the corresponding space on the gameboard. If the player guesses correctly, he or she takes another turn. If the player guesses incorrectly, or if no correct answer space is left on the board, he or she loses that turn and the next player proceeds.
- For games 7–8, all players take a card and read them aloud. The player with the highest number moves his or her game marker up one space on the gameboard. If the numbers are equal, all markers remain at their current position.
- Continue playing until the object of the game is reached.

Games

1. Four Together (Page 243; use game card set A, B, C, D, E, or F)

2. The Vine Game (Page 244; use game card set A, B, C, D, E, or F)

3. Add-a-Dino! (Page 245; use game card set A, B, C, D, E, or F)

Object for games 1–3: To be the first player to place four of his or her game markers next to each other on the gameboard.

4. Dinosaur Park (Page 246; use game card set A, B, C, D, E, or F)

5. Tyrannosaurus Trail (Page 247; use game card set A, B, C, D, E, or F)

6. Dinosaur Trail (Page 248; use game card set A, B, C, D, E, or F)

7. Capture the Dinosaur Bone (Page 249; use game card set G or H)

8. Stepping Stones (Page 250; use game card set G or H)

Object for games 4–8: To be the first player to place his or her game marker on the designated end of the gameboard.

Four Together

| 9 | 6 | 1 | 8 | 3 | 4 | 7 | 8 |

5							2
4							5
3							8
10							6
6							4
2							2
0							5
7							10
1							4

Object: To be the first player to place four game markers next to each other on the game board.

Game Cards: A, B, C, D, E, or F

| 5 | 9 | 7 | 6 | 3 | 7 | 9 | 1 |

The Vine Game

Object: To be the first player to place four game markers next to each other on the game board.

Game Cards: A, B, C, D, E, or F

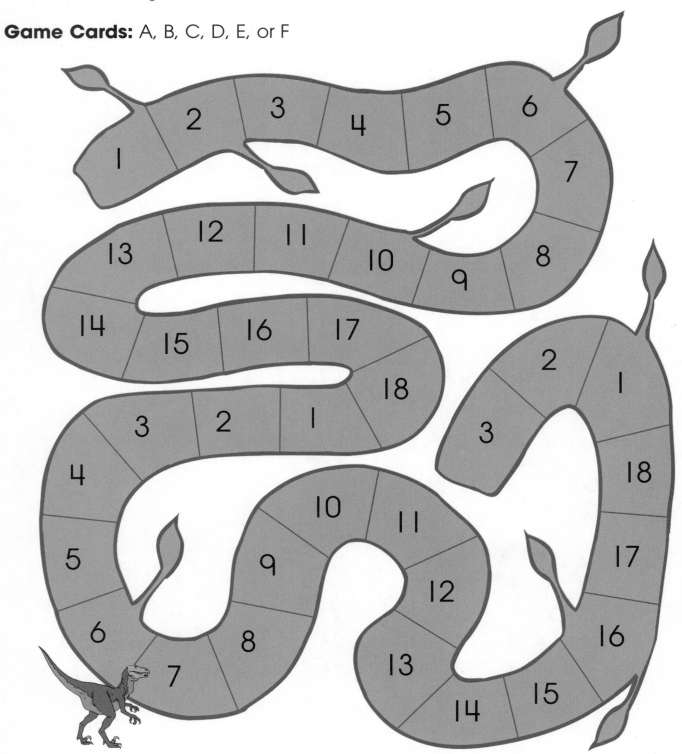

Add-a-Dino!

Object: To be the first player to place four game markers next to each other on the gameboard.

Game Cards: A, B, C, D, E, or F

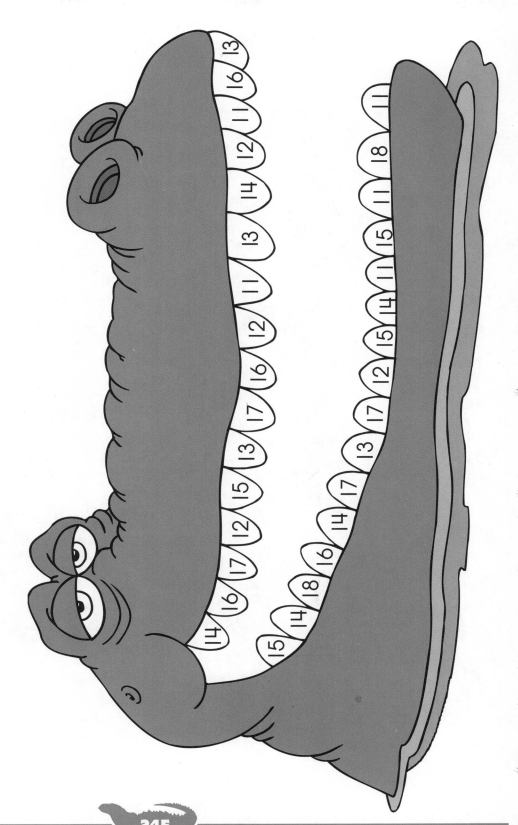

Dinosaur Park

Object: To be the first player to place his or her game marker on "X."

Game Cards: A, B, C, D, E, or F

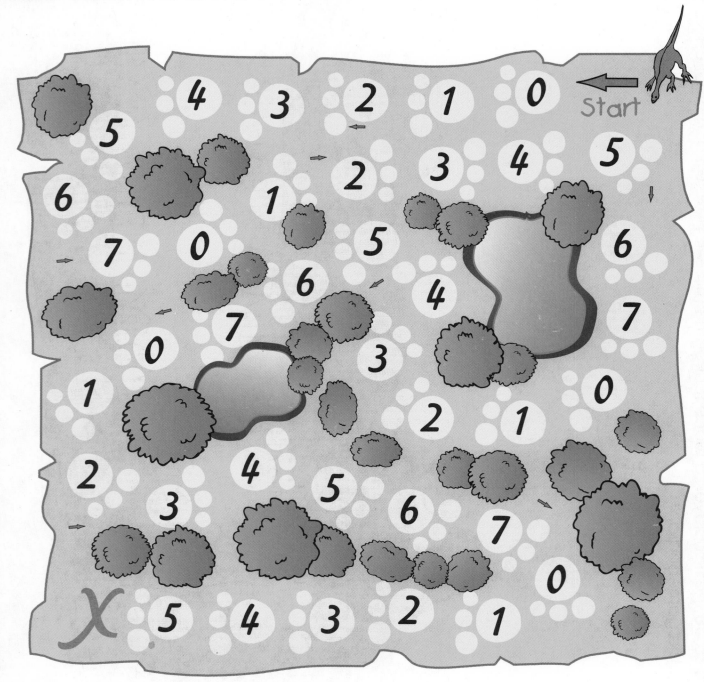

Tyrannosaurus Trail

Object: To be the first player to place his or her game marker on "Stop."

Game Cards: A, B, C, D, E, or F

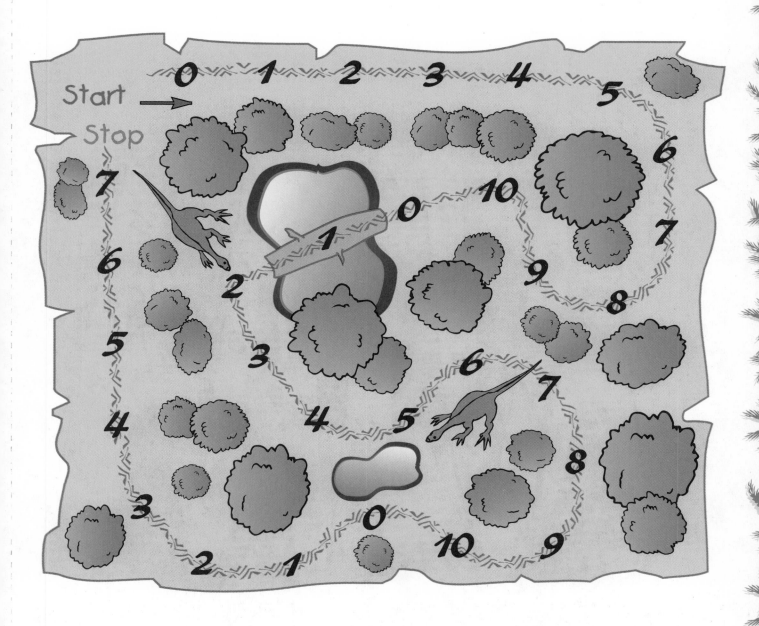

The Dinosaur Trail

Object: To be the first player to place his or her game marker on "Stop."

Game Cards: A, B, C, D, E, or F

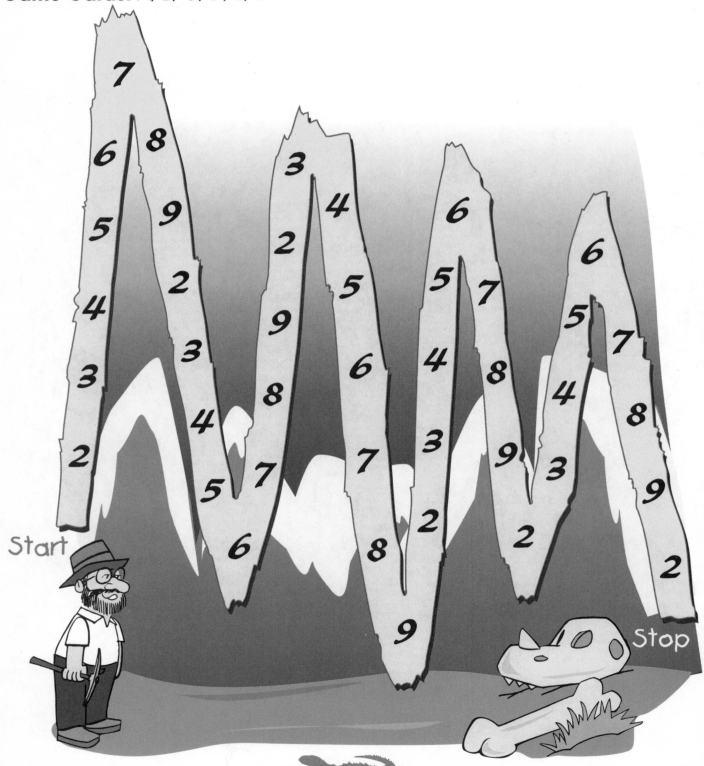

Capture the Dinosaur Bone

Object: To be the first player to place his or her marker on the number "12" at the top of the mountain.

Game Cards: G or H

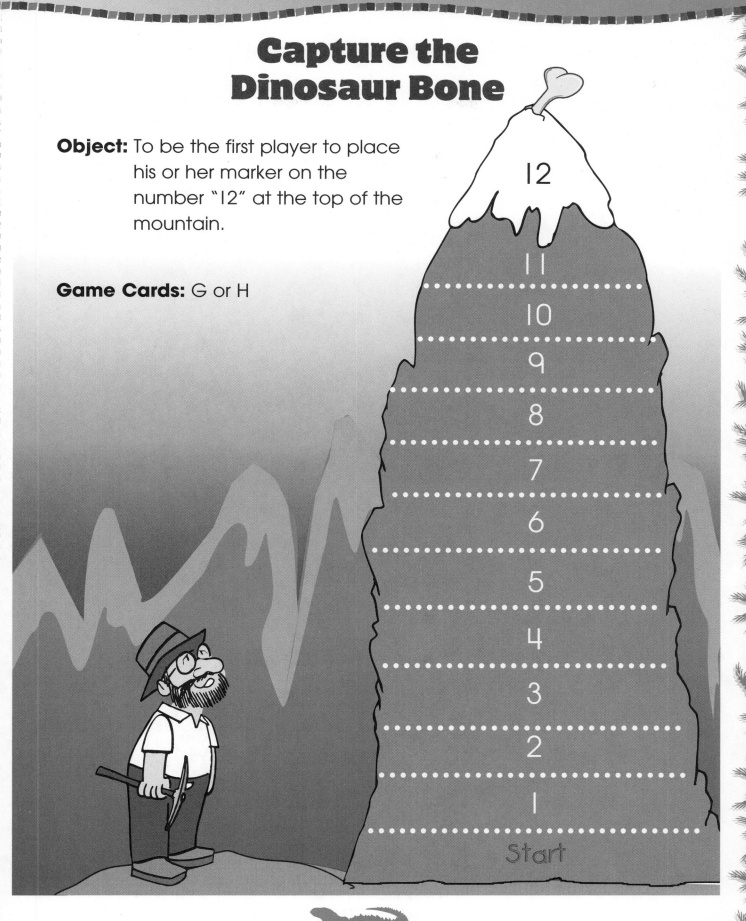

12

11

10

9

8

7

6

5

4

3

2

1

Start

Stepping Stones

Object: To be the first player to place his or her game marker on the "End" stone. **Game Cards:** G or H

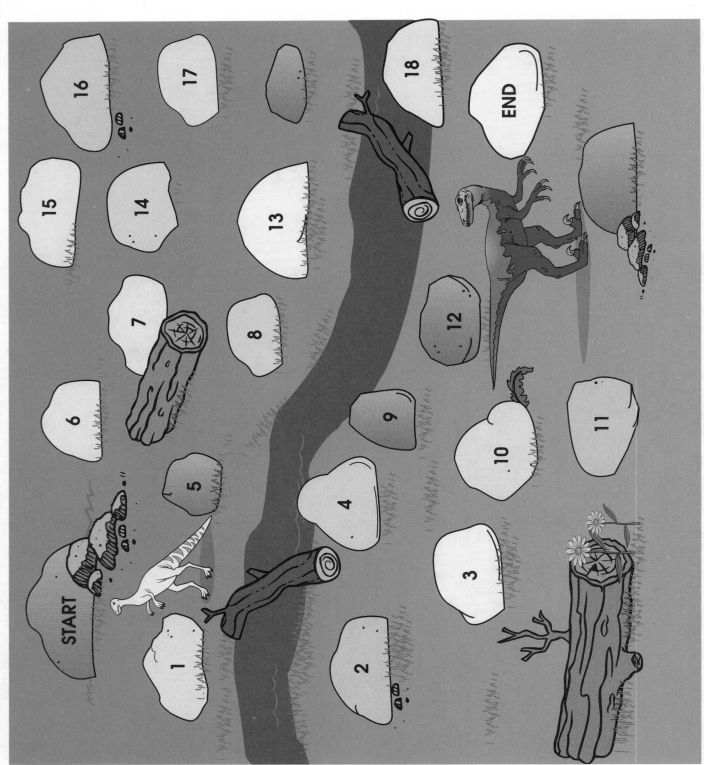

Game Cards A

5 + 0 A	1 + 1 A	7 + 1 A	5 + 2 A	5 + 3 A	5 + 5 A
4 + 0 A	10 + 0 A	6 + 1 A	4 + 2 A	4 + 3 A	6 + 4 A
3 + 0 A	9 + 0 A	5 + 1 A	3 + 2 A	3 + 3 A	5 + 4 A
2 + 0 A	8 + 0 A	4 + 1 A	2 + 2 A	8 + 2 A	4 + 4 A
1 + 0 A	7 + 0 A	3 + 1 A	9 + 1 A	7 + 2 A	7 + 3 A
0 + 0 A	6 + 0 A	2 + 1 A	8 + 1 A	6 + 2 A	6 + 3 A

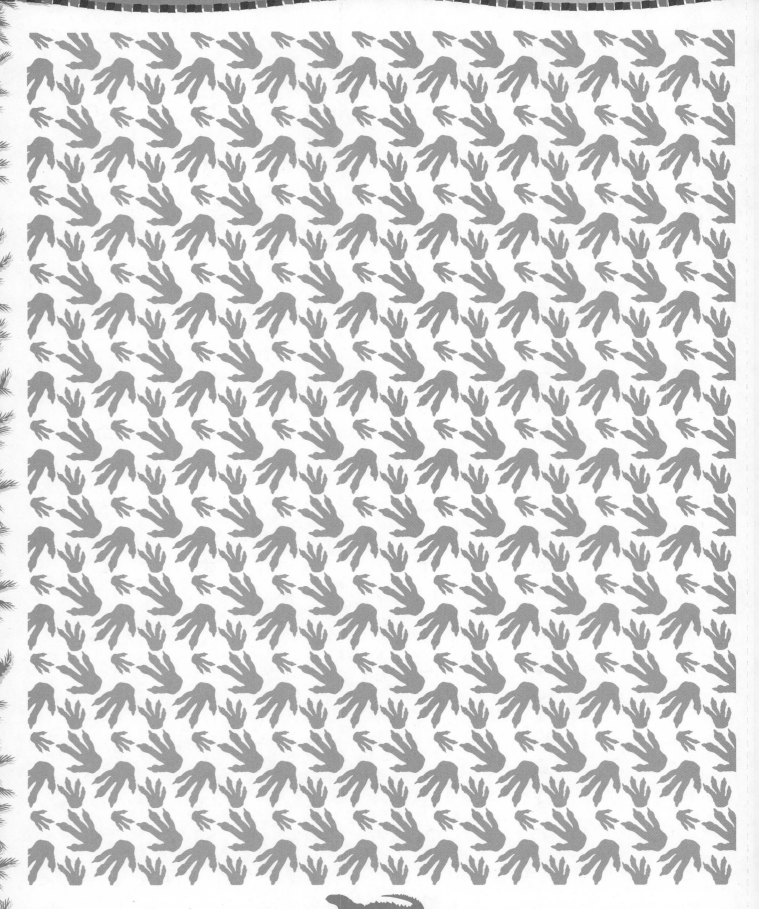

0 + 5 ^B	1 + 1 ^B	1 + 7 ^B	2 + 5 ^B	3 + 5 ^B	5 + 5 ^B
0 + 4 ^B	0 + 10 ^B	1 + 6 ^B	2 + 4 ^B	3 + 4 ^B	4 + 6 ^B
0 + 3 ^B	0 + 9 ^B	1 + 5 ^B	2 + 3 ^B	3 + 3 ^B	4 + 5 ^B
0 + 2 ^B	0 + 8 ^B	1 + 4 ^B	2 + 2 ^B	2 + 8 ^B	4 + 4 ^B
0 + 1 ^B	0 + 7 ^B	1 + 3 ^B	1 + 9 ^B	2 + 7 ^B	3 + 7 ^B
0 + 0 ^B	0 + 6 ^B	1 + 2 ^B	1 + 8 ^B	2 + 6 ^B	3 + 6 ^B

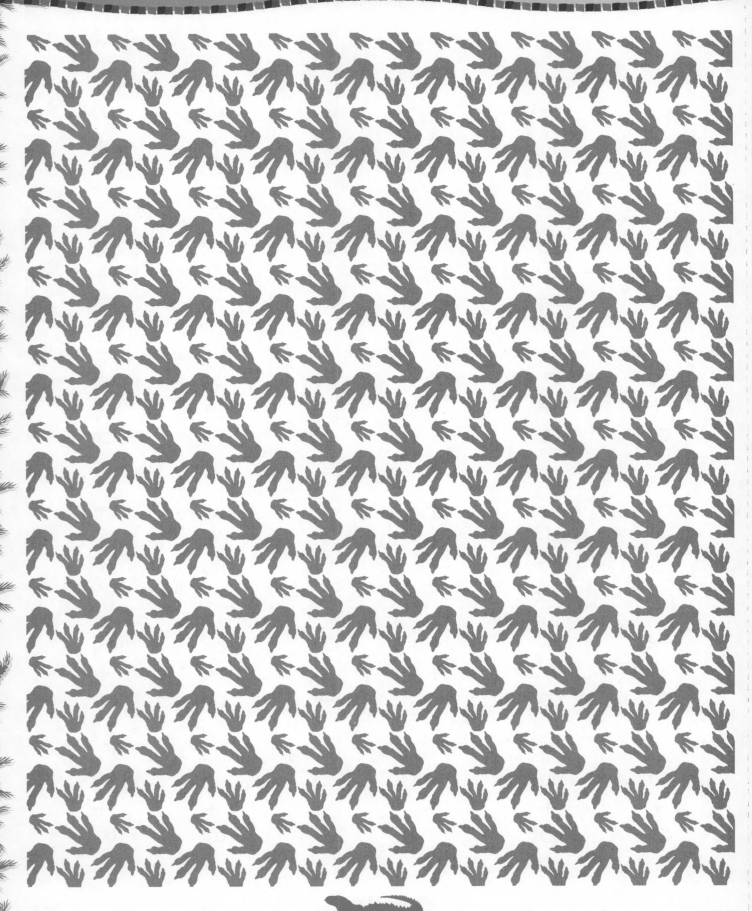

2 − 2 ᶜ	4 − 1 ᶜ	5 − 2 ᶜ	6 − 2 ᶜ	7 − 1 ᶜ	7 − 7 ᶜ
2 − 1 ᶜ	4 − 0 ᶜ	5 − 1 ᶜ	6 − 1 ᶜ	7 − 0 ᶜ	7 − 6 ᶜ
2 − 0 ᶜ	3 − 3 ᶜ	5 − 0 ᶜ	6 − 0 ᶜ	6 − 6 ᶜ	7 − 5 ᶜ
1 − 1 ᶜ	3 − 2 ᶜ	4 − 4 ᶜ	5 − 5 ᶜ	6 − 5 ᶜ	7 − 4 ᶜ
1 − 0 ᶜ	3 − 1 ᶜ	4 − 3 ᶜ	5 − 4 ᶜ	6 − 4 ᶜ	7 − 3 ᶜ
0 − 0 ᶜ	3 − 0 ᶜ	4 − 2 ᶜ	5 − 3 ᶜ	6 − 3 ᶜ	7 − 2 ᶜ

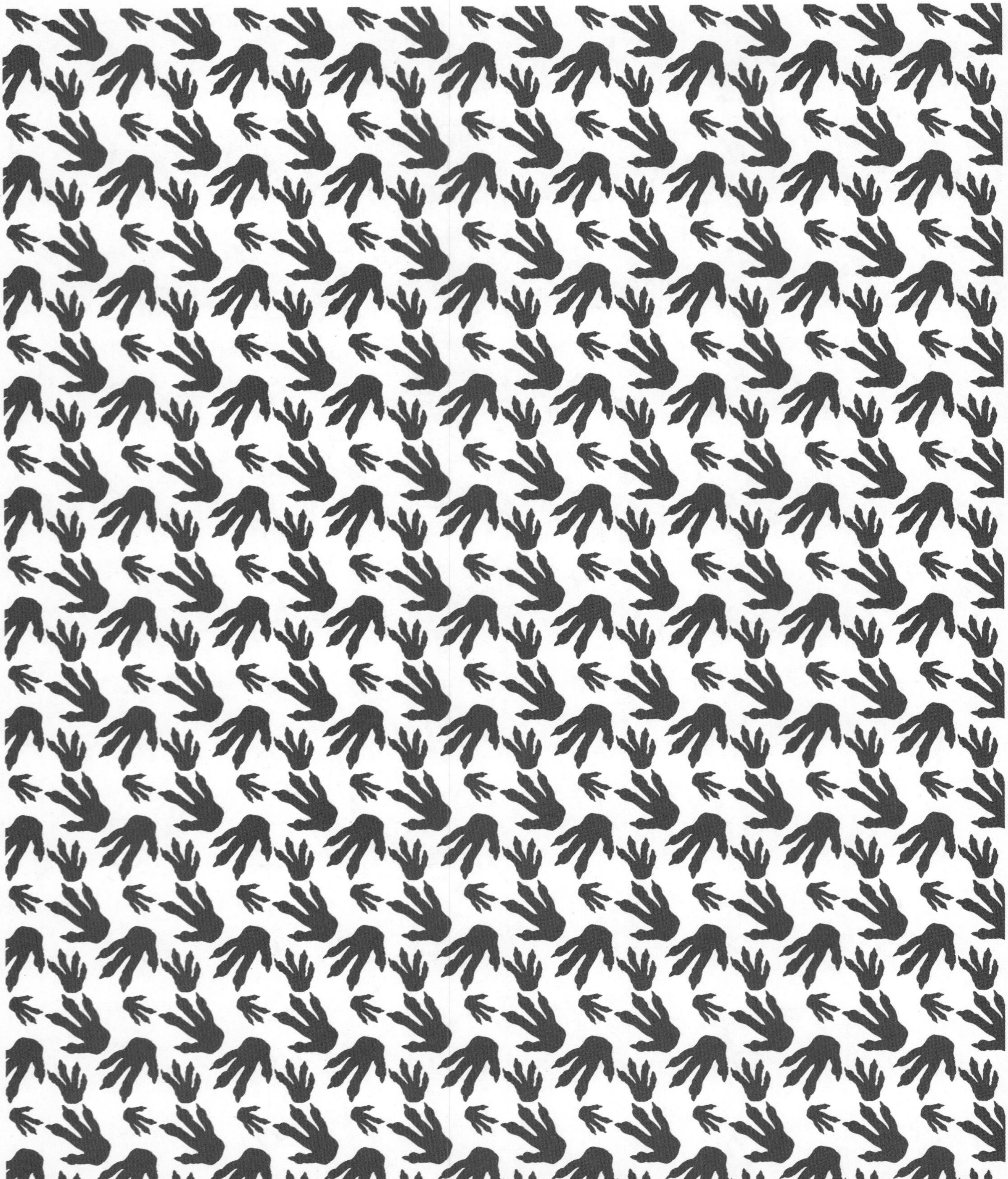

Game Cards D

8 − 5 D	9 − 2 D	9 − 8 D	10 − 4 D	10 − 10 D	10 − 4 D
8 − 4 D	9 − 1 D	9 − 7 D	10 − 3 D	10 − 9 D	10 − 5 D
8 − 3 D	9 − 0 D	9 − 6 D	10 − 2 D	10 − 8 D	10 − 6 D
8 − 2 D	8 − 8 D	9 − 5 D	10 − 1 D	10 − 7 D	10 − 7 D
8 − 1 D	8 − 7 D	9 − 4 D	10 − 0 D	10 − 6 D	10 − 8 D
8 − 0 D	8 − 6 D	9 − 3 D	9 − 9 D	10 − 5 D	10 − 9 D

4 + 7 E	6 + 6 E	7 + 6 E	7 + 7 E	6 + 9 E	9 + 9 E
5 + 6 E	7 + 5 E	8 + 5 E	8 + 6 E	7 + 8 E	8 + 9 E
6 + 5 E	8 + 4 E	9 + 4 E	9 + 5 E	8 + 7 E	9 + 8 E
7 + 4 E	9 + 3 E	3 + 9 E	4 + 9 E	9 + 6 E	7 + 9 E
8 + 3 E	2 + 9 E	4 + 8 E	5 + 8 E	5 + 9 E	8 + 8 E
9 + 2 E	3 + 8 E	5 + 7 E	6 + 7 E	6 + 8 E	9 + 7 E

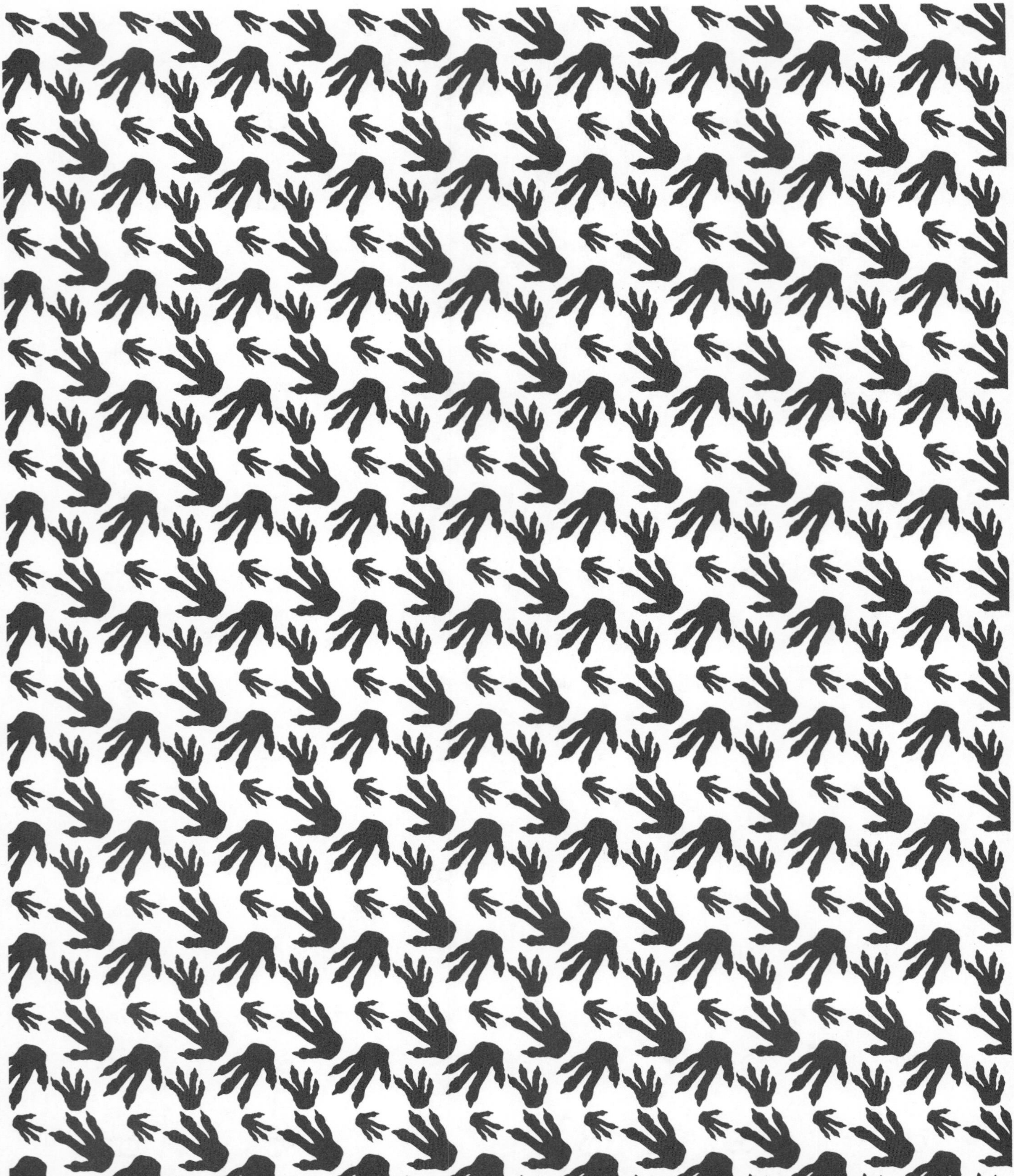

11 − 4 F	12 − 6 F	13 − 7 F	14 − 7 F	15 − 6 F	18 − 9 F
11 − 5 F	12 − 7 F	13 − 8 F	14 − 8 F	15 − 7 F	17 − 8 F
11 − 6 F	12 − 8 F	13 − 9 F	14 − 9 F	15 − 8 F	17 − 9 F
11 − 7 F	12 − 9 F	12 − 3 F	13 − 4 F	15 − 9 F	16 − 7 F
11 − 8 F	11 − 2 F	12 − 4 F	13 − 5 F	14 − 5 F	16 − 8 F
11 − 9 F	11 − 3 F	12 − 5 F	13 − 6 F	14 − 6 F	16 − 9 F

G	G	G	G	G	G
6	12	18	6	12	18
G	G	G	G	G	G
5	11	17	5	11	17
G	G	G	G	G	G
4	10	16	4	10	16
G	G	G	G	G	G
3	9	15	3	9	15
G	G	G	G	G	G
2	8	14	2	8	14
G	G	G	G	G	G
1	7	13	1	7	13

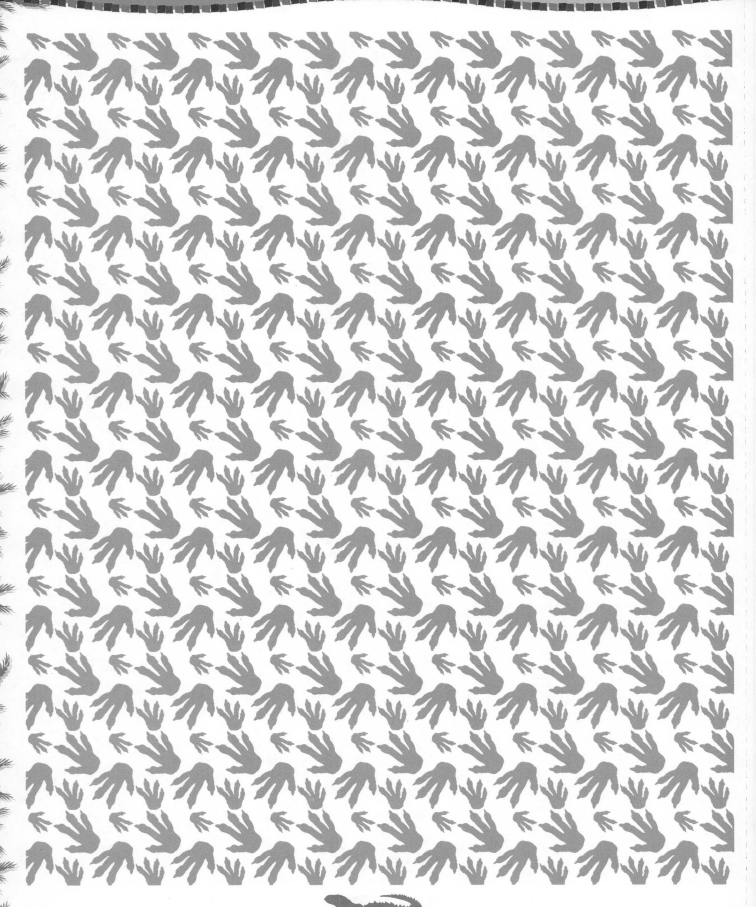

six	five	four	three	two	one
twelve	eleven	ten	nine	eight	seven
eighteen	seventeen	sixteen	fifteen	fourteen	thirteen
卌 I	卌	IIII	III	II	I
卌 卌 II	卌 卌 I	卌 卌	卌 IIII	卌 III	卌 卌
卌 卌 卌 III	卌 卌 卌 II	卌 卌 卌 I	卌 卌 卌	卌 卌 IIII	卌 卌 III

Can You Count It?

Help the mother dinosaur find her baby!

To Play:

1. Use the gameboard on page 268.

2. Cut out the game cards on page 269, mix them up, and place them in a pile facedown next to the gameboard.

3. Each player draws a card and then counts the number of dots on it. If the player counts correctly, he or she moves his or her game marker forward one space.

4. The first player to reach the stone marked "Finish" wins!

START

END

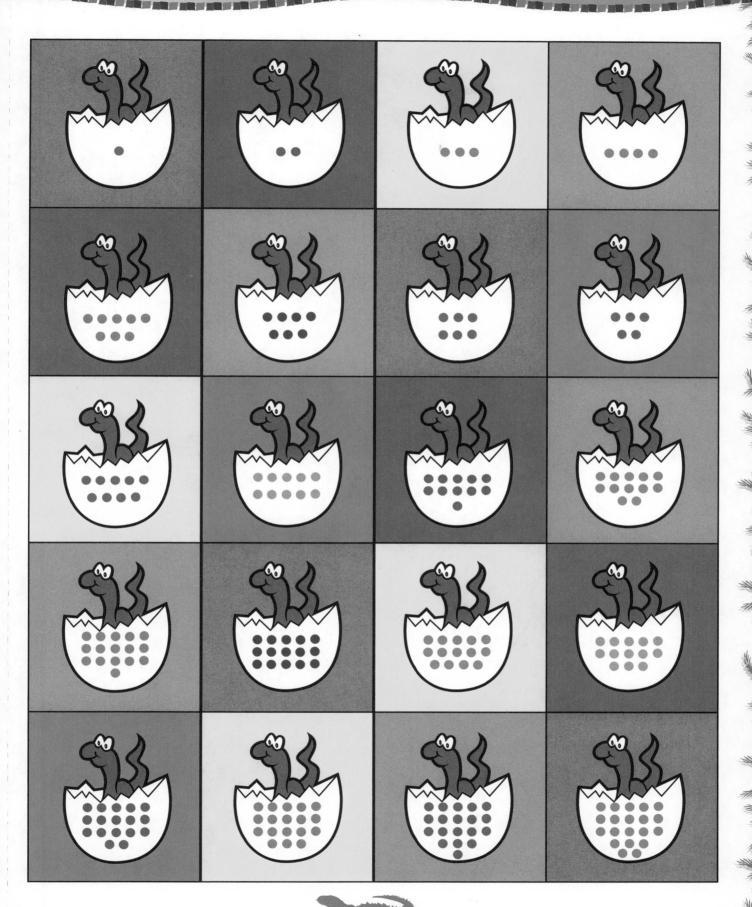

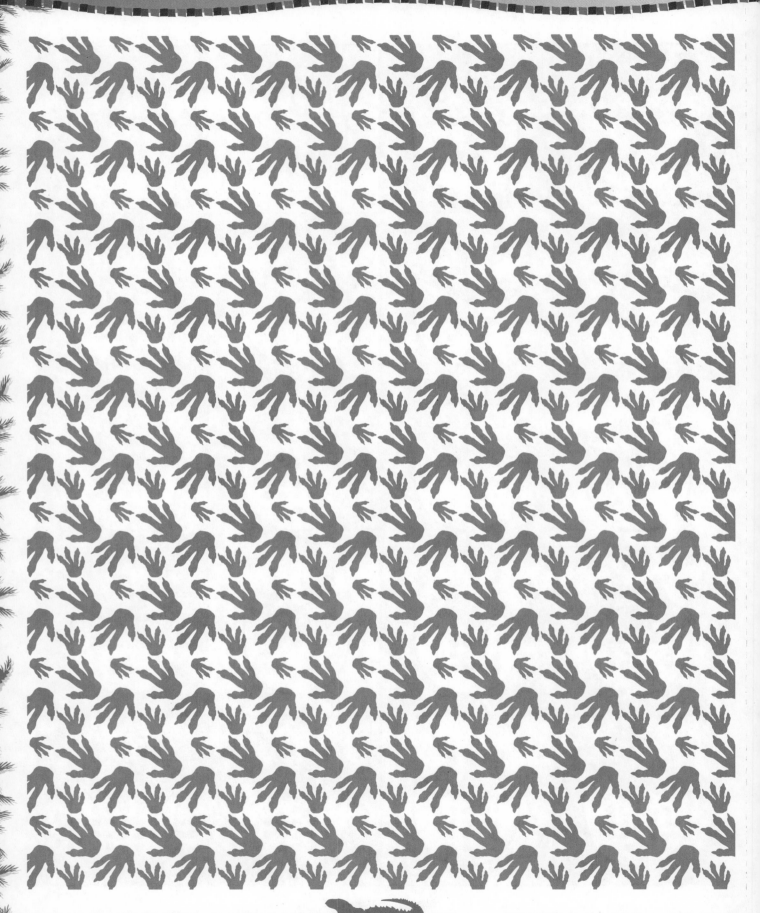

Dinosaur Memory Match

Object: To improve concentration and visual memory skills while having fun and learning about dinosaurs!

Beginning Activities:

1. Tear out pages 273–279 from the book and lay out all the pages in front of you.

2. Look at the pictures and say the name of each dinosaur.

3. Name any interesting facts about these dinosaur that you remember learning from this book.

4. Carefully cut out the cards.

How to Play:

1. Mix up and spread out all the cards facedown in front of you on a flat surface.

2. The first player turns over two cards. If the cards match, the player puts the pair of cards in a pile in front of him or her. The player continues playing until the cards he or she turns over do not match. The player returns the unmatched cards to the game pile.

3. Each player follows the same procedure. When all the game cards are gone, the player with the most cards in his or her pile wins.

Hint: Each player should try to remember where the unmatched cards have been placed so they can be located if a match is found.

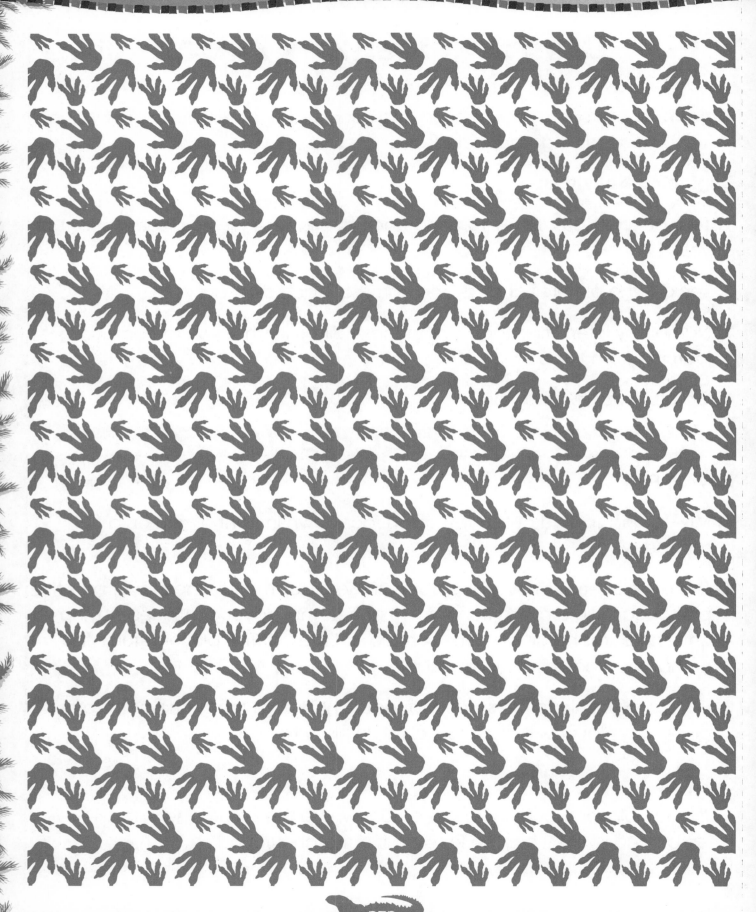

Corythosaurus

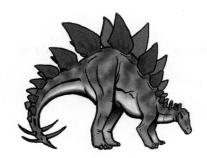

Stegosaurus

Apatosaurus

Corythosaurus

Stegosaurus

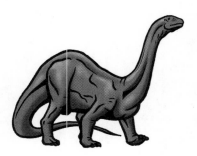

Apatosaurus

Corythosaurus

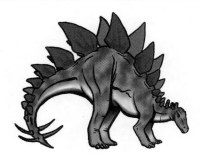

Stegosaurus

Apatosaurus

Corythosaurus

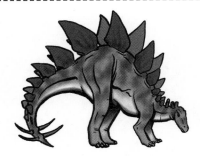

Stegosaurus

Apatosaurus

Maiasaura

Ceratosaurus

Protoceratops

Maiasaura

Ceratosaurus

Protoceratops

Maiasaura

Ceratosaurus

Protoceratops

Maiasaura

Ceratosaurus

Protoceratops

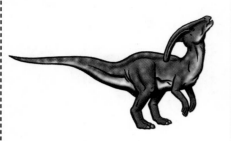

Parasaurolophus

Brachiosaurus

Compsognathus

Parasaurolophus

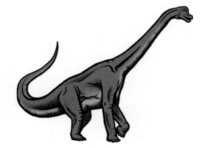

Brachiosaurus

Compsognathus

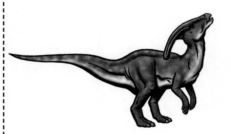

Parasaurolophus

Brachiosaurus

Compsognathus

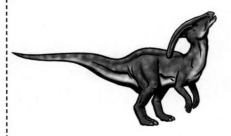

Parasaurolophus

Brachiosaurus

Compsognathus

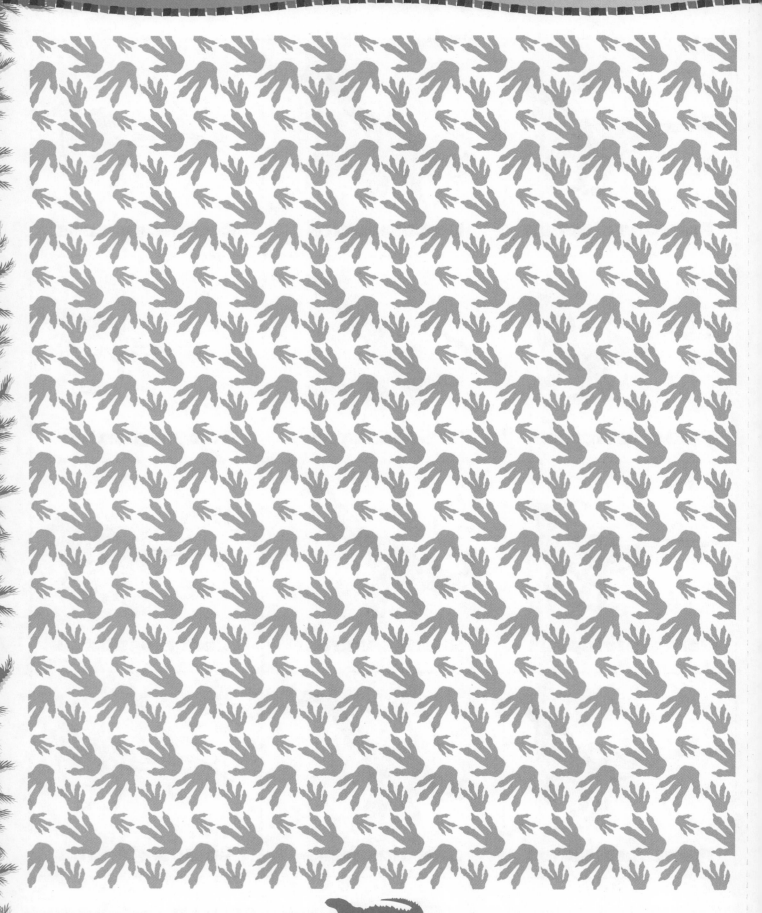

Tyrannosaurus

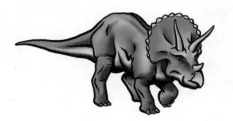

Triceratops

Allosaurus

Tyrannosaurus

Triceratops

Allosaurus

Tyrannosaurus

Triceratops

Allosaurus

Tyrannosaurus

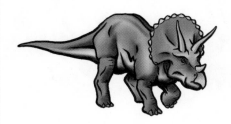

Triceratops

Allosaurus

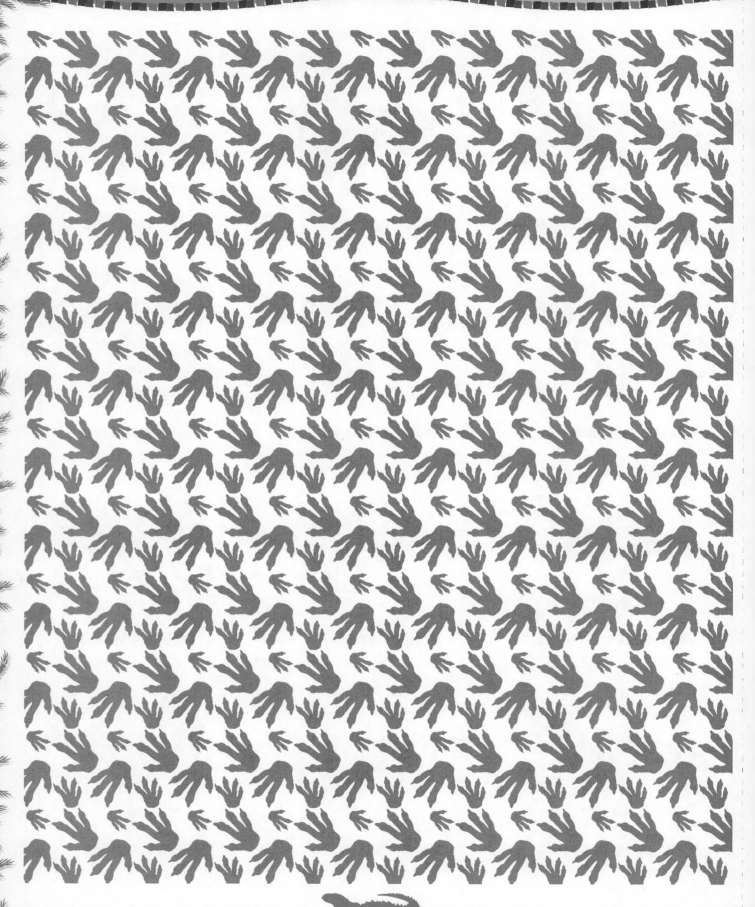

Dinosaur Dominoes

Object: To be the first player to be out of dominoes

To Play:

1. Tear out pages 283–289 from the book.

2. Carefully cut out the dominoes.

3. Mix up the dominoes and put them facedown on the playing surface in a draw pile.

4. Each player takes seven dominoes. Be careful not to let the other players see your dominoes!

5. Now take turns placing a domino on the playing surface so that the touching ends have matching dinosaurs.

6. If you can't make a match, take a domino from the draw pile. If you still can't make a match, your turn is over and the next player proceeds.

7. The first player to be out of dominoes is the winner.

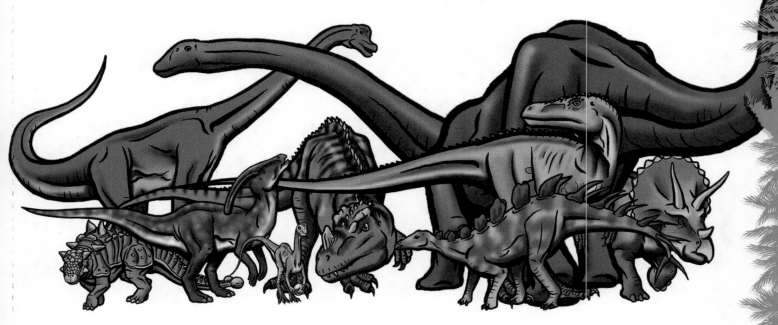

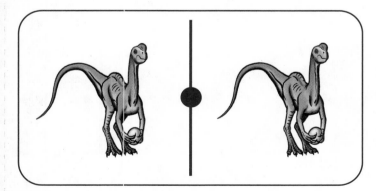

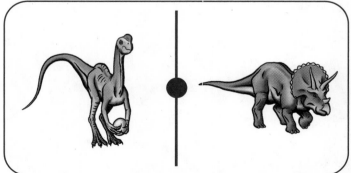

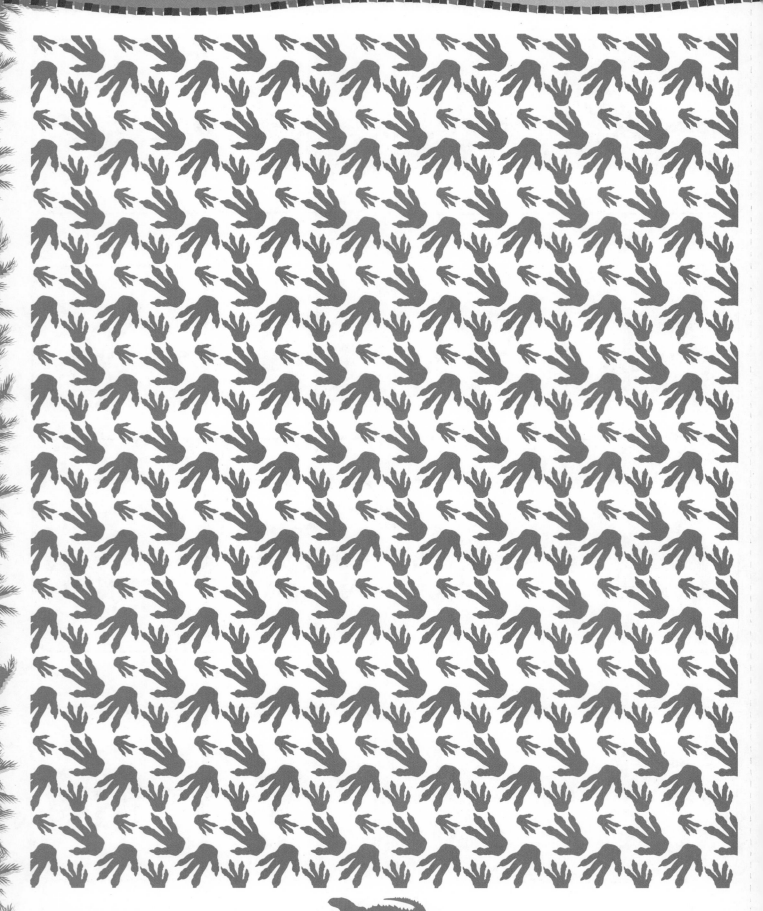

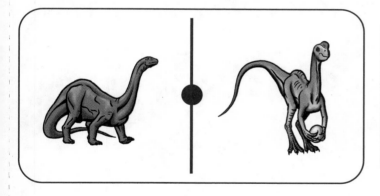

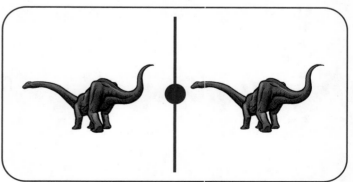

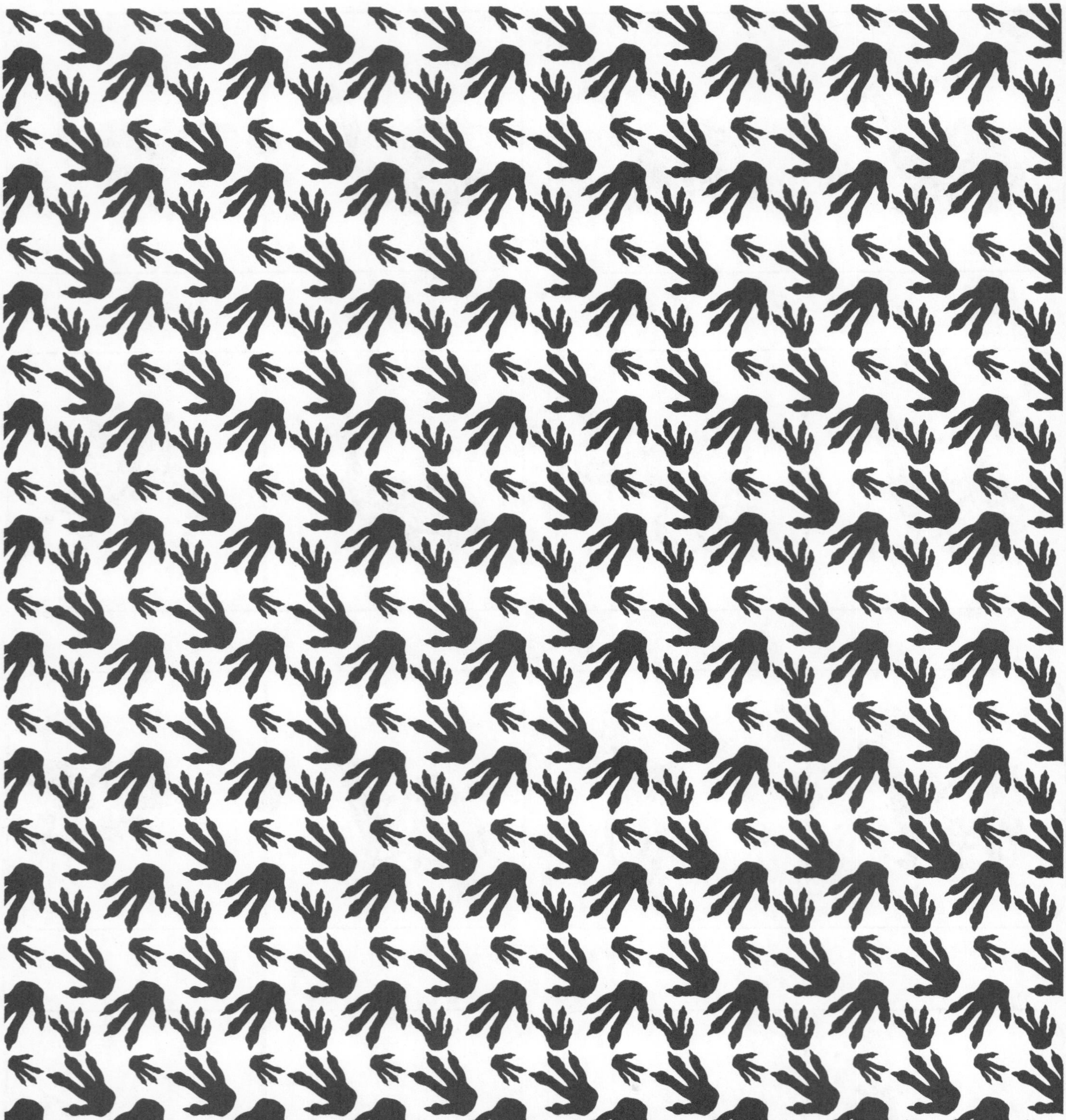

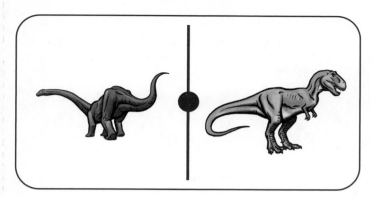

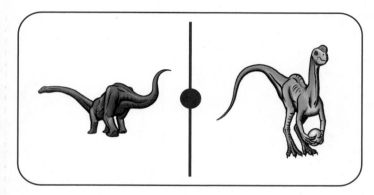

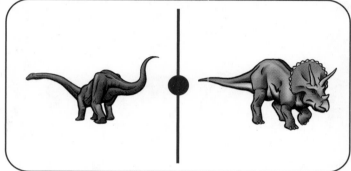

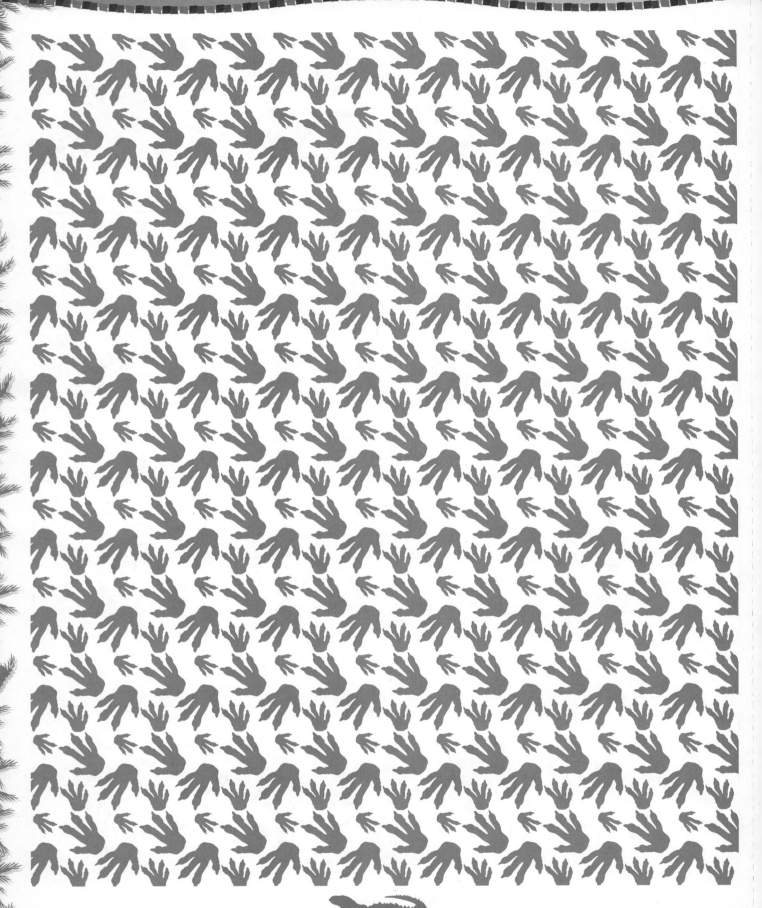

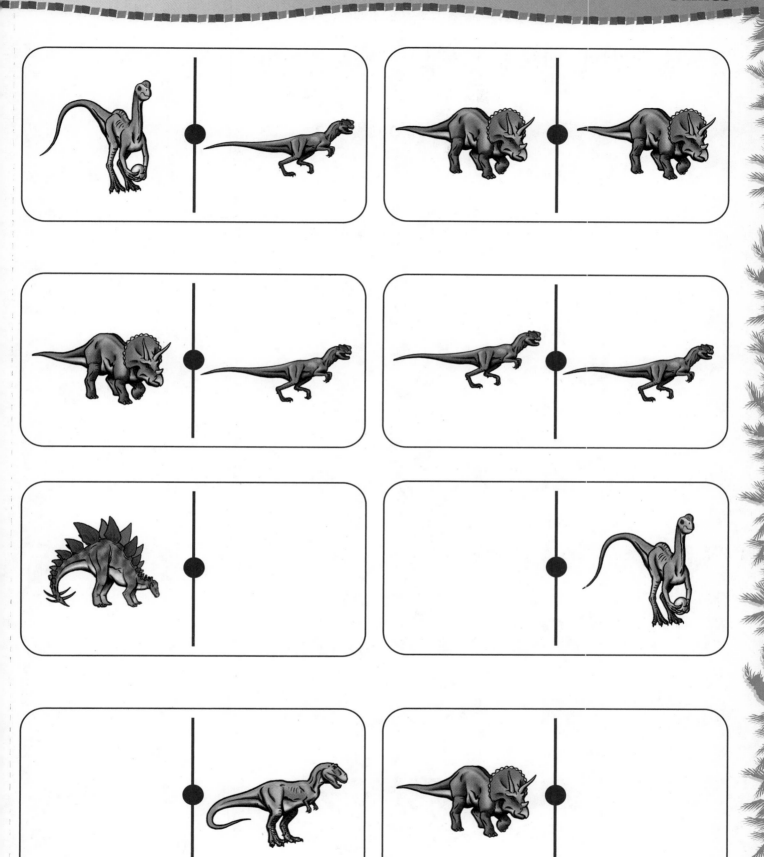

Dino-Mite!

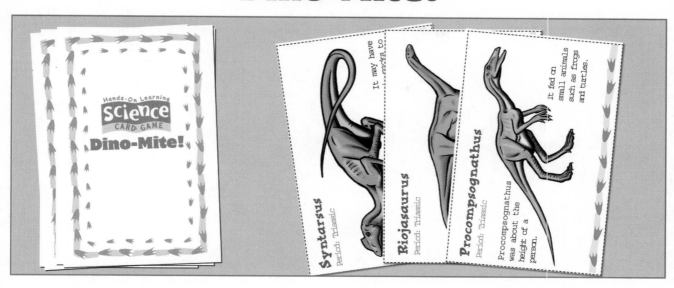

Object: To be the player who has collected the most cards.

To Play:

1. Tear out pages 293–309 from the book. Carefully cut out the cards.

2. One player mixes up the cards and deals all of them face down to the other players. Players keep their cards facedown and do not look at them.

3. The first player lays one card face up to start the discard pile. Then players take turns laying a card face up on top of this pile.

4. If two cards are played right after each other that both feature dinosaurs from the same time period, the first player to slap his or her hand on the pile and call out "Dino!" collects all of the cards in the pile. That round ends, and whoever has the next turn lays down a card to begin the discard pile again.

5. If a player slaps the pile in error, then he or she gives each of the other players one card from his or her "winnings" as a penalty.

6. The game ends when all the cards have been played. The player who has collected the most cards wins.

This page is intentionally left blank.

Triceratops
Period: Cretaceous

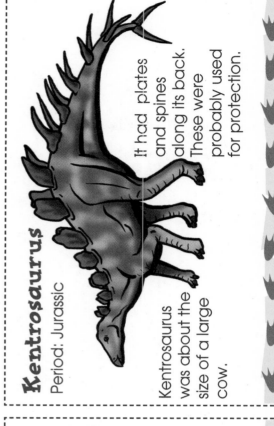

Triceratops was about the size of an elephant. It had three horns on its large head. Its bony frill protected its neck.

Kentrosaurus
Period: Jurassic

It had plates and spines along its back. These were probably used for protection.

Kentrosaurus was about the size of a large cow.

Eoraptor
Period: Triassic

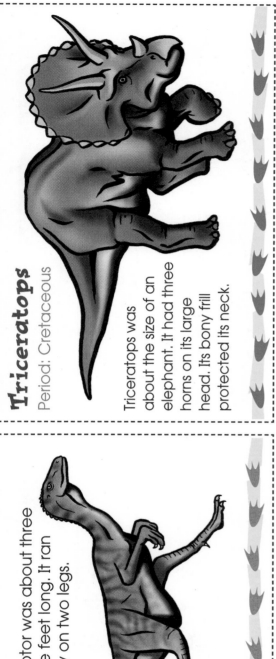

Eoraptor was about three to five feet long. It ran swiftly on two legs.

Herrerasaurus
Period: Triassic

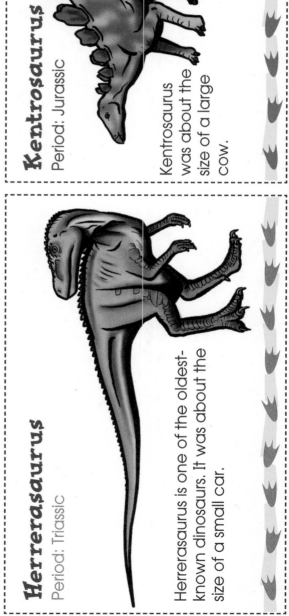

Herrerasaurus is one of the oldest-known dinosaurs. It was about the size of a small car.

Procompsognathus
Period: Triassic

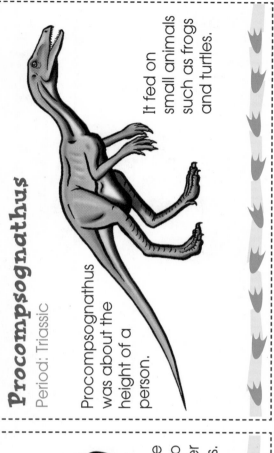

Procompsognathus was about the height of a person.

It fed on small animals such as frogs and turtles.

Coelophysis
Period: Triassic

Coelophysis was only about nine feet long. Its slim body and long legs were built for speed.

Syntarsus
Period: Triassic

Syntarsus was a small meat-eating dinosaur.

It may have hunted in packs to attack larger dinosaurs.

Riojasaurus
Period: Triassic

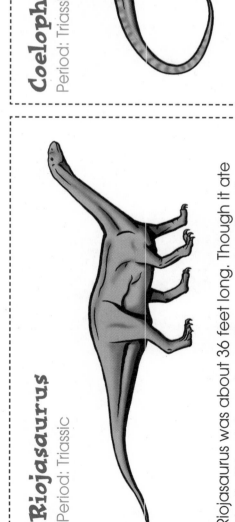

Riojasaurus was about 36 feet long. Though it ate plants, it had sharp fangs like a meat-eating dinosaur.

Plateosaurus
Period: Triassic

Plateosaurus was about 26 feet long. It ate plants near the ground or stood on its hind legs to feed from treetops.

Staurikosaurus
Period: Triassic

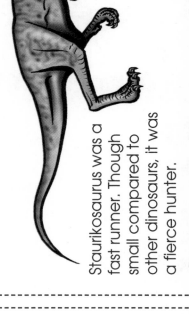

Staurikosaurus was a fast runner. Though small compared to other dinosaurs, it was a fierce hunter.

Scelidosaurus
Period: Jurassic

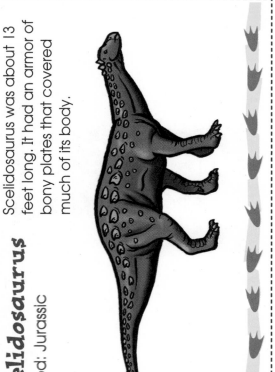

Scelidosaurus was about 13 feet long. It had an armor of bony plates that covered much of its body.

Massospondylus
Period: Triassic

Massospondylus was about as long as a car. It was a plant-eating dinosaur.

Brachiosaurus

Period: Jurassic

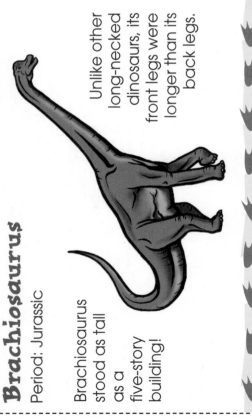

Brachiosaurus stood as tall as a five-story building!

Unlike other long-necked dinosaurs, its front legs were longer than its back legs.

Apatosaurus

Period: Jurassic

Apatosaurus was about 70 feet in length. It may have used its long, whiplike tail to defend itself.

Allosaurus

Period: Jurassic

Allosaurus was about 35 feet long. Its teeth had sawlike edges. Its front legs had sharp, curved claws for holding its prey.

Stegosaurus

Period: Jurassic

Stegosaurus used its spiky tail against enemies. Scientists think the plates on its back helped keep it cool or warm.

Diplodocus
Period: Jurassic

Much of its length came from its neck and tail.

Diplodocus was almost 90 feet long—longer than a tennis court!

Megalosaurus
Period: Jurassic

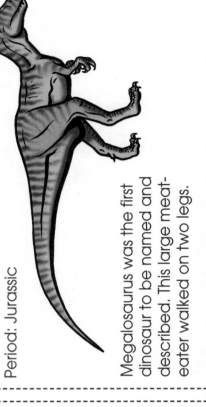

Megalosaurus was the first dinosaur to be named and described. This large meat-eater walked on two legs.

Heterodontosaurus
Period: Jurassic

Heterodontosaurus was a plant eater. Unlike most dinosaurs that had only one kind of tooth, it had three kinds of teeth.

Dilophosaurus
Period: Jurassic

Dilophosaurus was one of the earliest meat-eating dinosaurs. It had a bony crest on its head that looked like two plates standing on edge.

Ceratosaurus
Period: Jurassic

Ceratosaurus was almost 20 feet in length. It had bony ridges over its eyes and a small horn on its snout.

Compsognathus
Period: Jurassic

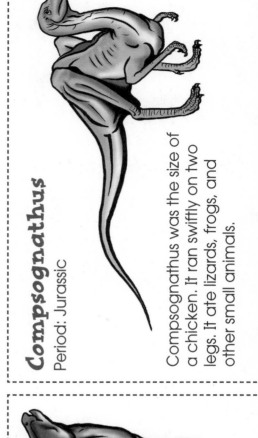

Compsognathus was the size of a chicken. It ran swiftly on two legs. It ate lizards, frogs, and other small animals.

Lesothosaurus
Period: Jurassic

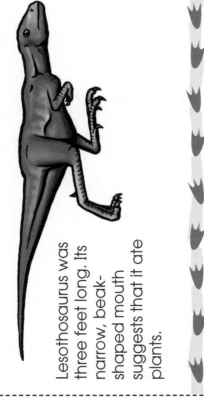

Lesothosaurus was three feet long. Its narrow, beak-shaped mouth suggests that it ate plants.

Parasaurolophus
Period: Cretaceous

Parasaurolophus had a long head crest that curved backwards. Scientists think this dinosaur blew air through the crest to make noises.

Maiasaura
Period: Cretaceous

Maiasaura was about 30 feet long. This plant-eater had a long face and a flat, ducklike beak.

Corythosaurus
Period: Cretaceous

Corythosaurus had a hollow crest on its head. The crest was shaped like a dinner plate. Scientists think it may have been used to make sounds.

Deinonychus
Period: Cretaceous

Deinonychus was a fast-moving dinosaur. It slashed its prey with its long, sharp claws.

Struthiomimus
Period: Cretaceous

Struthiomimus looked somewhat like an ostrich. It had a small head, beaklike jaw, and long, powerful back legs.

Tyrannosaurus
Period: Cretaceous

Tyrannosaurus was the largest of the meat-eating dinosaurs. It was about 46 feet long and 19 feet tall. Its jaws were lined with teeth that were seven inches long.

Oviraptor
Period: Cretaceous

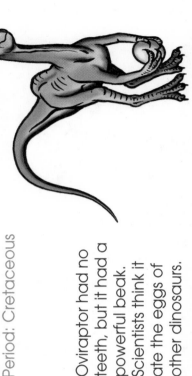

Oviraptor had no teeth, but it had a powerful beak. Scientists think it ate the eggs of other dinosaurs.

Psittacosaurus
Period: Cretaceous

Psittacosaurus had a beaked face that looked like that of a parrot. Its strong beak could slice through woody stems and crack seeds and nuts.

Iguanodon
Period: Cretaceous

Iguanodon was a large plant-eating dinosaur. It had a spiked thumb on each hand that may have been used for defense.

Velociraptor
Period: Cretaceous

Velociraptor was a fierce meat-eating dinosaur. It had long legs, a narrow head, and sharp teeth and claws.

Edmontosaurus
Period: Cretaceous

Edmontosaurus lived in herds. The front of its snout was toothless, but it had about 1,000 teeth in its cheek region for shredding plants.

Protoceratops
Period: Cretaceous

Protoceratops was one of the first horned dinosaurs. Instead of true horns, it had bony lumps on its skull. It also had a shield of bone around its neck.

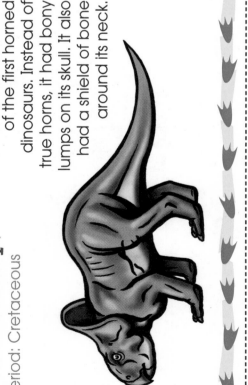

Euoplocephalus
Period: Cretaceous

Euoplocephalus had a body covered by an armor of bony plates and spikes. Its heavy tail club was a powerful weapon.

How to Draw Dinosaurs

Draw Allosaurus

Allosaurus was a powerful meat-eating predator that dominated the earth long before Tyrannasaurus rex lived.

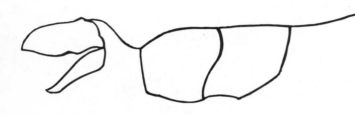

1. Draw the outline of Allosaurus's head, body, and hip. Attach the top of its neck and tail.

2. Begin to add its arms and legs, and finish its neck and tail. Add facial features, including the two small horns atop its head.

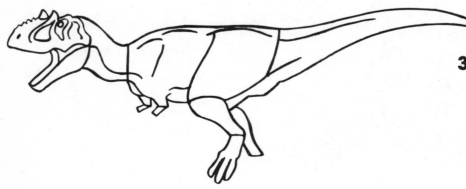

3. Add more detail to its face, as well as muscle definition along its body. Further render its legs, including one foot.

4. Draw its other foot, its front claws, and more muscle lines. Also, add the scales running down its neck and tail. Erase any unneeded lines.

5. To finish, render the dinosaur's teeth, and make its skin appear scaly and its feet bony.

Draw Ankylosaurus

Ankylosaurus was a plant-eating dinosaur covered with armored plates.

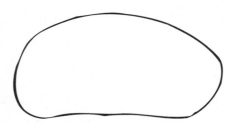

I. First draw a rounded rectangle for the body of Ankylosaurus.

2. Now draw a triangular head using curved lines as shown. Extend a curved tail line past the body. Draw a circle at the end of the tail to form a club shape.

3. Next, indicate the tail's rounded tip and underside. Draw in the four sturdy legs.

4. Add the upper and lower necklines. Next draw the eye, the nostril, the mouth, and the triangular spikes around the head. Sketch in the feet.

5. Pencil in the toes and claws. Erase all unnecessary lines on your creature and detail the tail club as shown. Draw curved lines from the head to the tail to indicate the separate rows of armor plates.

6. Now it's time to add armor. Cross the lines you've already drawn with shorter lines running from the top of the body to the underside. Draw a backward-curving spike inside each square as shown. Note that the spikes are smaller toward the tail. Crosshatch around the legs, face, and tail. Shade the spikes and the tail club, and fill in the eye and nostril. Give the tail texture by adding tiny triangles in the lower portion as shown

Draw Brachiosaurus

Brachiosaurus may have been 46 feet tall, 73 feet long, and could have weighed up to 160,000 pounds.

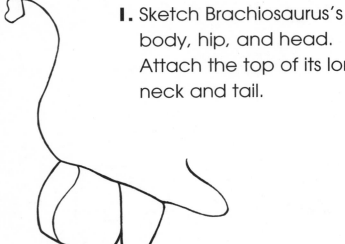

I. Sketch Brachiosaurus's body, hip, and head. Attach the top of its long neck and tail.

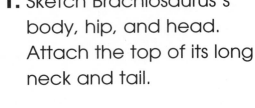

2. Add facial detail, and complete its neck and tail. Begin to form its legs as shown.

3. Render muscle definition on its neck and body, and complete two of its legs.

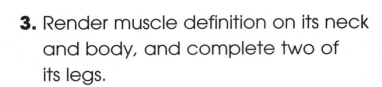

4. Add its eye pupil and more muscle lines. Create its other two legs, and erase unneeded lines.

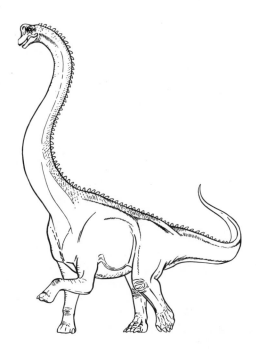

5. Draw its spikes, and detail its legs and feet as shown. Also, add wrinkles as shown. Erase any other unneeded lines.

Draw Coelophysis

Coelophysis was a small but vicious carnivore that, on occasion, even ate its own young.

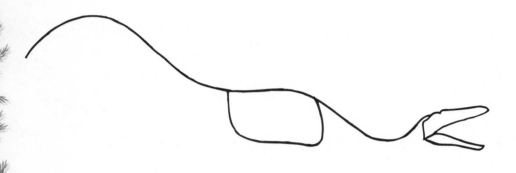

I. Outline its head and body, and then attach the top of its long, slender neck and tail.

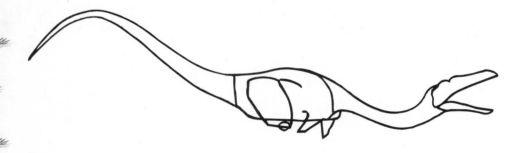

2. Complete its neck and tail, and begin to form its arms and legs.

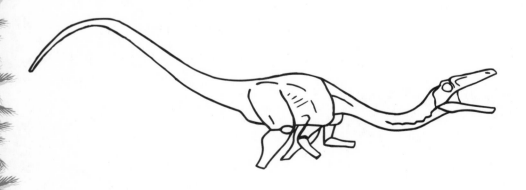

3. Sketch some facial features and the lower section of its arms and legs. Add muscle definition, and erase the line between its body and tail.

4. Draw more muscle definition
and Coelophysis's hands
and feet. Insert its eye pupil,
and erase unneeded lines.

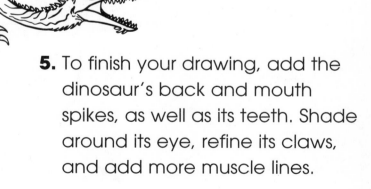

5. To finish your drawing, add the
dinosaur's back and mouth
spikes, as well as its teeth. Shade
around its eye, refine its claws,
and add more muscle lines.

Draw Giganotosaurus

Giganotosaurus is the only meat-eating dinosaur discovered to be larger than Tyrannosaurus rex.

I. Start by drawing the top of this dinosaur's neck, body, and tail.

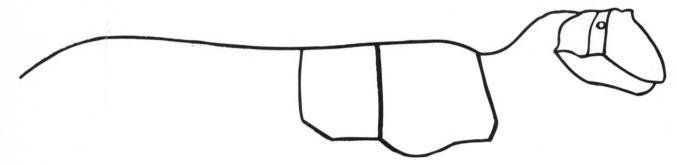

2. Add the rest of its body with the hip, as well as its head. Sketch its eye.

3. Further define its head, and begin to render its arms and legs.

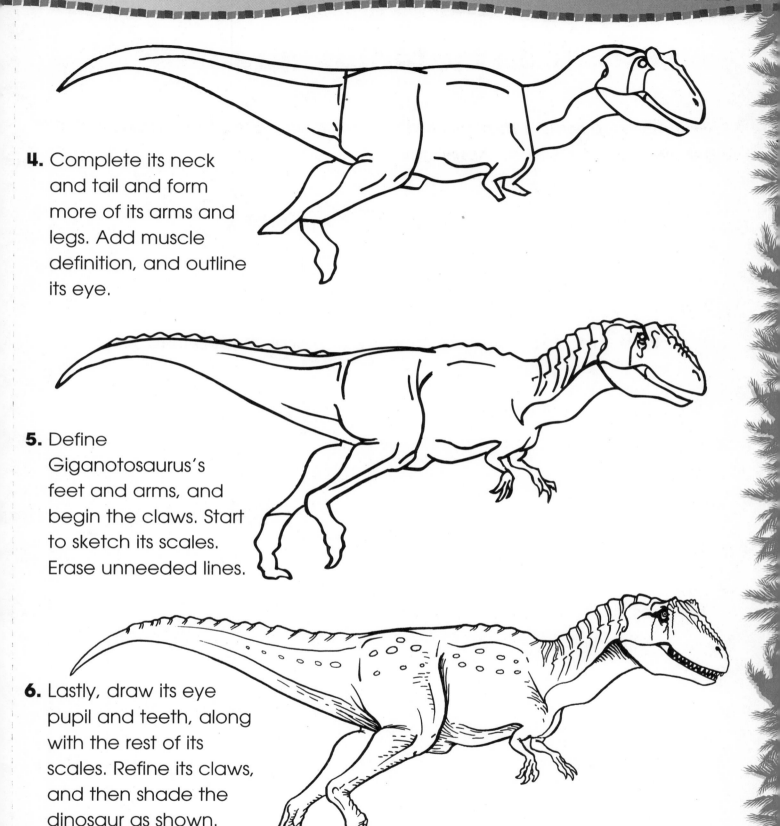

4. Complete its neck and tail and form more of its arms and legs. Add muscle definition, and outline its eye.

5. Define Giganotosaurus's feet and arms, and begin the claws. Start to sketch its scales. Erase unneeded lines.

6. Lastly, draw its eye pupil and teeth, along with the rest of its scales. Refine its claws, and then shade the dinosaur as shown. Erase additional unneeded lines.

Draw Maiasaura

Fossils have revealed that the Maiasaura took care of its babies long after they hatched from their eggs.

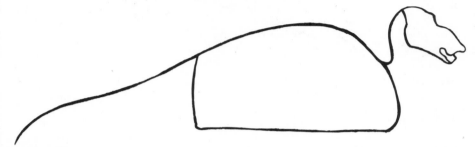

I. Sketch the dinosaur's head and body, as well as the top of its neck and back.

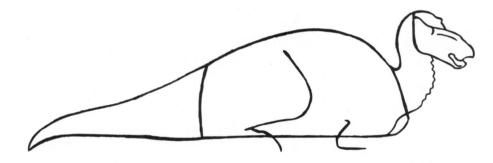

2. Complete its neck and tail, and begin to define its legs. Also, add facial features.

3. Further form its legs. Add more facial features, as well as muscle lines where indicated.

4. Finish outlining its legs, and then define the ridge on top of its head. Erase any unneeded lines.

5. To complete your Maiasaura, refine the head ridge, and sketch the ridges along its neck. Draw wrinkles where shown, and add its claws.

Draw Stegosaurus

Stegosaurus, one of the most famous dinosaurs, used its flexible, spiked tail as a weapon.

1. First draw the top of Stegosaurus's neck, body, and tail.

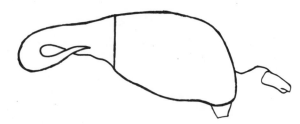

2. Sketch the outline of its head, and complete its body and tail. Begin to form one of its legs.

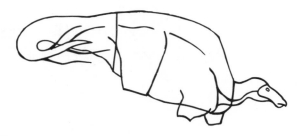

3. Draw the upper section of its other front leg and its visible hip. Add detail to its face, muscle lines on its body, and some of its tail spikes.

4. Sketch the rest of its tail spikes, as well as the spikes along its back and neck. Continue to render its facial features and its legs.

5. Complete its spikes so they look thick and powerful. Refine its legs. Add feet and toes, and erase any unneeded lines.

6. To finish your drawing, erase the ankle lines, and refine the feet. Also, detail the body and spikes as shown.

Draw Stygimoloch

Stygimoloch was a smaller version of Pachycephalosaurus with long horns on its head.

I. Begin by outlining Stygimoloch's head, body, and hip. Add the top of its neck and tail.

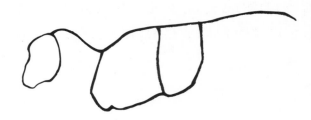

2. Sketch its eye, mouth, and the small horns growing around its skull. Complete its neck and tail, adding muscle lines. Begin to form its arms and legs, adding its front paws.

3. Attach the large horns jutting from the top of its head. Add its feet and more muscle definition. Erase unneeded lines.

4. Finish by drawing spines down Stygimoloch's back and refining the details on its arms and legs. Also, add the spots and wrinkles on its body where shown.

Amphibians – Animals that can live on land but must keep their skin wet and return to the water to lay eggs.

Armor – The protective covering on the body of an animal.

Archaeopteryx – The oldest known bird thought to have lived about 150 million years ago. Although it is believed that Archaeopteryx developed from a dinosaur, it is not a dinosaur.

Asteroid – A small planet or celestial body that orbits a sun; nearly all asteroids are rocky.

Asteroid Crash Theory – The belief by some scientists that a huge asteroid crashed into the earth, creating a massive dust cloud that blocked the sun. This caused the earth to become cold and the dinosaurs to starve and freeze.

Buckland, Professor William – Discovered and named Megalosaurus, the first dinosaur ever to be described scientifically.

Carnivores – Animals that eat other animals; also called meat-eaters.

Cenozoic Era – Also known as the "Age of Mammals." The Cenozoic Era began about 65 million years ago and has continued to the present day.

Climate Theory – The belief that the movement of the continents and shrinking oceans separated the land and made the earth cooler. This caused the dinosaurs to freeze and starve.

Cold-Blooded – Animals that do not produce enough heat from their body processes to keep their body temperature high, such as crocodiles and lizards. These animals need to absorb heat from their environment to be active.

Crest – A fan or tube-shaped top on some duck-billed dinosaurs' heads that may have been used as an echo chamber to help the dinosaur make sounds. Other scientists believe that it may have helped the dinosaur smell.

Cretaceous Period – The third and final period during the Mesozoic Era, lasting from 144 million years ago to 65 million years ago.

Defend – To protect against danger or an attack.

Evolution – Development by a species from one generation to another.

Extinction – The action of dying out by a group of species.

Frill – A sheet of bone on the heads of some dinosaurs, such as Triceratops, that protected their necks.

Fossils – Remnants, impressions, or traces of organisms of the past that have been preserved as rock in the earth's crust.

Gastroliths – Stones or small pebbles used by some dinosaurs to crush food in their stomachs.

Hatch – To emerge from an egg when ready to be born.

Hadrosaurs – Dinosaurs that had wide, duck-like mouths and rows of teeth in their cheeks.

Herbivores – Animals that eat plants, also called plant-eaters.

Herd – A group of animals of one kind that live or travel together.

Impression – A form or shape that can occur when one object touches another.

Jurassic Period - The second period during the Mesozoic Era, lasting from 208 million years ago to 144 million years ago.

Mantell, Dr. Gideon – One of the first fossil hunters; he named Iguanodon.

Mate – Either member of a pair of animals that can produce babies together.

Mesozoic Era – Also known as the "Age of Reptiles." This era lasted from 245 million years ago to 65 million years ago. There were three periods during the Mesozoic Era: Triassic, Jurassic, and Cretaceous.

Migration – To travel from one place to another.

Omnivore – Animals that eat plants and meat.

Ornithischia – Dinosaurs whose hips were like the hips of birds, with the two lower hipbones close together and pointing backward. Only herbivores could be Ornithischia.

Ornithomimosaurs – Meat-eating dinosaurs with beaks, small heads, long necks, and long legs.

Paleontologists – Scientists who study fossil remains to learn about the earth and its inhabitants of long ago.

Pangaea – A "super continent." When dinosaurs first appeared, all of earth's continents were joined together as one. They slowly broke apart into the formation that we know today.

Plates – Pieces of armor, or protective covering, on an animal's body usually made of bone. They may have also been used to adjust body temperature.

Plesiosaurs – Ocean-dwelling reptiles that lived during the Mesozoic Era. They were not dinosaurs.

Predator – An animal that hunts other animals for food.

Primates – Mammals that are the ancestors of monkeys, apes, and human beings.

Psittacosaurs – Dinosaurs that had long beaks at the front of their mouths.

Pterosaurs – Featherless, flying reptiles that lived during the Mesozoic Era. They were not dinosaurs.

Saurischia – Dinosaurs whose hips were like the hips of lizards, with their two lower hipbones separated, one pointing forward and one pointing backward. Both plant-eaters and meat-eaters could be Saurischia.

Sauropods – Plant-eating dinosaurs that had long necks and tails.

Scales – Sections of clearly marked, small, flattened, and hard areas on an animal's external body covering.

Scavenger – Animals that eat the meat of an animal they did not kill.

Sediments – Mud, sand, and gravel that hardens together to form stone. Most dinosaur fossils are found in sedimentary rocks.

Skeleton – The strong protective structure that supports an animal's body. It may be inside or outside the body.

Skulls – The hard, bony structure inside the heads of animals that have an internal skeleton. The skull encloses and protects the brain and chief sense organs and supports the jaws.

Thecodonts – An ancient group of lizards believed to have evolved into dinosaurs.

Triassic Period – The first period during the Mesozoic Era, lasting from 245 million years ago to 208 million years ago.

Volcano Theory – The belief that volcanic eruptions over thousands of years ago created dust clouds that blocked the sun. This caused the dinosaurs to freeze and starve.

Warm-Blooded – Animals that produce enough heat from their body processes to keep their body temperature high, such as mammals and bird. These animals can be active all the time.

Page 10

Get to Know Dinosaurs

What Species of Animal Were Dinosaurs?

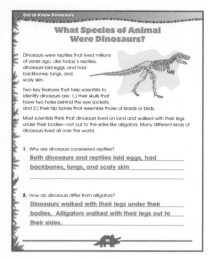

Dinosaurs were reptiles that lived millions of years ago. Like today's reptiles, dinosaurs laid eggs, and had backbones, lungs, and scaly skin.

Two key features that help scientists to identify dinosaurs are: 1.) their skulls that have two holes behind the eye sockets, and 2.) their hip bones that resemble those of lizards or birds.

Most scientists think that dinosaurs lived on land and walked with their legs under their bodies—not out to the sides like alligators. Many different kinds of dinosaurs lived all over the world.

1. Why are dinosaurs considered reptiles?
   Both dinosaurs and reptiles laid eggs, had
   backbones, lungs, and scaly skin

2. How do dinosaurs differ from alligators?
   Dinosaurs walked with their legs under their
   bodies. Alligators walked with their legs out to
   their sides.

10

Page 11

Get to Know Dinosaurs

3. What two features help scientists identify dinosaurs?
   The two features that help scientists identify
   dinosaurs are the two holes behind the eye
   sockets in their skulls and certain bones in their
   hips that resemble those of lizards or birds.

4. Name some reptiles that are living today.
   Sample answers: Snakes, turtles, lizards, iguanas,
   crocodiles, and alligators.

5. Which living reptile do you think looks most like a dinosaur? Why?
   Answers will vary.

6. Name some other animals that walk with their legs under their bodies.
   Sample answers: Cats, dogs, horses, birds, and
   pigs.

11

Page 12

Get to Know Dinosaurs

Where Did Dinosaurs Come From?

Scientists believe the ancestors, or early relatives, of dinosaurs developed from amphibians. Amphibians, such as frogs and salamanders, can live on land, but they must keep their skin wet and return to water to lay eggs.

Amphibians that lived long ago looked like big salamanders. Over millions of years, some of them developed into animals with stronger skeletons, tougher skins, and hard eggs. These new animals were the first reptiles.One ancient group of reptiles, called thecodonts, were slim and fast. In time, they developed into dinosaurs.

Answer the questions below by filling in the correct answers. The first one has been done for you.

1. Which animal is an amphibian?
   Ⓐ a cat
   Ⓑ an elephant
   Ⓒ a thecodont
   Ⓓ a frog

2. What does ancient mean?
   Ⓐ wet skin
   Ⓑ five years old
   Ⓒ very old
   Ⓓ young

12

Page 13

Get to Know Dinosaurs

3. How did some ancient amphibians develop into reptiles?
   Ⓐ They walked more on the ground.
   Ⓑ They developed stronger skeletons, tougher skins, and harder eggs.
   Ⓒ They laid their eggs in the water.
   Ⓓ They became slim and fast.

4. Which animals lived first?
   Ⓐ amphibians
   Ⓑ dinosaurs
   Ⓒ alligators
   Ⓓ mice

5. What was one of the first groups of reptiles called?
   Ⓐ rats
   Ⓑ thecodonts
   Ⓒ salamanders
   Ⓓ frogs

6. Over time, Thecodonts developed into _____.
   Ⓐ frogs
   Ⓑ amphibians
   Ⓒ dinosaurs
   Ⓓ salamanders

13

Page 14

Get to Know Dinosaurs

How Long Ago Did Dinosaurs Live?

The history of the earth is divided into eras, or time periods. Dinosaurs lived during the Mesozoic Era, which is also called the *Age of Reptiles*.

The Mesozoic Era began 245 million years ago and ended 65 million years ago. It is divided into three periods—the Triassic, the Jurassic, and the Cretaceous Periods. The landscape and vegetation of the earth changed from one period to another, as did life for the dinosaurs.

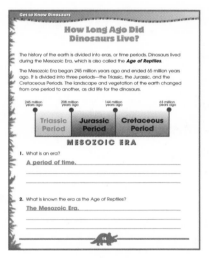

245 million years ago	208 million years ago	144 million years ago	65 million years ago
Triassic Period	**Jurassic Period**	**Cretaceous Period**	

MESOZOIC ERA

1. What is an era?
   A period of time.

2. What is known the era as the Age of Reptiles?
   The Mesozoic Era.

14

Page 15

Get to Know Dinosaurs

3. Name the three periods in the Age of Reptiles.
   The Triassic Period, the Jurassic Period, and the
   Cretaceous Period.

4. When did that era begin and end?
   The Mesozoic Era began 245 million years ago
   and ended 65 million years ago.

5. If you had a time machine that could take you back to that era, would you go? Why or why not?
   Answers will vary.

6. Dinosaurs are prehistoric animals. What does prehistoric mean?
   Prehistoric means the time before recorded
   history began.

15

Page 16

Get to Know Dinosaurs

What Was the World Like When Dinosaurs Lived?

The world's *climate*, or long-term weather, was generally warm during the Mesozoic Era. In the early part of the era, there were many evergreen trees and shrubs, and ferns. Later, gingko trees with fan-shaped leaves appeared. These were followed by flowering plants, which added flecks of color to the earth.

Just like today's earth, some places in the Mesozoic world had tropical rain forests, while others had sandy deserts or great plains. Different kinds of dinosaurs lived in each of these habitats, or areas.

1. What does climate mean?
   Ⓐ a period of time
   Ⓑ lived long ago
   Ⓒ long-term weather
   Ⓓ favored over another

2. What was the climate like when dinosaurs lived?
   Ⓐ hot and humid
   Ⓑ warm
   Ⓒ rainy
   Ⓓ overcast

16

Page 17

Get to Know Dinosaurs

3. During the early Mesozoic Era, the main types of plants were _____.
   Ⓐ oak and willow trees
   Ⓑ evergreen trees and shrubs, and ferns
   Ⓒ little shrubs
   Ⓓ roses and daisies

4. In what order did these plants appear in the Mesozoic Era?
   Ⓐ evergreen trees and shrubs, flowering plants, ginkgo trees
   Ⓑ ginkgo trees, flowering plants, ferns
   Ⓒ flowering plants, ferns, ginkgo trees
   Ⓓ evergreens and shrubs, ginkgo trees, flowering plants

5. What is a habitat?
   Ⓐ a manner of behavior
   Ⓑ an area where something lives
   Ⓒ a sandy desert
   Ⓓ a great plain

6. What type of habitat was not typical during the Mesozoic Era?
   Ⓐ sandy deserts
   Ⓑ tropical rain forests
   Ⓒ great plains
   Ⓓ icy mountains

17

Page 18

Get to Know Dinosaurs

Where Did Dinosaurs Live?

Most scientists think that when dinosaurs first appeared, the earth's continents were all joined together as one supercontinent called *Pangaea*, which means "all the land." Dinosaurs roamed all over the giant *landmass*, or large area of land. About 150 million years ago, Pangaea began to split into separate landmasses that looked like our modern-day continents. Dinosaurs traveled with the moving landmasses. As a result, dinosaurs lived on every continent on the earth.

Pangaea
(about 250 million years ago)

Pangaea splitting
(about 150 million years ago)

1. What was Pangaea?
   Pangaea was land made up of all the
   landmasses on earth.

2. Why was Pangaea called a supercontinent?
   Pangaea was called a supercontinent because it
   was the only land on earth.

18

Page 19

3. When did Pangaea begin to break apart?

Pangaea began to break up about 150 million years ago.

4. Why did dinosaurs live on every continent on the earth?

Dinosaurs traveled with the continents as Pangaea broke apart.

5. What do you think surrounded Pangaea?

Sample answer: One large body of water called Panthalassa.

6. How many continents are there on modern-day earth? Name them.

There are seven continents. North America, South America, Antarctica, Africa, Europe, Asia and Australia.

19

Page 20

Did Dinosaurs Migrate?

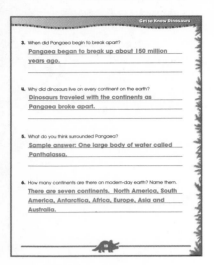

Scientists believe some dinosaurs *migrated,* or traveled from place to place, in search of food. One reason they believe this is because the fossils of the large, horned, plant-eater, Pachyrhinosaurus have been found in the Arctic, Alaska, and Canada. Just like today, Arctic winters were long and dark in the Mesozoic Era. Plants would not have lived due to the lack of sunshine. Scientists think Arctic dinosaurs may have migrated south in winter and north in spring to have a steady supply of food.

- - - - - - : migration route of Pachyrhinosaurus

Pachyrhinosaurus

1. What does migrate mean?
- Ⓐ travel to space
- Ⓑ search for food
- Ⓒ travel from place to place
- Ⓓ long, dark winter

2. Why did some dinosaurs migrate?
- Ⓐ They were looking for a house.
- Ⓑ They were looking for food.
- Ⓒ They were looking for other dinosaurs.
- Ⓓ They were outgrowing their habitats.

20

Page 21

3. Where have the bones of Pachyrhinosaurus not been found?
- Ⓐ The Arctic
- Ⓑ Alaska
- Ⓒ Africa
- Ⓓ Canada

4. Arctic winters in the Mesozoic Era were _____.
- Ⓐ warm, short, and sunny
- Ⓑ rainy and windy
- Ⓒ hot and humid
- Ⓓ cold, long, and dark

5. Why were plants not able to live in the Mesozoic Era Arctic?
- Ⓐ There was not enough light.
- Ⓑ There were not enough dinosaurs.
- Ⓒ There was no wind.
- Ⓓ There was not enough water.

6. Which modern-day animals migrate south in the winter and north in the spring?
- Ⓐ lions
- Ⓑ birds
- Ⓒ ants
- Ⓓ dogs

21

Page 22

Word Search Activity

Use the word list to help you find the words about dinosaurs that are hidden in the block below. Some of the words are hidden backward or diagonally.

WORD LIST

AGE OF REPTILES	EVOLVED	PANGAEA
AMPHIBIANS	HABITAT	PREHISTORIC
ANCIENT	JURASSIC	REPTILES
CLIMATE	LANDMASS	SUPERCONTINENT
CRETACEOUS	MESOZOIC ERA	THECODONTS
ERA	MIGRATE	TRIASSIC

22

Page 23

Get a Clue!

Unscramble the words below. Then, use the words as clues to fill in the answers to the questions.

geA fo ptsRelie	Age of Reptiles
hpminasbia	amphibians
ecmilat	climate
sariscuJ	Jurassic
dlgmrtae	migrated
tscoineupnnter	supercontinent

1. Dinosaurs are believed to have _____migrated_____, much like birds do today.

2. The Mesozoic Era is also known as the _____Age of Reptiles_____.

3. Pangaea was a _____supercontinent_____ that split apart into separate continents during the Mesozoic Era.

4. _____Amphibians_____ are animals that must keep their skin wet and return to the water to lay their eggs.

5. The _____Jurassic_____ Period lasted from 208 million years ago to 144 million years ago.

6. Plants were able to flourish during the Mesozoic Era because the world's _____climate_____ was generally warm.

23

Page 24

What Was the Biggest Dinosaur?

The largest known meat-eating dinosaur was Giganotosaurus, from what is now Argentina. Giganotosaurus measured 45 feet in length—as long as three cars—and weighed 8 tons, or slightly more than an African elephant. It walked on two legs and had long, sharp teeth.

The largest known plant-eating dinosaur was the four-legged long-neck Argentinosaurus, also from what is now Argentina. It measured 115 feet in length—almost as long as eight cars—and weighed 100 tons, or as much as fourteen African elephants.

Argentinosaurus

1. What was the biggest known plant-eating dinosaur?

The biggest known plant-eating dinosaur was Argentinosaurus.

2. What was the biggest known meat-eating dinosaur?

The biggest known meat-eating dinosaur was Giganotosaurus.

24

Page 25

3. Was the largest known dinosaur a meat-eater or a plant-eater?

The largest known dinosaur was a plant-eater.

4. Which of these two biggest dinosaurs do you think moved faster? Why?

Sample answer: Giganotosaurus moved faster because it weighed less than Argentinosaurus.

5. Why do you think Argentinosaurus walked on four legs instead of two?

Sample answer: Argentinosaurus walked on four legs because it needed the extra help to carry its weight.

6. How many Giganotosauruses would need to be lined up to equal the length of one Argentinosaurus?

There would need to be just over two Giganotosaurus to be the same length as one Argentinosaurus.

25

Page 26

What Was the Smallest Dinosaur?

Compsognathus was one of the smallest known dinosaurs. This meat-eater was about as big as a turkey and weighed about as much as a newborn human baby. Scientists think Compsognathus was a fast runner that chased down small lizards and other prey.

Compsognathus

Heterodontosaurus, also about as big as a turkey, was among the smallest known plant-eaters. It had several kinds of teeth, which it may have used to bite, tear, and grind plants.

1. What was the smallest known plant-eating dinosaur?
- Ⓐ Compsognathus
- Ⓑ Giganotosaurus
- Ⓒ Heterodontosaurus
- Ⓓ Argentinosaurus

2. What was the smallest known meat-eating dinosaur?
- Ⓐ Argentinosaurus
- Ⓑ Compsognathus
- Ⓒ Giganotosaurus
- Ⓓ Heterodontosaurus

26

Page 27

3. Compsognathus and Heterodontosaurus were about the same size as _____.
- Ⓐ a mouse
- Ⓑ a horse
- Ⓒ a newborn baby
- Ⓓ a turkey

4. Scientists think that Compsognathus was a _____.
- Ⓐ fast runner
- Ⓑ quick eater
- Ⓒ newborn baby
- Ⓓ turkey

5. Heterodontosaurus had many different types of _____.
- Ⓐ feet
- Ⓑ scales
- Ⓒ teeth
- Ⓓ eyes

6. What was Compsognathus believed to have eaten?
- Ⓐ rats
- Ⓑ plants
- Ⓒ small lizards
- Ⓓ large birds

27

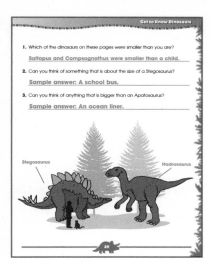

Page 29 — Get to Know Dinosaurs

1. Which of the dinosaurs on these pages were smaller than you are?

Saltopus and Compsognathus were smaller than a child.

2. Can you think of something that is about the size of a Stegosaurus?

Sample answer: A school bus.

3. Can you think of anything that is bigger than an Apatosaurus?

Sample answer: An ocean liner.

Stegosaurus   Hadrosaurus

29

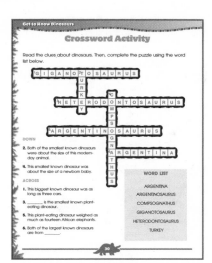

Page 30 — Get to Know Dinosaurs

Crossword Activity

Read the clues about dinosaurs. Then, complete the puzzle using the word list below.

GIGANOTOSAURUS
TURKEY
HETERODONTOSAURUS
COMPSOGNATHUS
ARGENTINOSAURUS
ARGENTINA

DOWN

2. Both of the smallest known dinosaurs were about the size of this modern-day animal.

4. This smallest known dinosaur was about the size of a newborn baby.

ACROSS

1. This biggest known dinosaur was as long as three cars.

3. _____ is the smallest known plant-eating dinosaur.

5. This plant-eating dinosaur weighed as much as fourteen African elephants.

6. Both of the largest known dinosaurs are from _____.

WORD LIST
ARGENTINA
ARGENTINOSAURUS
COMPSOGNATHUS
GIGANOTOSAURUS
HETERODONTOSAURUS
TURKEY

30

Page 31

How Long Were Dinosaurs?

Dinosaurs varied greatly in size. Some were up to 90 feet long! Use the charts on pages 130, 140, and 154 to find the lengths of some dinosaurs. Write the names of the dinosaurs along the bottom of the line graph. Color in the lengths (in feet) with different colored pencils or crayons.

Answers will vary.

Dinosaur Length in Feet
55 50 45 40 35 30 25 20 15 10 5

Dinosaur Names

31

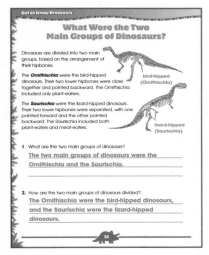

Page 32 — Get to Know Dinosaurs

What Were the Two Main Groups of Dinosaurs?

Dinosaurs are divided into two main groups, based on the arrangement of their hipbones.

The **Ornithischia** were the bird-hipped dinosaurs. Their two lower hipbones were close together and pointed backward. The Ornithischia included only plant-eaters.

bird-hipped (Ornithischia)

The **Saurischia** were the lizard-hipped dinosaurs. Their two lower hipbones were separated, with one pointed forward and the other pointed backward. The Saurischia included both plant-eaters and meat-eaters.

lizard-hipped (Saurischia)

1. What are the two main groups of dinosaurs?

The two main groups of dinosaurs were the Ornithischia and the Saurischia.

2. How are the two main groups of dinosaurs divided?

The Ornithischia were the bird-hipped dinosaurs, and the Saurischia were the lizard-hipped dinosaurs.

32

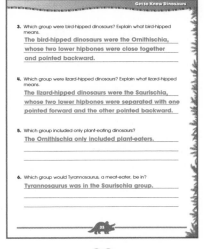

Page 33

3. Which group were bird-hipped dinosaurs? Explain what bird-hipped means.

The bird-hipped dinosaurs were the Ornithischia, whose two lower hipbones were close together and pointed backward.

4. Which group were lizard-hipped dinosaurs? Explain what lizard-hipped means.

The lizard-hipped dinosaurs were the Saurischia, whose two lower hipbones were separated with one pointed forward and the other pointed backward.

5. Which group included only plant-eating dinosaurs?

The Ornithischia only included plant-eaters.

6. Which group would Tyrannosaurus, a meat-eater, be in?

Tyrannosaurus was in the Saurischia group.

33

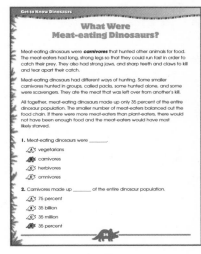

Page 34 — Get to Know Dinosaurs

What Were Meat-eating Dinosaurs?

Meat-eating dinosaurs were **carnivores** that hunted other animals for food. The meat-eaters had long, strong legs so that they could run fast in order to catch their prey. They also had strong jaws, and sharp teeth and claws to kill and tear apart their catch.

Meat-eating dinosaurs had different ways of hunting. Some smaller carnivores hunted in groups, called packs, some hunted alone, and some were scavengers. They ate the meat that was left over from another's kill.

All together, meat-eating dinosaurs made up only 35 percent of the entire dinosaur population. The smaller number of meat-eaters balanced out the food chain. If there were more meat-eaters than plant-eaters, there would not have been enough food and the meat-eaters would have most likely starved.

1. Meat-eating dinosaurs were _____.
   - vegetarians
   - **carnivores**
   - herbivores
   - omnivores

2. Carnivores made up _____ of the entire dinosaur population.
   - 75 percent
   - 35 billion
   - 35 million
   - **35 percent**

34

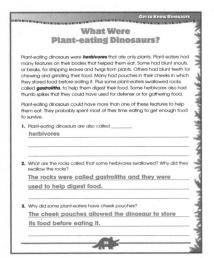

Page 35

What Were Plant-eating Dinosaurs?

Plant-eating dinosaurs were **herbivores** that ate only plants. Plant-eaters had many features on their bodies that helped them eat. Some had blunt snouts, or beaks, for stripping leaves and twigs from plants. Others had blunt teeth for chewing and grinding their food. Many had pouches in their cheeks in which they stored food before eating it. Plus some plant-eaters swallowed rocks, called **gastroliths**, to help them digest their food. Some herbivores also had thumb spikes that they could have used for defense or for gathering food.

Plant-eating dinosaurs could have more than one of these features to help them eat. They probably spent most of their time eating to get enough food to survive.

1. Plant-eating dinosaurs are also called _____.

herbivores

2. What are the rocks called that some herbivores swallowed? Why did they swallow the rocks?

The rocks were called gastroliths and they were used to help digest food.

3. Why did some plant-eaters have cheek pouches?

The cheek pouches allowed the dinosaur to store its food before eating it.

35

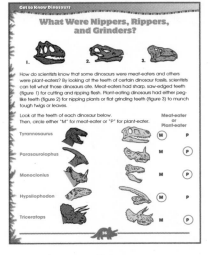

Page 36

What Were Nippers, Rippers, and Grinders?

1.   2.   3.

How do scientists know that some dinosaurs were meat-eaters and others were plant-eaters? By looking at the teeth of certain dinosaur fossils, scientists can tell what those dinosaurs ate. Meat-eaters had sharp, saw-edged teeth (figure 1) for cutting and ripping flesh. Plant-eating dinosaurs had either peg-like teeth (figure 2) for nipping plants or flat grinding teeth (figure 3) to munch tough twigs or leaves.

Look at the teeth of each dinosaur below.
Then, circle either "M" for meat-eater or "P" for plant-eater.

	Meat-eater or Plant-eater
Tyrannosaurus	**M** P
Parasaurolophus	M **P**
Monoclonius	M **P**
Hypsilophodon	**M** P
Triceratops	M **P**

36

Page 37 — Get to Know Dinosaurs

What Is the Difference?

1. Which of the two dinosaur skulls shown below do you think belongs to a meat-eater? Circle your answer.

2. How do you know?

The dinosaur skull on the right was a meat-eater because it has sharp teeth.

3. How else can you tell the difference between a carnivore and an herbivore?

Carnivores usually have claws. Herbivores usually do not have sharp claws.

4. What do you think the dinosaur pictured below ate?

It ate meat.

Velociraptor

37

Answer Key

Which Was Which?

Circle the dinosaurs pictured below and on the next page that you think were meat-eaters. Put a square around the plant-eaters.

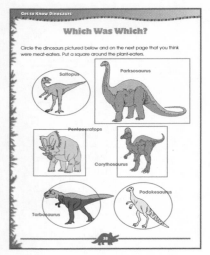

Saltopus
Parksosaurus
Pentaceratops
Corythosaurus
Tarbosaurus
Podokesaurus

38

Parasaurolophus
Velociraptor
Saltasaurus
Protoceratops
Deinonychus
Tyrannosaurus

39

What Did Dinosaurs Use Their Claws For?

Hunters, or predators, such as Utahraptor used the huge, knifelike claws on their hands and feet to kill prey. The crocodile-jawed Baryonyx may have used its enormous thumb claws to scoop fish out of the water for food. Most plant-eating dinosaurs, such as Iguanodon, used their broad, flat claws to dig up plants and to protect themselves from attackers.

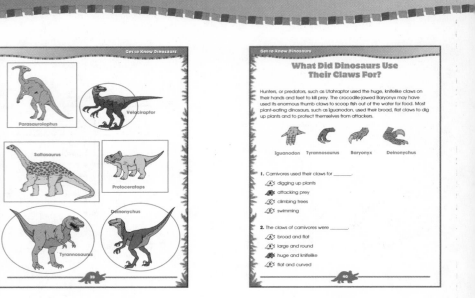

Iguanodon   Tyrannosaurus   Baryonyx   Deinonychus

1. Carnivores used their claws for _____.
   - digging up plants
   - **attacking prey**
   - climbing trees
   - swimming

2. The claws of carnivores were _____.
   - broad and flat
   - large and round
   - **huge and knifelike**
   - flat and curved

40

---

3. Herbivores used their claws for _____.
   - swimming
   - climbing trees
   - attacking prey
   - **digging up plants**

4. The claws of herbivores were _____.
   - flat and curved
   - **broad and flat**
   - huge and knifelike
   - large and round

5. A predator is something that _____.
   - is hunted by another
   - eats a lot of food
   - **hunts other animals**
   - scoops fish out of the water

6. Prey is something that _____.
   - is hatched from eggs
   - uses its claws for defense
   - **is hunted by another**
   - eats its own kind

41

Story will vary.

43

Why Did Some Dinosaurs Have Armor Plates?

Some plant-eating dinosaurs, called **ankylosaurs**, had hard scales and bony plates all over their bodies—even their eyelids! This **armor** protected them from the bites and claws of meat-eaters. Only their underbellies were unprotected, so predators would have to flip them over to bite or claw them.

Ankylosaurus, for example, was covered with thick plates and bony spikes that a predator couldn't bite through. It also had a bony club on its tail that it used as a weapon.

Daspletosaurus

Ankylosaurus

1. What are the hard scales and bony plates on some dinosaurs called?
   <u>The hard scales and bony plates on some dinosaurs are called armor.</u>

2. What kind of dinosaurs had hard scales and bony plates?
   <u>Ankylosaurs had hard scales and bony plates.</u>

44

---

3. Why did these dinosaurs have armor?
   <u>The armor would protect them from bites and claws from meat-eaters.</u>

4. What was the only part of ankylosaurs that did not have armor?
   <u>They did not have armor on their bellies.</u>

5. Some small plant-eaters had no horns or armor. How do you think they avoided being eaten by predators?
   <u>They were small, which would make them hard to see, and they were fast.</u>

6. Name some modern-day animals that have armor or horns.
   <u>Sample answer: Turtles and bulls.</u>

45

What Are Frills?

Besides armor plates, some plant-eating dinosaurs had other ways to defend themselves against meat-eaters. Some dinosaurs had sharp horns on their faces, spikes on their bodies, or a hard bony collar, called a **frill**, on their heads to protect their necks.

Color the frill on this dinosaur red.
Color the horns blue.

Triceratops

Color the spikes on this dinosaur green.

Ankylosaurus

Which type of body defense feature do you think was the most useful for the plant-eating dinosaurs? Explain. <u>Sample answer: The spikes were the best kind of defense, because they would hurt the meat-eating dinosaurs. The armor is the best kind of defense, because it would protect the plant-eating dinosaur.</u>

46

How Do I Defend Myself?

Look at the plant-eating dinosaurs below. Find the features of their bodies that gave them protection from their enemies. Explain in the space provided.

Stegosaurus
<u>Sample answer: The plates would protect it from bites. It would use its tail to attack the meat-eaters.</u>

Ankylosaurus
<u>Sample answer: It may have defended itself with the sharp spikes on its back and club on its tail.</u>

Triceratops
<u>Sample answer: Its sharp horns could have speared enemies.</u>

47

Page 48

Get to Know Dinosaurs

What Did Dinosaurs Use Their Tails For?

Plant-eating dinosaurs used their tails to defend themselves. Long-necked dinosaurs, such as Diplodocus, had whiplike tails that they used to lash out at meat-eaters. They also used their tails for balance when they walked.

Diplodocus

Armored dinosaurs had dangerous tails. For example, Stegosaurus had spikes on its tail as long as baseball bats. When slammed into a predator, its tail would have caused serious wounds.

Some meat-eaters such as Deinonychus probably used their tails for balance when they ran.

Stegosaurus

1. What kind of dinosaurs had dangerous tails?
   - A. long-necked dinosaurs
   - B. meat-eating dinosaurs
   - C. armored dinosaurs
   - D. plant-eating dinosaurs

2. _____ had a long neck and a whiplike tail.
   - A. Deinonychus
   - B. Herbivore
   - C. Stegosaurus
   - D. Diplodocus

Deinonychus

Page 49

3. Deinonychus used its tail for _____.
   - A. balance when it ran
   - B. clearing away trees from a path
   - C. attracting a mate
   - D. holding onto food

4. _____ is an armored dinosaur.
   - A. Diplodocus
   - B. Deinonychus
   - C. Tyrannosaurus
   - D. Stegosaurus

5. Long-necked dinosaurs used their tail for defense and for _____.
   - A. swinging from vine to vine
   - B. balance when they walked
   - C. catching fish in the water
   - D. holding up their heads

6. Stegosaurus had spikes on its tail as long as a _____.
   - A. toothpick
   - B. pencil
   - C. baseball bat
   - D. banana

Page 50

Get to Know Dinosaurs

Did Dinosaurs Live Alone or In Groups?

Scientists think that many plant-eating dinosaurs lived in groups to protect themselves from predators. Proof of this has been found in fossil beds containing many Maiasaura, both young and adult.

Coelophysis dinosaurs

Clusters of fossil bones from some meat-eaters, such as Coelophysis, show that they formed groups as well. Other meat-eaters may have formed temporary packs for hunting, but many predatory dinosaurs hunted alone.

1. Why do scientists think that many plant-eating dinosaurs lived in groups?
   Scientists think that many plant-eaters lived in groups for protection.

2. How do scientists know that some dinosaurs lived in groups?
   Fossil remains of many Maiasaura have been found in the same spot.

Page 51

Get to Know Dinosaurs

3. Why do scientists theorize that some meat-eating dinosaurs formed groups?
   Meat-eaters may have formed groups to hunt.

4. Why do scientists feel that some meat-eating dinosaurs hunted by themselves?
   Sample answer: So that the dinosaur could sneak up on its prey.

5. What are some modern-day animals that live in groups?
   Sample answer: Horses and cows.

6. People sometimes form groups called *clubs*. If you formed a dinosaur fan club, what would you call it?
   Answers will vary.

Page 52

Get to Know Dinosaurs

What Is a Group of Dinosaurs Called?

The groups that some dinosaurs lived in are called herds. Fossil tracks show that when some herds migrated, or moved, they kept their young dinosaurs in the middle of the pack.

Why would this be a good way for some dinosaurs to protect their young?
Dinosaur babies were smaller, slower, and weaker than them, so they would have been easier to kill. By herding together, the adults could protect the young dinosaurs.

Color the picture below any way you like.

Page 53

Get to Know Dinosaurs

What Is the Secret Word?

Cross out the letters that spell the name of each of these items pictured below. Then, use the remaining letters to complete the sentence.

Some dinosaurs, such as this sauropod, travel in a
h e r d for safety.

Page 54

Get to Know Dinosaurs

How Fast Did Dinosaurs Run?

Some dinosaurs protected themselves by running away from other dinosaurs. Running fast also helped some carnivores catch slow-moving dinosaurs. Scientists figured out the speed that a dinosaur ran by measuring the distance between its tracks and by studying the length of its legs. Scientists found that dinosaurs with long legs could probably run faster than dinosaurs with short legs.

The graph below shows how fast some dinosaurs may have been able to run. Use the graph to answer the questions below.

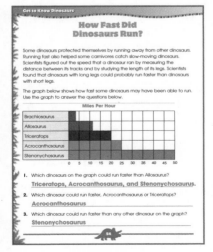

Miles Per Hour

	0	5	10	15	20	25	30	35	40	45	50
Brachiosaurus											
Allosaurus											
Triceratops											
Acrocanthosaurus											
Stenonychosaurus											

1. Which dinosaurs on the graph could run faster than Allosaurus?
   Triceratops, Acrocanthosaurus, and Stenonychosaurus.

2. Which dinosaur could run faster, Acrocanthosaurus or Triceratops?
   Acrocanthosaurus

3. Which dinosaur could run faster than any other dinosaur on the graph?
   Stenonychosaurus

Page 55

Get to Know Dinosaurs

Word Search Activity

Use the word list to help you find the words about dinosaurs that are hidden in the block below. Some of the words are hidden backward or diagonally.

```
M Z N X B E R O V I N R A C S
L A K S J O H D H F S G P O C O
I S E U N R E Y T Z L C A B M
U D G W J Y L Q R T A L S E T
A U O H A P X V N D V E F I H J
I C W O R L S I P S M B C R J Z
H L J R G A C P D A P I Y E R
C O R N I T H I S C H I A S W N
V X S K E H F S O U R E M T E
S I Q X V N S S E F H K W M R G A
R Y I K A L S D K D J F O F O
U P Q O W H E R B I V O R E T C K
E U R Y T Z M N R T G I S
S R E D N I R G Y R U E I W O S
Q P L R I P P E R S A K S J J D
H F G V M Z N S R E P P I N X V
```

WORD LIST

ARMOR	GRINDERS	PACKS
BONY PLATES	HERBIVORE	RIPPERS
CARNIVORE	HERDS	SAURISCHIA
CLAWS	HORNS	SCALES
DEFENSE	NIPPERS	SPIKES
FRILLS	ORNITHISCHIA	TAILS

Page 56

Get to Know Dinosaurs

How Did Dinosaurs Reproduce?

Dinosaurs laid eggs in nests on the ground. Scientists think that some dinosaurs stayed with their eggs until they hatched. Small dinosaurs, such as Oviraptor, may have sat on their eggs much like chickens do. Many dinosaurs, though, probably covered their eggs with sand and plants to keep them warm and left them behind.

Dinosaur eggs ranged in size. Some were the size of golf balls. Others were the size of footballs. Eggs could not have been too large or too thick. Air had to pass through the shells and young dinosaurs had to break out. That is why some scientists think giant dinosaurs may have given birth to live young as big as adult pigs.

Oviraptor

1. How did dinosaurs reproduce?
   - A. They laid eggs in the water.
   - B. They gave birth.
   - C. They laid eggs in caves.
   - D. They laid eggs in nests.

2. Why did some dinosaurs sit on their eggs?
   - A. to hide the color of their eggs
   - B. to keep their eggs warm until they hatched
   - C. to alert predators of the eggs
   - D. to keep them clean

Page 57

3. Where did dinosaurs make their nests?
- (A) in tree branches
- (B) in the water
- (C) on the ground
- (D) in a cave

4. Why couldn't dinosaur eggs be too large or too thick?
- (A) so air could get in the shells and babies could break out
- (B) so the eggs could be hidden easily
- (C) so the eggs would not roll around
- (D) because no big, thick eggs have been found

5. Why did scientists think that giant dinosaurs gave birth to live babies?
- (A) They thought the eggs would have been fossilized.
- (B) They never found the remains of dinosaur eggs.
- (C) The eggs would have been too large and too thick for the babies to hatch.
- (D) They thought only birds laid eggs.

6. What modern-day animals lay eggs?
- (A) tigers
- (B) elephants
- (C) turtles
- (D) hamsters

57

Page 58

Did Dinosaurs Take Care of Their Young?

Scientists think that some dinosaurs simply covered their eggs and walked away. They also think that other dinosaurs protected their eggs and cared for their young. Fossilized nests of Maiasaura, a plant-eater, have been found containing the fossils of many helpless baby dinosaurs. Scientists think that one or both parents protected these youngsters and brought them food.

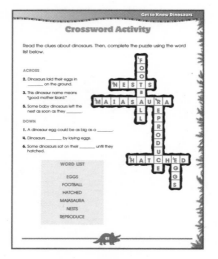

Maiasaura

Other baby dinosaurs hatched with well-developed legs. Scientists believe these youngsters left the nest as soon as they hatched to find their own plants to eat.

1. What proof do scientist have that some dinosaurs took care of their young?
Scientists have found fossilized nests with Maiasaura babies in them.

2. Why do scientists believe that some babies left their nests as soon as they were born?
Some baby dinosaurs were born with well-developed legs and probably left the nest as soon as they hatched to find their own food.

58

Page 59

3. Maiasaura means "good mother lizard." Why do you think scientists chose this name?
Sample answer: Remains of adult Maiasaura have been found with their nest.

4. Of the dinosaurs that did not care for their young, do you think there were more or less of them than the dinosaurs that protected their young? Why?
Sample answer: There were fewer, because meat-eaters were able to eat the babies while in the egg or just after they were born.

5. Name some modern-day animals that take care of their young.
Sample answer: Cats and birds.

6. How did your parents take care of you when you were a baby?
Sample answer: Feeding, cleaning, and keeping warm.

59

Page 60

Did Baby Dinosaurs Look Like Their Parents?

Most dinosaurs looked very much like their parents when they were born, but some features, such as horns and frills, took time to develop. This is how an adult Protoceratops looked.

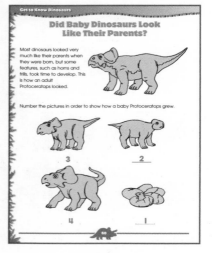

Number the pictures in order to show how a baby Protoceratops grew.

3

2

4

1

60

Page 61

Crossword Activity

Read the clues about dinosaurs. Then, complete the puzzle using the word list below.

ACROSS

2. Dinosaurs laid their eggs in _____ on the ground.
3. This dinosaur name means "good mother lizard."
5. Some baby dinosaurs left the nest as soon as they _____.

DOWN

1. A dinosaur egg could be as big as a _____.
4. Dinosaurs _____ by laying eggs.
6. Some dinosaurs sat on their _____ until they hatched.

Crossword answers: FOOTBALL, NESTS, MAIASAURA, REPRODUCE, HATCHED, EGGS

WORD LIST

EGGS
FOOTBALL
HATCHED
MAIASAURA
NESTS
REPRODUCE

61

Page 62

When Were Dinosaurs First Discovered?

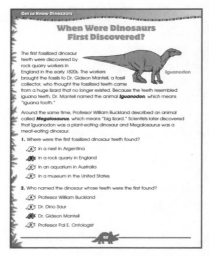

Iguanodon

The first fossilized dinosaur teeth were discovered by rock quarry workers in England in the early 1820s. The workers brought the fossils to Dr. Gideon Mantell, a fossil collector, who thought the fossilized teeth came from a huge lizard that no longer existed. Because the teeth resembled iguana teeth, Dr. Mantell named the animal *Iguanodon*, which means "iguana tooth."

Around the same time, Professor William Buckland described an animal called *Megalosaurus*, which means "big lizard." Scientists later discovered that Iguanodon was a plant-eating dinosaur and Megalosaurus was a meat-eating dinosaur.

1. Where were the first fossilized dinosaur teeth found?
- (A) in a nest in Argentina
- (B) in a rock quarry in England
- (C) in an aquarium in Australia
- (D) in a museum in the United States

2. Who named the dinosaur whose teeth were the first found?
- (A) Professor William Buckland
- (B) Dr. Dino Saur
- (C) Dr. Gideon Mantell
- (D) Professor Pal E. Ontologist

62

Page 63

3. Why was the first named dinosaur called Iguanodon?
- (A) Because it looked like an iguana.
- (B) Because it looked like a lizard.
- (C) Because its teeth looked like those of an iguana.
- (D) Because it was found next to an Iguanodon nest.

4. What dinosaur did Professor William Buckland first describe?
- (A) Iguanodon
- (B) Tyrannosaurus
- (C) Megalosaurus
- (D) Troödon

5. Why were dinosaurs originally called lizards?
- (A) They had scales like lizards.
- (B) Their bones were fossilized.
- (C) They were green.
- (D) Their teeth and bones resembled those of lizards.

6. Which animal's name means "big lizard"?
- (A) Troödon
- (B) Iguanodon
- (C) Tyrannosaurus
- (D) Megalosaurus

63

Page 64

How Are Dinosaurs Named?

Names for new animals are usually created from Latin or Greek words. Giganotosaurus, for example, was a huge dinosaur found in South America. Its name comes from the Greek words *gigas* (giant), *notos* (south), and *sauros* (lizard).

Dinosaurs can also be named for people. Zuniceratops christopheri, found in New Mexico, was named for the Zuni Indians and for nine-year-old Christopher Wolfe who helped discover the fossils.

1. What languages are usually used to name new animals?
Latin and Greek.

2. What does the name Giganotosaurus mean?
Giant South Lizard.

64

Page 65

3. Has a dinosaur ever been named after a person? If so, name the dinosaur and the person, or persons, it was named for.
Yes, Zuniceratops christopheri was named after Christopher Wolfe and the Zuni Indians.

4. Are dinosaurs found all over the world? If so, why?
Yes, because they moved with the breaking up of Pangaea.

5. Do you think dinosaurs have different names in different countries? Explain.
No, they have the same name all around the world so that no one gets confused.

6. If a dinosaur was named after you, what would you want it to be called?
Answers will vary.

65

66

What Is In a Name?

Did you know that most dinosaur names tell us something about the animal? Look at the list of name meanings and the pictures on this page and the next. Match the correct meaning to the dinosaur names. Write the letters in the boxes next to the dinosaur names.

Name Meanings

A. Plated or Roofed Creature
B. Fish Creature
C. Three-horned Face Creature
D. Terrible Creature
E. Duck Creature
F. Helmet Creature
G. Armored Creature
H. Pretty Jaw
I. Spiked Creature
J. Single-horned Creature

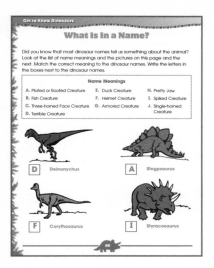

D Deinonychus
A Stegosaurus
F Corythosaurus
I Styracosaurus

67

C Triceratops
G Panoplosaurus
B Ichthyosaurus
J Monoclonius
E Anatosaurus
H Compsognathus

68

What Were Duck-billed Dinosaurs?

Hadrosaurs, or duck-billed dinosaurs, were plant-eaters that lived in many parts of the world. They had wide, duck-like mouths and rows of teeth in their cheeks. Scientists believe duckbills were able to make honking or bellowing noises.

Different kinds of duckbills had different head ornaments. Some had tall spines, while others had crests or bony lumps. Some had no ornaments at all. Scientists think that duckbills cared for their young and traveled in herds.

Corythosaurus

Lambeosaurus

1. The group of duck-billed dinosaurs is called _____.
Ⓐ Parasaurolophus
Ⓑ hadrosaurs
Ⓒ Corythosaurus
Ⓓ Tsinataosaurus

Parasaurolophus

2. What kind of noises did duck-billed dinosaurs make?
Ⓐ honking or bellowing
Ⓑ barking or quacking
Ⓒ howling or singing
Ⓓ chirping or whistling

Saurolophus

Tsintaosaurus

69

3. Hadrosaurs were _____.
Ⓐ herbivores
Ⓑ carnivores
Ⓒ siblings
Ⓓ friends

4. Why were hadrosaurs called duckbills?
Ⓐ They had webbed feet.
Ⓑ They had feathers.
Ⓒ They had duck-like mouths.
Ⓓ They liked to be around water.

5. Duckbills had these types of head ornaments.
Ⓐ horns or spikes
Ⓑ frills, armor plates, or curled horns
Ⓒ crests, bony lumps, or spines
Ⓓ crests or egg-shaped bumps

6. Duckbills traveled _____.
Ⓐ with a buddy
Ⓑ by themselves
Ⓒ as a herd
Ⓓ when the wind changed

70

What Were Parrot-beaked Dinosaurs?

Psittacosaurs, or parrot-beaked dinosaurs, had a long beak at the front of their mouths. Psittacosaurs were plant-eaters and used their beak and teeth to snip off vegetation. They could not chew well, so they used **gastroliths**, or stomach stones, to crush food. All known parrot-beaked dinosaurs lived in what is now Asia, and none were longer than about 6 feet. Psittacosaurs are related to dinosaurs that have horns and bony frills around their necks, such as Triceratops.

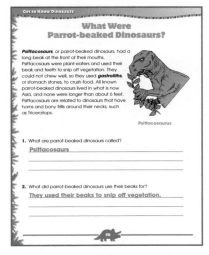

Psittacosaurus

1. What are parrot-beaked dinosaurs called?
Psittacosaurs

2. What did parrot-beaked dinosaurs use their beaks for?
They used their beaks to snip off vegetation.

71

3. How did psittacosaurs use gastroliths?
They were used to help digest food.

4. Do you think that parrot-beaked dinosaurs would have problems eating if they were carnivores? Why?
Sample answer: Yes. They could not chew well.

5. Where did parrot-beaked dinosaurs live?
They lived in modern-day Asia.

6. What other kinds of dinosaurs are psittacosaurs related to?
They were related to dinosaurs that had horns and bony frills.

72

What Were Long-Necks?

Sauropods, or long-necks, were plant-eating dinosaurs with long necks and tails. Found all over the world, long-necks were the largest known dinosaurs.

The longest sauropod may have been Seismosaurus, from what is now Mexico. Seismosaurus was about 150 feet in length—as long as 10 cars—and weighed around 30 tons, or more than four African elephants. Sauropods walked on four legs and usually had no armor. Scientists think that their enormous size and herding habits kept them safe from meat-eaters.

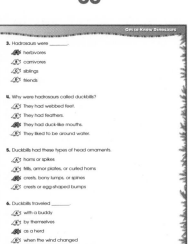

Seismosaurus

1. Long-necked dinosaurs are also known as _____.
Ⓐ Seismosaurus
Ⓑ African elephants
Ⓒ hadrosaurs
Ⓓ sauropods

2. Long-necks were _____.
Ⓐ carnivores with short tails
Ⓑ herbivores with long necks and tails
Ⓒ carnivores with long necks and tails
Ⓓ herbivores with short tails

73

3. How long was Seismosaurus?
Ⓐ about 70 feet
Ⓑ as long as 15 cars
Ⓒ about 150 feet
Ⓓ about 110 feet

4. How much did Seismosaurus weigh?
Ⓐ 100 tons
Ⓑ 100 pounds
Ⓒ 30 tons
Ⓓ 300 pounds

5. What kept sauropods safe from predators?
Ⓐ their size and herding habits
Ⓑ their clubbed tails
Ⓒ their speed
Ⓓ their long necks

6. What modern-day animals have long necks?
Ⓐ African elephants
Ⓑ giraffes
Ⓒ snakes
Ⓓ zebras

74

What Were Ostrich Dinosaurs?

Ornithomimosaurs were meat-eating dinosaurs with beaks, small heads, long necks, and long legs. Scientists think that ornithomimosaurs looked and ran like ostriches and sometimes call them **ostrich dinosaurs**. Struthiomimus, an ornithomimosaur from what is now North America, was probably one of the smartest and fastest dinosaurs. It was about 12 feet long and as tall as a human adult.

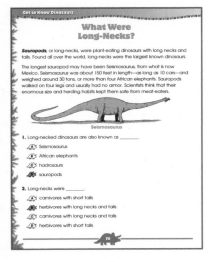

Struthiomimus

1. Why are ornithomimosaurs called ostrich dinosaurs?
Ornithomimosaurs looked and ran like ostriches.

2. Describe how ornithomimosaurs looked.
They had small heads with beaks, long necks, and long legs.

Page 75

Get to Know Dinosaurs

3. What features helped ornithomimosaurs catch its prey?
They were very fast and smart.

4. Were ornithomimosaurs herbivores or carnivores?
They were meat-eaters.

5. Where was Struthiomimus from?
Struthiomimus has been found in North America.

6. How long and tall was Struthiomimus?
Struthiomimus was 12 feet.

Page 76

Get to Know Dinosaurs

What Were Curved-claw Dinosaurs?

Velociraptors belonged to a group of meat-eating dinosaurs called dromaeosaurs. Dromaeosaurs had an enormous curved claw on the second toe of each foot for attacking prey. They also had birdlike skeletons, and scientists think they were closely related to birds. Found in what is now Asia, Velociraptor was about 6 feet in length. It was probably intelligent, fast, had good eyesight, and may have hunted in packs.

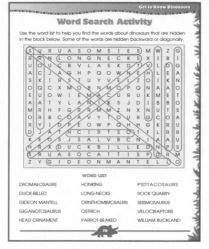
Velociraptor
Thescelosaurus

1. Curved-claw dinosaurs are called _____.
   - Struthiomimus
   - **dromaeosaurs**
   - ornithomimosaurs
   - Triceratops

2. They had a curved claw on _____.
   - the second finger of each hand
   - their right hands only
   - **the second toe of each foot**
   - the end of their tails

Page 77

Get to Know Dinosaurs

3. Their curved claw was used for _____.
   - digging up plants
   - breaking open fruit
   - **attacking prey**
   - building shelter

4. Scientists think that the dromaeosaurs were closely related to _____.
   - tigers
   - **birds**
   - crocodiles
   - elephants

5. Dromaeosaurs had birdlike _____.
   - wings
   - **skeletons**
   - hips
   - beaks

6. Velociraptor is a dromaeosaur that was from _____.
   - Australia
   - England
   - **Asia**
   - South Africa

Page 78

Get to Know Dinosaurs

Get a Clue!

Unscramble the words below. Then, use the words to fill in the answers to the questions.

Scrambled	Answer
shroadusra	**Hadrosaurs**
undigaoon	**Iguanodon**
ekerG	**Greek**
tsgtliohsar	**gastroliths**
psarousdo	**sauropods**
rmusttthSiomul	**Struthiomimus**
vrudec wcla	**curved claw**
ssgaleauMrou	**Megalosaurus**

1. The first dinosaur teeth found were from ___**Iguanodon**___.
2. Dinosaur names are created from Latin or ___**Greek**___ words.
3. ___**Hadrosaurs**___ had wide, duck-like mouths and rows of teeth in their cheeks.
4. Psittacosaurs used ___**gastroliths**___ to crush food in their stomachs.
5. Long-necked dinosaurs are called ___**sauropods**___.
6. ___**Struthiomimus**___ an ostrich dinosaur, was one of the smartest and fastest dinosaurs.
7. Velociraptors had an enormous ___**curved claw**___ on the second toe of each of their feet.
8. Professor William Buckland described a dinosaur called___**Megalosaurus**___

Page 79

Get to Know Dinosaurs

Word Search Activity

Use the word list to help you find the words about dinosaurs that are hidden in the block below. Some of the words are hidden backward or diagonally.

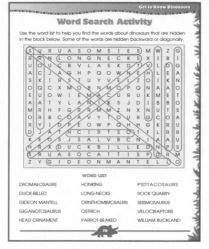

WORD LIST

DROMAEOSAURS	HONKING	PSITTACOSAURS
DUCK-BILLED	LONG-NECKS	ROCK QUARRY
GIDEON MANTELL	ORNITHOMIMOSAURS	SEISMOSAURUS
GIGANOTOSAURUS	OSTRICH	VELOCIRAPTORS
HEAD ORNAMENT	PARROT-BEAKED	WILLIAM BUCKLAND

Page 80

Get to Know Dinosaurs

What Are Fossils?

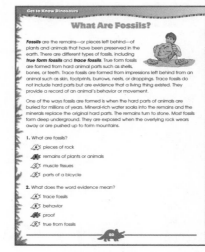

Fossils are the remains—or pieces left behind—of plants and animals that have been preserved in the earth. There are different types of fossils, including **true form fossils** and **trace fossils**. True form fossils are formed from hard animal parts such as shells, bones, or teeth. Trace fossils are formed from impressions left behind from an animal such as skin, footprints, burrows, nests, or droppings. Trace fossils do not include hard parts but are evidence that a living thing existed. They provide a record of an animal's behavior or movement.

One of the ways fossils are formed is when the hard parts of animals are buried for millions of years. Mineral-rich water soaks into the remains and the minerals replace the original hard parts. The remains turn to stone. Most fossils form deep underground. They are exposed when the overlying rock wears away or are pushed up to form mountains.

1. What are fossils?
   - pieces of rock
   - **remains of plants or animals**
   - muscle tissues
   - parts of a bicycle

2. What does the word evidence mean?
   - trace fossils
   - behavior
   - **proof**
   - true from fossils

Page 81

Get to Know Dinosaurs

3. Where do most fossils form?
   - on hills
   - in trees
   - **deep underground**
   - in water

4. What are true from fossils?
   - **hard animal parts**
   - soft animal parts
   - plants
   - footprint impressions

5. What are trace fossils?
   - hard animal parts
   - **impressions**
   - bones
   - teeth

6. Trace fossils are evidence that a living thing _____.
   - danced
   - sang
   - ate
   - **existed**

Page 82

Get to Know Dinosaurs

What Do Trace Fossils Look Like?

The pictures below are examples of different kinds of trace fossils. Draw a line from the description of the kind of trace fossil to its picture.

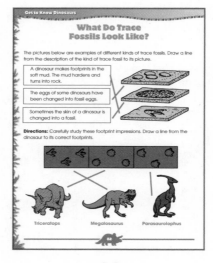

A dinosaur makes footprints in the soft mud. The mud hardens and turns into rock.

The eggs of some dinosaurs have been changed into fossil eggs.

Sometimes the skin of a dinosaur is changed into a fossil.

Directions: Carefully study these footprint impressions. Draw a line from the dinosaur to its correct footprints.

Triceratops   Megalosaurus   Parasaurolophus

Page 83

Get to Know Dinosaurs

What Do Fossils Tell Us?

It's exciting when a scientist finds a dinosaur fossil. The fossil might be from a dinosaur no one has ever discovered before.

It might take years for scientists to put together most of a dinosaur's bones. The lumps, bumps, and scars on the bones give them clues as to what the dinosaur might have looked like. These marks on the bones show where muscles were attached. By looking at the whole skeleton and the lumps, bumps, and scars on each bone, scientists can come up with a theory about the shape of the dinosaur's body.

The two skeletons below are make-believe dinosaurs that nobody has ever found. Study the skeletons. Use colored pencils, crayons, or markers to draw right over the skeleton to show what these dinosaurs might have looked like. Then, name your dinosaurs.

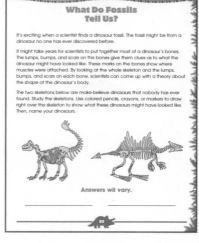

Answers will vary.

Page 84

What Are Scientists Who Study Dinosaurs Called?

Scientists who study **fossils** are called **paleontologists**. Dinosaur paleontologists search for dinosaur remains all over the world. When they discover dinosaur fossils, paleontologists make notes about their find and map the area where they made their find. Then they carefully remove the fossils, pack them in plaster jackets, and take them to laboratories for study.

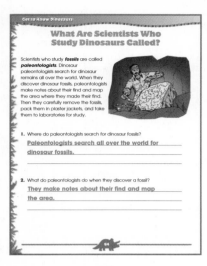

1. Where do paleontologists search for dinosaur fossils?
   <u>Paleontologists search all over the world for dinosaur fossils.</u>

2. What do paleontologists do when they discover a fossil?
   <u>They make notes about their find and map the area.</u>

Page 85

3. Do paleontologists only study dinosaur fossils? If not, what else do they study?
   <u>No. Paleontologists study many different kinds of animals and plants.</u>

4. Why do you think fossils are wrapped in plaster jackets before they are sent to laboratories?
   <u>So that the fossils are protected when being shipped.</u>

5. Why do you think it is important for scientists to take notes about their finds?
   <u>Sample answer: So they know exactly what they found and where.</u>

6. What kind of tools do you think paleontologists use while hunting for fossils?
   <u>Sample answers: Shovels, pick-axes, and brushes.</u>

Page 86

Where Do Paleontologists Look for Dinosaur Fossils?

Paleontologists look for dinosaur fossils all over the world. Most fossils are found in **sedimentary rocks**. Sedimentary rocks are made from layers of **sediments**—mud, sand, and gravel—that harden into stone. When dinosaurs died, their remains were sometimes covered with windblown sand or washed into rivers or lakes. If the remains were quickly covered with sediments, the bones were preserved. As the sediments hardened into rock, the bones became fossils.

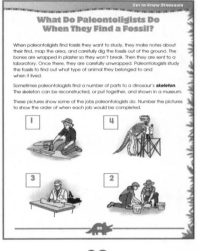

1. Most fossils are found in _____.
   A. water
   B. trees
   C. leaves
   D. ● sedimentary rocks

2. Sedimentary rocks can be made up of any of these sediments except _____.
   A. mud
   B. ● tree bark
   C. sand
   D. gravel

Page 87

3. To have a chance of becoming fossils, dinosaur bodies had to be _____ after they died.
   A. cleaned
   B. left out in the sun
   C. kept warm
   D. ● covered quickly

4. As sediments hardened into rocks, the bones became _____.
   A. sedimentary rocks
   B. ● fossils
   C. rocks
   D. sandstone

5. Some dinosaur remains were washed into _____.
   A. ● rivers or lakes
   B. mountains
   C. rocks
   D. sand

6. Why did bones need to be covered by sediments to become fossils?
   A. to keep them out of the way
   B. ● to preserve them
   C. to slow the fossil process down
   D. so that scientists could find them

Page 88

To What Group Do Dinosaurs Belong?

Before the 1800s, people who found dinosaur bones and teeth did not know what they were. Little by little, scientists realized that these fossils were different from those of any other group of animals. These animals were somewhat like lizards, a type of reptile, but were generally much bigger. They decided to call this group **Dinosauria**. The name **dinosaur** comes from this word, which means "terrible lizards."

Why do you think "terrible lizards" was chosen for the name of dinosaurs? What do you think paleontologists knew about dinosaurs at this time?
<u>Sample answer: They believed that dinosaurs were huge and powerful relatives of modern-day lizards.</u>

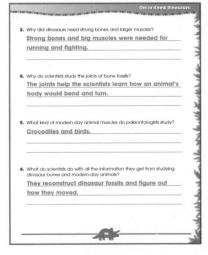

Over the years, paleontologists have been able to learn a lot about dinosaurs and other animals that lived a long time ago.

Why do you think paleontologists and other people continue to look for fossils today?
<u>Sample answer: They hope to discover new fossils that will help them learn more about dinosaurs and what earth was like when dinosaurs lived.</u>

Page 89

What Do Paleontoligists Do When They Find a Fossil?

When paleontologists find fossils they want to study, they make notes about their find, map the area, and carefully dig the fossils out of the ground. The bones are wrapped in plaster so they won't break. Then they are sent to a laboratory. Once there, they are carefully unwrapped. Paleontologists study the fossils to find out what type of animal they belonged to and when it lived.

Sometimes paleontologists find a number of parts to a dinosaur's **skeleton**. The skeleton can be reconstructed, or put together, and shown in a museum.

These pictures show some of the jobs paleontologists do. Number the pictures to show the order of when each job would be completed.

1	4
3	2

Page 90

How Do Paleontologists Know How Dinosaurs Moved?

Paleontologists figure out how dinosaurs moved by studying their bones. **Muscle scars** on dinosaur bones show where muscles were attached to the bones, and how big they were. Strong bones and larger muscles were needed for running and fighting. Studying **joints**, the places where bones come together, gives scientists an idea of how an animal's body could bend and turn.

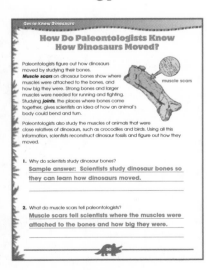
muscle scars

Paleontologists also study the muscles of animals that were close relatives of dinosaurs, such as crocodiles and birds. Using all this information, scientists reconstruct dinosaur fossils and figure out how they moved.

1. Why do scientists study dinosaur bones?
   <u>Sample answer: Scientists study dinosaur bones so they can learn how dinosaurs moved.</u>

2. What do muscle scars tell paleontologists?
   <u>Muscle scars tell scientists where the muscles were attached to the bones and how big they were.</u>

Page 91

3. Why did dinosaurs need strong bones and larger muscles?
   <u>Strong bones and big muscles were needed for running and fighting.</u>

4. Why do scientists study the joints of bone fossils?
   <u>The joints help the scientists learn how an animal's body would bend and turn.</u>

5. What kind of modern-day animal muscles do paleontologists study?
   <u>Crocodiles and birds.</u>

6. What do scientists do with all the information they get from studying dinosaur bones and modern-day animals?
   <u>They reconstruct dinosaur fossils and figure out how they moved.</u>

Page 92

What Was Dinosaur Skin Like?

Impressions of dinosaur skin are sometimes preserved in rocks. They show that most dinosaurs probably had tough, scaly, waterproof skin, like other reptiles. Polacanthus was an armored plant-eater. It had bumpy skin with bony spikes and plates for extra protection. Meat-eaters such as Carnotaurus had smooth scales, like that of a lizard. Some small meat-eaters may have had feathers like birds.

Scientists cannot determine the color of a dinosaur's skin from its fossils. They theorize though, that dinosaurs had various patterns and colors, just like today's reptiles.

1. Impressions of dinosaur skin can be preserved in _____
   A. water
   B. ● rocks
   C. trees
   D. sand

2. The impressions show that most dinosaur scales were like _____
   A. bird feathers
   B. ● those of other reptiles
   C. lion fur
   D. seal skin

Page 93

3. What kind of dinosaur was Polacanthus?
- (A) an unarmored herbivore
- (B) a carnivore with armor
- (C) a carnivore
- **(D) an armored herbivore**

4. The skin of a Carnotaurus was _____.
- (A) bumpy
- **(B) smooth and scaly**
- (C) rough and dry
- (D) orange

5. Scientists think that some small meat-eaters may have had _____.
- (A) armor plates
- (B) spikes
- (C) fur
- **(D) feathers**

6. Paleontologists theorize that dinosaur skin _____.
- **(A) could have been different colors**
- (B) was brown
- (C) was green and brown
- (D) was green

93

Page 95

Word Search Activity

Use the word list to help you find the words about dinosaurs that are hidden in the block below. Some of the words are hidden backward or diagonally.

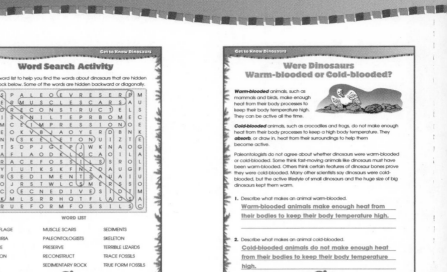

WORD LIST

CAMOUFLAGE	MUSCLE SCARS	SEDIMENTS
DINOSAURIA	PALEONTOLOGISTS	SKELETON
EVIDENCE	PRESERVE	TERRIBLE LIZARDS
IMPRESSION	RECONSTRUCT	TRACE FOSSILS
JOINTS	SEDIMENTARY ROCK	TRUE FORM FOSSILS

95

Page 96

Were Dinosaurs Warm-blooded or Cold-blooded?

Warm-blooded animals, such as mammals and birds, make enough heat from their body processes to keep their body temperature high. They can be active all the time.

Cold-blooded animals, such as crocodiles and frogs, do not make enough heat from their body processes to keep a high body temperature. They **absorb**, or draw in, heat from their surroundings to help them become active.

Paleontologists do not agree about whether dinosaurs were warm-blooded or cold-blooded. Some think fast-moving animals like dinosaurs must have been warm-blooded. Others think certain features of dinosaur bones prove they were cold-blooded. Many other scientists say dinosaurs were cold-blooded, but the active lifestyle of small dinosaurs and the huge size of big dinosaurs kept them warm.

1. Describe what makes an animal warm-blooded.
   Warm-blooded animals make enough heat from their bodies to keep their body temperature high.

2. Describe what makes an animal cold-blooded.
   Cold-blooded animals do not make enough heat from their bodies to keep their body temperature high.

96

Page 97

3. Name some modern-day animals that are warm-blooded.
   Sample answer: Human beings, rabbits, mice, and birds.

4. Name some modern-day animals that are cold-blooded.
   Sample answer: Snakes, crocodiles, and lizards.

5. Why do some paleontologists think that dinosaurs were warm-blooded?
   Because some dinosaurs moved fast.

6. Why do some paleontologists think that dinosaurs were cold-blooded?
   Some scientists think that dinosaur bones prove they were cold-blooded.

97

Page 98

Did Dinosaurs Have Good Eyesight?

Paleontologists study a dinosaur's skull to figure out how big different parts of its brain were. Large "sight areas" in the brain mean that a dinosaur had good eyesight. Leaellynasaura was a meat-eater that had sharp vision, perhaps to help it see in the dark. Velociraptor and Oviraptor also had good vision and may have hunted at night. It is likely that not all dinosaurs had good eyesight. Some plant-eating dinosaurs probably had a better sense of smell than of sight.

1. What do paleontologists study to figure out how big different parts of a dinosaur's brain were?
- (A) their eyes
- (B) their size
- (C) their tail length
- **(D) their skulls**

2. What is a sight area?
- (A) An area in which everything is viewed.
- (B) A dinosaur's field of vision.
- (C) An area where dinosaurs have been found.
- **(D) An area in the brain that controls the sense of sight.**

98

Page 99

3. A large sight area in a dinosaur's skull meant _____.
- (A) it had bad eyesight
- **(B) it had good eyesight**
- (C) it had more than two eyes
- (D) it could not see color

4. Some paleontologists believe that Leaellynasaura could _____.
- (A) not see at all
- (B) see only during the day
- **(C) see in the dark**
- (D) see with only one eye

5. Scientists think that Oviraptor hunted _____.
- (A) only during the day
- **(B) at night**
- (C) in the water
- (D) from the branches of trees

6. Did all dinosaurs have good eyesight?
- (A) Yes, all dinosaurs had large sight areas.
- (B) No, only carnivores had large sight areas.
- (C) No, only herbivores had good eyesight.
- **(D) No, some dinosaurs had a better sense of smell.**

99

Page 100

Did Dinosaurs Make Sounds?

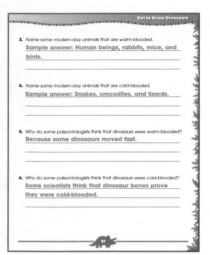

Skull bones show that many dinosaurs probably made sounds. Young dinosaurs may have squeaked or squealed, and older dinosaurs may have croaked, barked, or roared. The skulls of some duck-billed dinosaurs have fan-shaped or tube-shaped **crests**, or tops. Paleontologists think these crests may have been echo chambers that helped the dinosaurs make sounds. Duckbills may have bellowed to attract mates, like a modern moose would.

Corythosaurus

1. What part of a dinosaur's remains did scientists use to determine how dinosaurs made sounds?
   Scientists use skull bones to determine if dinosaurs made noises.

2. What kinds of sounds might some young dinosaurs have made?
   A young dinosaur may have squeaked or squealed.

100

Page 101

3. What kinds of sounds might some older dinosaurs have made?
   An older dinosaur may have croaked, barked, or roared.

4. Paleontologists think that the crests on duck-billed dinosaurs may have been used as what?
   The crests may have been used as echo chambers that helped the dinosaurs make sounds.

5. Why do scientists think that duckbills made sounds?
   Duckbills may have made sounds to attract mates.

6. Name some modern-day animals that make sounds to attract mates.
   Sample answer: Birds, dogs, and cats.

101

Page 102

How Smart Were Dinosaurs?

To figure out how smart a dinosaur was, paleontologists compare the size of its brain to the size of its body. Scientists think dinosaurs that had large brains compared to their bodies were smart. Small, nimble meat-eaters, such as Troödon and Oviraptor, had big brains. Both guarded their eggs, and paleontologists think they were among the smartest dinosaurs. Giant long-necks, such as Brachiosaurus, had rather small brains. They probably walked slowly and performed only simple activities.

Troödon

1. To figure out how smart a dinosaur was paleontologists compare the size of its brain to the size of its _____.
- (A) head
- (B) feet
- (C) tail
- **(D) body**

2. The larger the size of a dinosaur's brain compared to the size of its body meant that _____.
- **(A) the dinosaur was smarter than other dinosaurs**
- (B) the dinosaur could only walk slowly
- (C) the dinosaur performed only simple activities
- (D) the dinosaur could not slow down

102

Page 103

Get to Know Dinosaurs

3. Small, nimble carnivores had _____.
- small brains
- **large brains**
- average-sized brains
- no brains

4. Scientists think that Troödon and Oviraptor did all of these except _____.
- guard their eggs
- **eat plants**
- run quickly and nimbly
- hunt other dinosaurs

5. To what group of dinosaurs does Brachiosaurus belong?
- **long-necks**
- duckbills
- curved-claws
- parrot-beaked

6. Which sentence does not describe what paleontologists believe about long-necks?
- They walked slowly.
- **They had big brains.**
- They had small brains.
- They performed only simple tasks.

103

Page 104

Am I Smart?

Which of the dinosaurs below do you think would have been "smart" dinosaurs? Circle the correct pictures.

Podokesaurus, Pentaceratops, Corythosaurus, Tarbosaurus, Saltopus, Parksosaurus

104

Page 105

Get to Know Dinosaurs

Crossword Activity

Read the clues about dinosaurs. Then, complete the puzzle using the word list below.

DOWN
1. Animals whose bodies do not produce enough heat to keep them warm are called _____
3. Animals that make enough body heat to keep their body temperatures high are called _____
5. If a dinosaur had large _____, then it was believe to have had excellent sight.

ACROSS
2. Cold-blooded animals _____ heat from their surroundings.
4. Scientists that _____ may have bellowed to attract mates.
6. Some duck-billed dinosaurs had _____ on the tops of their heads.

WORD LIST
COLD-BLOODED
SIGHT
WARM-BLOODED
CRESTS
ABSORB
DUCKBILLS

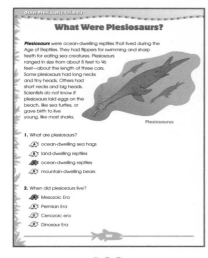

105

Page 106

Other Prehistoric Animals

What Other Kinds of Animals Lived When Dinosaurs Lived?

Many kinds of animals were alive during the Age of Reptiles—the time when dinosaurs lived. The oceans were filled with sponges, jellyfish, crabs, shrimp, snails, oysters, corals, sea stars, sea urchins, squid, and fish. The seas also contained swimming reptiles, like *pliosaurs*, *plesiosaurs*, and *ichthyosaurs*. The land provided homes for insects, spiders, centipedes, salamander-like amphibians, crocodiles, and turtles. Flying reptiles, like *pterosaurs*, filled the air. Lizards, snakes, small mammals, and birds also appeared during this time.

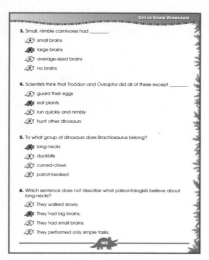

Enchodus
Kuehneosaurus

1. What kinds of animals lived in the oceans and seas when dinosaurs lived?
Sample answer: Sponges, jellyfish, crabs, shrimp, and snails.

2. What kinds of animals lived on land when dinosaurs lived?
Sample answer: insects, spiders, centipedes, salamander-like amphibians, and crocodiles.

106

Page 107

Other Prehistoric Animals

3. What kinds of flying animals lived when dinosaurs lived?
Pterosaurs.

4. Do you think any of these different kinds of animals are alive today? If so, name them.
Sample answer: Yes. Jellyfish, crabs, and crocodiles.

5. What kinds of animals first appeared during the Mesozoic Era?
Sample answer: Lizards, snakes, small mammals, and birds.

6. What kind of defense did these animals have against the dinosaurs?
Sample answer: Dinosaurs could not fly or swim. The land animals were probably very small and quick.

107

Page 108

Other Prehistoric Animals

What Were Plesiosaurs?

Plesiosaurs were ocean-dwelling reptiles that lived during the Age of Reptiles. They had flippers for swimming and sharp teeth for eating sea creatures. Plesiosaurs ranged in size from about 8 feet to 46 feet—about the length of three cars. Some plesiosaurs had long necks and tiny heads. Others had short necks and big heads. Scientists do not know if plesiosaurs laid eggs on the beach, like sea turtles, or gave birth to live young, like most sharks.

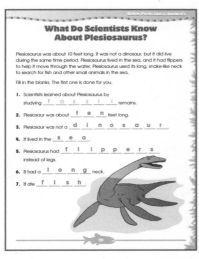

Plesiosaurus

1. What are plesiosaurs?
- ocean-dwelling sea hags
- land-dwelling reptiles
- **ocean-dwelling reptiles**
- mountain-dwelling bears

2. When did plesiosaurs live?
- **Mesozoic Era**
- Permian Era
- Cenozoic era
- Dinosaur Era

108

Page 109

Other Prehistoric Animals

3. How did plesiosaurs swim?
- **with their flippers**
- with a partner
- with scuba gear
- with a surf board

4. Plesiosaurs could be as long as _____.
- 2 cars
- 8 feet
- **46 feet**
- 1 car

5. How do scientists think plesiosaurs reproduced?
- They laid eggs.
- They gave birth.
- They cloned themselves.
- **Scientists are unsure.**

6. Which statement about plesiosaurs is correct?
- They all had long necks.
- They all laid their eggs on the beach.
- **Some were short, and some were long.**
- They gave birth to live young in the sea.

109

Page 110

Other Prehistoric Animals

What Did Water-dwelling Creatures Look Like?

To find out what the three prehistoric sea creatures below looked like, follow the correct path. The correct path will also give you some interesting facts to help you answer the questions at the bottom of the page.

Plesiosaurs   Ichthyosaurs   Pliosaurs

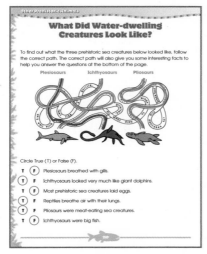

Circle True (T) or False (F).

- T **F** Plesiosaurs breathed with gills.
- **T** F Ichthyosaurs looked very much like giant dolphins.
- **T** F Most prehistoric sea creatures laid eggs.
- T **F** Reptiles breathe air with their lungs.
- **T** F Pliosaurs were meat-eating sea creatures.
- **T** F Ichthyosaurs were big fish.

110

Page 111

Other Prehistoric Animals

What Do Scientists Know About Plesiosaurus?

Plesiosaurus was about 10 feet long. It was not a dinosaur, but it did live during the same time period. Plesiosaurus lived in the sea, and it had flippers to help it move through the water. Plesiosaurus used its long, snake-like neck to search for fish and other small animals in the sea.

Fill in the blanks. The first one is done for you.

1. Scientists learned about Plesiosaurus by studying f o s s i l remains.
2. Plesiosaur was about t e n feet long.
3. Plesiosaur was not a d i n o s a u r.
4. It lived in the s e a.
5. Plesiosaurus had f l i p p e r s instead of legs.
6. It had a l o n g neck.
7. It ate f i s h.

111

341

Page 112

What Were Pterosaurs?

Pterosaurs were featherless, flying reptiles that lived during the Age of Reptiles. Though distantly related to dinosaurs, pterosaurs were not dinosaurs. Pterosaurs ranged from robin-sized creatures to large animals with wingspans of 35 feet. The leathery wings of pterosaurs extended back from rods made of arm and finger bones. Scientists believed that pterosaurs used all four limbs to walk. Pterosaurs probably ate fish and small animals.

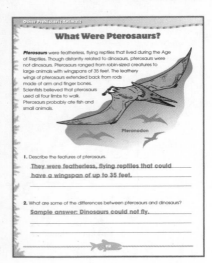

Pteranodon

1. Describe the features of pterosaurs.

   They were featherless, flying reptiles that could have a wingspan of up to 35 feet.

2. What are some of the differences between pterosaurs and dinosaurs?

   Sample answer: Dinosaurs could not fly.

112

Page 113

3. How did pterosaurs move when they were on the ground?

   Pterosaurs probably used all four limbs when walking.

4. What did pterosaurs eat?

   They probably ate fish and small animals.

5. How do you think pterosaurs were able to catch their prey?

   Sample answer: They could swoop down and pick up their food with their mouths.

6. What modern-day animals are similar to pterosaurs?

   Sample answer: Eagles, vultures, pelicans, and owls.

113

Page 114

What Was Archaeopteryx?

Archaeopteryx is the oldest known bird. It lived about 150 million years ago, during the Age of Reptiles. Archaeopteryx was about the size of a modern-day crow and had both bird and dinosaur features. Like a bird, it had wings, feathers, and a beak. Like a dinosaur, it had teeth and a bony tail. Its skeleton was also similar to those of some small dinosaurs. Most paleontologists think Archaeopteryx and other birds developed from a dinosaur ancestor and that modern birds are living dinosaurs.

Archaeopteryx

1. Archaeopteryx is the oldest known _____.
   - ⓐ dinosaur
   - ⓑ animal
   - **ⓒ bird**
   - ⓓ fish

2. It lived about _____ years ago.
   - ⓐ 75 million
   - ⓑ 256 million
   - ⓒ 14 million
   - **ⓓ 150 million**

114

Page 115

3. How big was an Archaeopteryx?
   - **ⓐ about the size of a modern-day crow**
   - ⓑ about the size of a modern-day eagle
   - ⓒ about the size of a modern-day chicken
   - ⓓ about the size of a modern-day vulture

4. Archaeopteryx had all of these features in common with a bird except _____.
   - ⓐ wings
   - **ⓑ teeth**
   - ⓒ feathers
   - ⓓ a beak

5. Archaeopteryx had all of these features in common with a dinosaur except _____.
   - ⓐ teeth
   - **ⓑ wings**
   - ⓒ a bony tail
   - ⓓ a similar skeleton to some small dinosaurs

6. Most paleontologists believe that _____.
   - **ⓐ modern birds are ancestors of dinosaurs**
   - ⓑ dinosaurs developed from ancient birds
   - ⓒ reptiles and birds are the same
   - ⓓ Archaeopteryx is a living bird

115

Page 116

Were There Any People When Dinosaurs Lived?

Dinosaurs lived long before people appeared on earth. However, the theory of evolution suggests that distant ancestors of human beings, the first **primates**, a kind of mammal, appeared at the end of the dinosaur age. The first primates were probably similar to tree shrews—squirrel-sized animals with pointed noses, long tails, and sharp claws. Most scientists think that over many millions of years, these early primates **evolved**, or developed, into advanced primates— monkeys, then apes, then humans. Scientists theorize that the first human beings appeared about 5 million years ago.

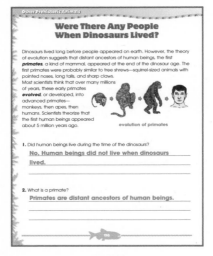

evolution of primates

1. Did human beings live during the time of the dinosaurs?

   No. Human beings did not live when dinosaurs lived.

2. What is a primate?

   Primates are distant ancestors of human beings.

116

Page 117

3. Describe the first primates.

   They were similar to tree shrews, about the same size as a squirrel with pointed noses, long tails, and sharp claws.

4. How did the first primates evolve into human beings?

   They developed from small mammals to more advanced primates.

5. Did the early primates evolve quickly or slowly? How do you know?

   It took many millions of years.

6. When did the first human beings appear on earth?

   The first humans appeared on earth about 5 million years ago.

117

Page 118

Why Did Dinosaurs Disappear?

Nobody knows exactly why dinosaurs became **extinct**, or died out. Below are a few theories that scientists have suggested. One or more of these events may have caused the extinction of the dinosaurs.

Asteroid Crash Theory: An asteroid, a large rocky object from space, smashed into the earth. The collision created a cloud of dust that surrounded the planet and blocked the sun. The earth grew cold, and most plants died. The dinosaurs froze or died from starvation.

Volcano Theory: Volcanic eruptions over millions of years produced clouds of dust that surrounded the earth. The dust blocked the sun. The planet grew cold, and most plants died. The dinosaurs froze and died from starvation.

Climate Theory: Continental movements and shrinking oceans broke up the areas where dinosaurs lived and made the climate cooler. The dinosaurs froze to death.

1. What does extinct mean?
   - **ⓐ to die out**
   - ⓑ to reappear
   - ⓒ to think of a theory
   - ⓓ to freeze

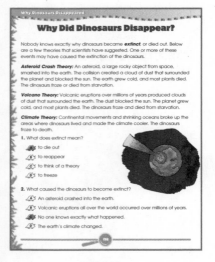

2. What caused the dinosaurs to become extinct?
   - ⓐ An asteroid crashed into the earth.
   - ⓑ Volcanic eruptions all over the world occurred over millions of years.
   - **ⓒ No one knows exactly what happened.**
   - ⓓ The earth's climate changed.

118

Page 119

3. The Asteroid Crash Theory suggests that _____.
   - ⓐ volcanoes erupted and the smoke blocked the sun
   - ⓑ the oceans grew smaller and the earth got cold
   - ⓒ aliens came to earth and took the dinosaurs away with them
   - **ⓓ an asteroid smashed into the earth and dust blocked the sun**

4. The Volcano Theory suggests that _____.
   - **ⓐ volcanoes erupted and the smoke blocked the sun**
   - ⓑ an asteroid smashed into the earth and dust blocked the sun
   - ⓒ the oceans grew smaller and the earth got cold
   - ⓓ dinosaurs lived near volcanoes, and when the volcanoes erupted, the dinosaurs were too close

5. The Climate Theory suggests that _____.
   - ⓐ an asteroid smashed into the earth
   - ⓑ the earth became hot and all the water disappeared
   - **ⓒ continental movements broke up the areas where dinosaurs lived**
   - ⓓ dust in the air blocked the sun

6. What do the three theories mentioned have in common?
   - ⓐ Asteroids hit the earth.
   - ⓑ Dust blocked the sun.
   - **ⓒ The dinosaurs froze.**
   - ⓓ The plants died.

119

Page 120

What Other Extinction Theories Have Been Suggested?

A few other theories of why the dinosaurs became extinct are listed below. Each theory has a **cause** and an **effect**. A cause is a change that happened on earth and an effect is what resulted from the change on earth.

Draw a line from each cause to its effect.

Cause	Effect
Small, fast mammals that liked to eat eggs quickly spread around the world.	Dinosaurs were cold-blooded. They couldn't find places to hibernate. They had no fur or feathers to keep themselves warm. They froze to death.
New kinds of flowering plants started to grow on the earth. These plants had poison in them that the dinosaurs could not taste.	Fewer and fewer baby dinosaurs were born.
When dinosaurs were living, the earth was warm all year long. Suddenly the earth became cooler with cold winter months.	The dinosaurs ate poison without even knowing it and they died.

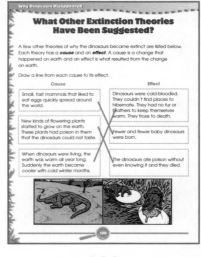

120

What Do You Think Happened to the Dinosaurs?

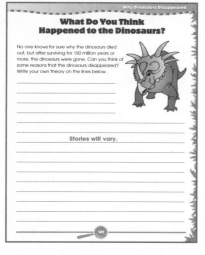

No one knows for sure why the dinosaurs died out, but after surviving for 150 million years or more, the dinosaurs were gone. Can you think of some reasons that the dinosaurs disappeared? Write your own theory on the lines below.

_____
_____
_____
_____

Stories will vary.

_____
_____
_____
_____
_____
_____

121

Are New Kinds of Dinosaurs Still Being Found?

Paleontologists are finding new kinds of dinosaurs all the time. Every year, they go on *dinosaur digs*, or fossil hunts, in areas that contain sedimentary rocks. Dinosaur digs have been done in Africa, Antarctica, Argentina, Canada, China, Madagascar, Mongolia, and the United States. Scientists think there are hundreds of kinds of dinosaurs still to be discovered.

1. In what countries have scientists dug for dinosaurs fossils?

Sample answer: Africa, Antarctica, Argentina, and Canada.

2. What areas do paleontologists look for fossils? Why do they look there?

They look in areas with sedimentary rocks.

122

---

3. Why do scientists think that there are still more kinds of dinosaurs to be found?

Sample answer: Because they haven't looked everywhere.

4. Why is a fossil hunt called a dinosaur dig?

Because paleontologists dig dinosaur bones out of rock.

5. Besides fossils, what do you think scientists find during a dinosaur dig?

Sample answer: Nests, eggs, gastroliths, and footprints.

6. If you could go on a fossil hunt in one of the countries mentioned above, which one would you go to? Why?

Answers will vary.

123

What Are Some Living Relatives of Dinosaurs?

All living reptiles, such as turtles, crocodiles, snakes, and lizards, are distantly related to dinosaurs. The closest relatives of dinosaurs, though, are birds. In fact, most paleontologists believe that birds are living dinosaurs.

In China, paleontologists discovered the fossils of dinosaurs that had feathers but could not fly, such as Caudipteryx. Scientists also discovered the fossils of an ancient bird that looked like a small dinosaur. They think some small dinosaurs developed wings and the ability to fly and then became birds.

Caudipteryx

1. What are the closest living relatives to dinosaurs?
- A. reptiles
- B. humans
- C. ants
- D. birds

2. Name the dinosaur that had feathers but could not fly.
- A. Caudipteryx
- B. Plesiosaurus
- C. Primates
- D. Archaeopteryx

124

---

3. Where was the dinosaur that had feathers but could not fly found?
- A. North America
- B. China
- C. Africa
- D. Japan

4. Paleontologists believe that birds are _____.
- A. flying cats
- B. living dolls
- C. swimming sharks
- D. living dinosaurs

5. Some small dinosaurs may have developed _____ and then became birds.
- A. wings
- B. beaks
- C. feathers
- D. eggs

6. How do scientists figure out which animals are closely related to each other and which are not?
- A. by comparing weight
- B. by comparing leg length
- C. by comparing appearance
- D. by comparing eye color

125

Keeping Up With the Dinosaurs

Read the dinosaur facts below. Then, write True (T) or False (F) in the blanks before the sentences at the bottom of the page.

Paleontologists believe that the first dinosaurs evolved on earth about 245 million years ago and became extinct about 65 million years ago. All dinosaurs were land-living creatures. The gigantic prehistoric sea creatures, such as ichthyosaurs and plesiosaurs, were not really dinosaurs. Pterosaurs were not really dinosaurs either. They were flying reptiles that looked like lizards with wings.

The word dinosaur means "terrible lizard," but dinosaurs were not lizards. Modern science now links dinosaurs to birds. Today's birds are thought to be the closest relatives to the dinosaurs. Crocodiles are also thought to be more distant relatives of the dinosaurs. Scientists believe all animals and plants living on earth today are descendants of creatures that lived when dinosaurs roamed the earth.

True (T) or false (F) ?

1. **F** The first dinosaurs evolved on earth about 65 million years ago.
2. **F** Ichthyosaurs were dinosaurs.
3. **T** Dinosaurs were not lizards.
4. **T** Scientists believe birds are related to dinosaurs.
5. **F** Some dinosaurs were flying reptiles.

126

A Dinosaur Tale

Study the prehistoric animals pictured below. Then, complete each category with words that you associate with these animals. A few examples are already written under each category. Use the words to compose a poem or short story about these animals.

Nouns	Verbs	Adjectives
tail	walk	huge
teeth	run	spiked
head	eat	sharp

Entries will vary.

Title: _____

Stories will vary.

127

Use the information from the previous page to answer the following questions.

1. The name Coelophysis means "hollow form" because it had **hollow** bones.

2. A two-legged herbivore that may have been able to use its hands for grasping was named **Plateosaurus**.

3. "Socket-toothed Lizard" had **Thecodontosaurus** teeth in distinct sockets.

4. Eoraptor was one of the **earliest** known dinosaurs.

5. **Riojasaurus** probably could not run.

6. Saltopus was only about two feet long and probably ate mainly **insects**.

7. Dinosaurus's name means **Terrifying Lizard**.

8. **Massospondylus** whose name means "Massive Vertibra," also lived during the early Jurassic Period.

131

Coelophysis

Coelophysis was a small, slender dinosaur that weighed only about 60 or 70 pounds. This little dinosaur was a meat-eater, and it had sharp teeth and a long jaw. It was also a fast runner. Coelophysis lived in *herds*, or family groups.

Connect the letters in alphabetical order to find a picture of Coelophysis. Then, color the picture any way you like.

132

133

Plateosaurus

Plateosaurus was a large herbivore that lived during the late Triassic Period. It weighed about 1,500 pounds and was 20-26 feet long. It was one of the early long-necked dinosaurs and probably stood up on its back legs to reach leaves in the trees. It probably ate small stones as well to help grind food in its stomach. Plateosaurus had short claws on its front legs that did not provide much defense from meat-eaters, so it probably ran away from predators rather than trying to attack them. Plateosaurus fossils have been found in Europe.

Use the passage above to answer the questions below.

1. Plateosaurus lived during the __Triassic__ Period.

2. It probably stood on its __back__ legs to reach leaves in the trees.

3. The __stones__ in its stomach helped grind up its food.

4. Plateosaurus only had small __claws__ on its front legs to use for defense.

5. Its fossils have been found in __Europe__.

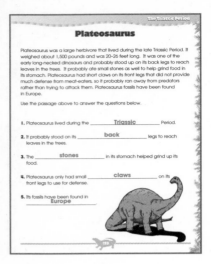

134

Saltopus

Very little is known about Saltopus, one of the earliest dinosaurs that lived during the late Triassic Period. It was a small carnivore, weighing about 2 pounds and was only about 2 feet long. It probably ate insects. Like Coelophysis, Saltopus had hollow bones, which allowed it to be a fast runner. Its jaw was lined with many sharp teeth. Saltopus had small claws on its hands. Saltopus's fossils have been found in Scotland.

Use the passage above to answer the questions below.

1. Saltopus was a small __carnivore__, and probably ate insects.

2. It only weighted about __2__ pounds.

3. Like Coelophysis, Saltopus also had __hollow__ bones.

4. It was also a __fast__ runner.

5. Saltopus's jaw was lined with __sharp__ teeth.

135

Name That Dinosaur!

Complete the puzzle below by writing a dinosaur's name across each letter. Remember that the name you choose must contain that letter. The first one has been done for you. If you need help, use the Word Bank at the bottom of the page.

Word Bank

Coelophysis
Dinosaurus
Eoraptor
Plateosaurus
Riojasaurus
Saltopus
Thecodontosaurus

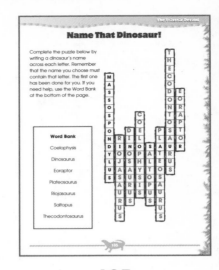

136

Dinosaur Diagram

A Venn diagram can be used to compare things. First, look at the picture to notice ways the two dinosaurs are the same. Then, look for how they are different.

Plateosaurus   Coelophysis

Complete the Venn diagram below by writing more ways Plateosaurus and Coelophysis are both alike and different.

Plateosaurus   Coelophysis

Answers will vary

Different   Same   Different

137

Who Am I?

Read the 16 clues below about a certain dinosaur. Use a science book or other resource materials and your own logical thinking to guess the name of the dinosaur. When you are finished, write your own clues about another dinosaur. Give it to someone else to see if he or she can guess the answer.

I am a dinosaur.

1. My name means "La Rioja Lizard."
2. I had a small head.
3. I had spoon-shaped teeth.
4. I ate plants.
5. I walked on all four legs.
6. I was 30-36 feet long.
7. I had a bulky body.
8. I lived during the Triassic Period.
9. I had claws on my feet.
10. My fossils were found in Argentina.
11. I was a Saurischian.
12. I had a long neck.
13. I probably could not run.
14. My backbone was hollow.
15. I had a long tail.
16. I was named by José F. Bonaparte in 1969.

I am __Riojasaurus__

I am a dinosaur.

I am _____

141

Use the information from the previous page to answer the following questions.

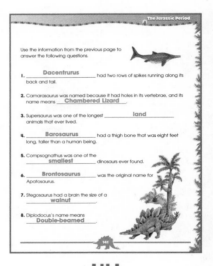

1. __Dacentrurus__ had two rows of spikes running along its back and tail.

2. Camarasaurus was named because it had holes in its vertebrae, and its name means __Chambered Lizard__.

3. Supersaurus was one of the longest __land__ animals that ever lived.

4. __Barosaurus__ had a thigh bone that was eight feet long, taller than a human being.

5. Compsognathus was one of the __smallest__ dinosaurs ever found.

6. __Brontosaurus__ was the original name for Apatosaurus.

7. Stegosaurus had a brain the size of a __walnut__.

8. Diplodocus's name means __Double-beamed__.

142

Apatosaurus

Apatosaurus was a very large dinosaur that walked on four feet. It was about 70 feet long! It had a long neck, which allowed it to munch on leaves from tall trees. It also had a long tail. This dinosaur had very strong bones to support its weight. Apatosaurus was covered with tough, leathery skin.

Create a rhyme about Apatosaurus. Fill in each blank below using the information given above.

Its neck was long.
Its bones were __strong__.

It reached with ease
To the tops of __trees__.

Its skin was __tough__.
And that's enough!

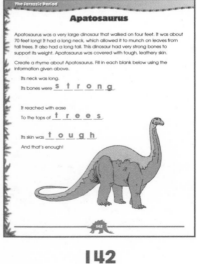

144

Camarasaurus

Camarasaurus was a fairly large four-footed plant-eater. It had a long neck and a very strong but short tail.

Carefully copy the lines in each numbered box into the square on the grid that has the same number. Then, color the finished drawing any way you like.

145

Compsognathus

Compsognathus was a tiny dinosaur that was no bigger than a chicken! Because it weighed about 5 pounds, Compsognathus was probably quick and light on its feet. It could chase down insects and other small animals, then use its sharp teeth and claws.

There are six of these tiny dinosaurs hiding in the picture below. Can you find them all? Circle each one.

146

Dacentrurus

Dacentrurus was a fairly small dinosaur. It was only 15 feet long, and it weighed about 1 ton. It had two rows of spikes on its back and tail. Dacentrurus walked on all four feet. It was a plant-eater.

How many different words can you make using the letters in the name Dacentrurus?

DACENTRURUS

_____

Answers will vary.

_____

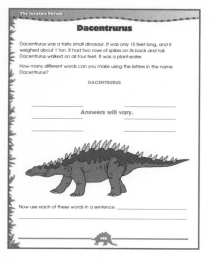

Now use each of these words in a sentence. _____

147

Diplodocus

Diplodocus was one of the longest dinosaurs. It was 85 to 100 feet long! Diplodocus had a very long neck and a small head. Its tail was about 45 feet long! Diplodocus probably swayed its tail back and forth to keep other dinosaurs away.

Connect the letters in alphabetical order to make a picture of Diplodocus. Then, color the picture any way you like.

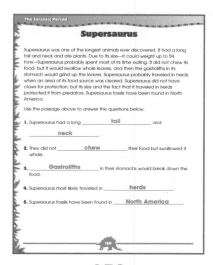

148

Stegosaurus

Stegosaurus had large bony plates on its neck, back, and tail. Scientists are not sure why the dinosaur had these plates. Perhaps the plates protected Stegosaurus, or maybe they helped it warm up and cool down.

Stegosaurus was about 25 feet long and weighed over 3 tons. It had a very small head and brain. Stegosaurus walked with its head close to the ground because its front legs were shorter than its back legs. Stegosaurus had sharp spikes on the end of its tail.

Color the Stegosaurus plates purple. Color the spikes red. Color the rest of the dinosaur any way you like.

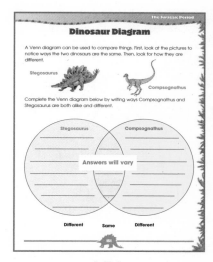

149

Use the information from the previous page to complete each sentence below.

Stegosaurus had a small **h e a d**.

Stegosaurus had sharp **s p i k e s** on the end of its tail.

Stegosaurus was about 25 **f e e t** long.

Stegosaurus weighed over 3 **t o n s**.

Stegosaurus had bony **p l a t e s** on its back.

Its head was close to the **g r o u n d**.

Unscramble the letters in the circles to find out what Stegosaurus liked to eat.

Stegosaurus ate **p l a n t s**.

150

Supersaurus

Supersaurus was one of the longest animals ever discovered. It had a long tail and neck and ate plants. Due to its size—it could weight up to 54 tons—Supersaurus probably spent most of its time eating. It did not chew its food, but it would swallow whole leaves, and then the gastroliths in its stomach would grind up the leaves. Supersaurus probably traveled in herds when an area of its food source was cleared. Supersaurus did not have claws for protection, but its size and the fact that it traveled in herds protected it from predators. Supersaurus fossils have been found in North America.

Use the passage above to answer the questions below.

1. Supersaurus had a long **tail** and **neck**.

2. They did not **chew** their food but swallowed it whole.

3. **Gastroliths** in their stomachs would break down the food.

4. Supersaurus most likely traveled in **herds**.

5. Supersaurus fossils have been found in **North America**.

151

Dinosaur Diagram

A Venn diagram can be used to compare things. First, look at the pictures to notice ways the two dinosaurs are the same. Then, look for how they are different.

Stegosaurus   Compsognathus

Complete the Venn diagram below by writing ways Compsognathus and Stegosaurus are both alike and different.

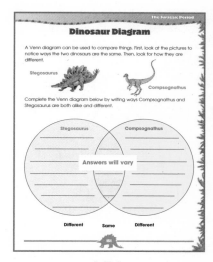

Stegosaurus   Compsognathus

Answers will vary

Different   Same   Different

155

Use the information from the previous page to answer the following questions.

1. **Ingenia** was a two-legged carnivore that protected its eggs.

2. Parasaurolophus had a long **crest** on its head that probably use to make a loud noise.

3. An armored dinosaur, Ankylosaurus ate **plants**.

4. **Saltasaurus** fossils were found in the Salta Province in Argentina.

5. Scientists believe that Troödon may have been the **smartest** dinosaur.

6. The fossils of the four-legged herbivore **Maiasaura** were the first to be found alongside its fossilized eggs and nest.

7. **Velociraptor** could run up to 40 miles an hour for short distances.

8. Corythosaurus had a flat, bony crest on its head that looked like a **helmet**.

9. Pachycephalosaurus, whose name means **Thick-headed Lizard**, probably ran away from danger before fighting.

10. Scientists believed that **Gallimimus** used its tail for balance as it ran.

11. **Pentaceratops** had the largest known skull of any land animal.

12. Tyrannosaurus Rex could have teeth up to **13** inches long.

156

Ankylosaurus

Ankylosaurus was about 35 feet long and weighed about 5 tons. It had a short neck and stubby legs. The body of Ankylosaurus was covered with thick, leathery skin and bony plates. It also had rows of knobs and spikes on its body. Ankylosaurus had a tail that ended in a big bony club, which could be used to fight off other dinosaurs. The dinosaur used its small teeth and jaws to eat plants near the ground.

Ankylosaurus weighed **f i v e   t o n s**
                        1   2   3   4   5   6   7   8

Ankylosaurus had a **s h o r t** neck.
                    8   9   6 10   5

Ankylosaurus had bony plates. **s p i k e s** and knobs for armor.
                              8 11 2 12   4   8

Ankylosaurus ate **p l a n t s**
                  11 13 14   7   5   8

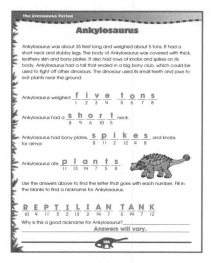

Use the answers above to find the letter that goes with each number. Fill in the blanks to find a nickname for Ankylosaurus.

R E P T I L I A N   T A N K
 10 4 11 12 3 12 14 7 12   1 14 7 12

Why is this a good nickname for Ankylosaurus? _____
Answers will vary.

157

Corythosaurus

Corythosaurus was fairly large. It was about 30 feet long and weighed more than 2 tons. It had bumpy skin and a hollow, rounded crest covering its head. Corythosaurus was a plant-eater, and it had many rows of teeth for grinding food. Scientists think it ate pine needles and leaves. Corythosaurus probably ran on two feet with its tail out for balance.

Corythosaurus was fairly large in **s i z e**
                                   1 2 3 4

In fact, it was about **t h i r t y   f e e t** long.
                       5 6 2 7 5 8   9 4 4 7

Corythosaurus had a large crest on its **h e a d**
                                        6 4 10 11

Its skin was **b u m p y**
              12 13 14 15 4

It probably ate **l e a v e s**
                 16 4 10 7 4 1

Use the answers above to find the letter that goes with each number. Fill in the blanks to find the meaning of this dinosaur's name.
H E L M E T   L I Z A R D
 6 4 16 14 4 7   16 2 3 10 11 1

Do you think this is a good name for Corythosaurus? Why? _____
Answers will vary.

158

The Cretaceous Period

Gallimimus

Gallimimus looked sort of like a giant ostrich. It had long, thin legs and could run fast. Its hands were probably not very strong. Gallimimus had a long neck and a small head. Scientists think that it had jaws that looked like a beak. Gallimimus did not have teeth. It probably ate eggs, plants, and fruit.

Fill in the blanks.

1. Gallimimus probably ate plants and **eggs**.
2. It did not have **teeth**.
3. Its **hands** were weak.
4. Gallimimus had jaws that looked like a **beak**.
5. Gallimimus looked somewhat like a giant **ostrich**.
6. It could **run** fast.
7. It had a **small** head.

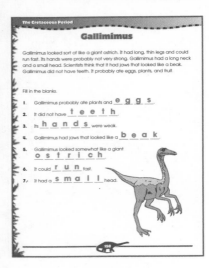

159

The Cretaceous Period

Ingenia

Ingenia was a small dinosaur. It weighed about 60 pounds and was less than 5 feet long. It probably ate insects and the eggs of other dinosaurs.

Color the path that Ingenia must take to get to its food.

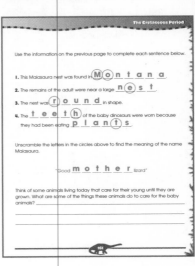

161

The Cretaceous Period

Use the information on the previous page to complete each sentence below.

1. This Maiasaura nest was found in **M o n t a n a**
2. The remains of the adult were near a large **n e s t**
3. The nest was **r o u n d** in shape.
4. The **t e e t h** of the baby dinosaurs were worn because they had been eating **p l a n t s**.

Unscramble the letters in the circles above to find the meaning of the name Maiasaura.

"Good **m o t h e r** lizard"

Think of some animals living today that care for their young until they are grown. What are some of the things these animals do to care for the baby animals? _____

162

The Cretaceous Period

Pachycephalosaurus

Pachycephalosaurus had a thick bone on the top of its head. Knobs and spikes stuck out from this dome and the dinosaur's nose. Pachycephalosaurus may have crashed heads with rival dinosaurs to become the leader of the herd or to win mates.

Circle the two pictures below that are exactly alike.

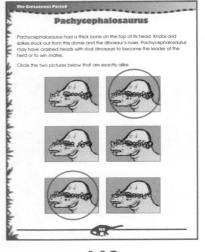

163

The Cretaceous Period

Parasaurolophus

Parasaurolophus had a long crest on the top of its head. This crest was about 5 feet long! Some paleontologists think that the tube helped the dinosaur smell. Others believe that the tube gave Parasaurolophus a loud voice.

Look at each Parasaurolophus shown below. Circle the two pictures that are exactly alike.

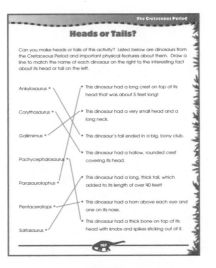

What is different about each of the other pictures? _____ **1 fewer spots, 1 more spots, 1 bigger crest**

165

The Cretaceous Period

Saltasaurus

Saltasaurus was a large dinosaur that walked on four feet. It had a fairly long neck and a long, thick tail. Saltasaurus was almost 40 feet long from nose to tail. Saltasaurus had rough plates, studs, and tiny spikes covering its back.

Cut a piece of string that is 40 feet long. Take the string outside and lay it out in a straight line on the sidewalk.

1. Was Saltasaurus bigger than a car? **Yes, Saltasaurus was bigger than a car.**

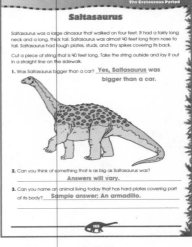

2. Can you think of something that is as big as Saltasaurus was? **Answers will vary.**
3. Can you name an animal living today that has hard plates covering part of its body? **Sample answer: An armadillo.**

166

The Cretaceous Period

Troödon

Troödon was a very fast and smart dinosaur. In fact, some scientists think it was the most intelligent of all the dinosaurs. It had sharp claws and could see well, so it was probably a good hunter.

Copy the lines in each numbered box into the square on the grid below that has the same number. Then, color the finished drawing any way you like.

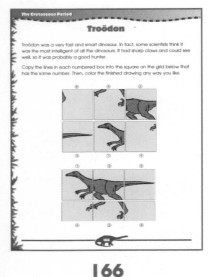

167

The Cretaceous Period

Heads or Tails?

Can you make heads or tails of this activity? Listed below are dinosaurs from the Cretaceous Period and important physical features about them. Draw a line to match the name of each dinosaur on the right to the interesting fact about its head or tail on the left.

Ankylosaurus •
Corythosaurus •
Gallimimus •
Pachycephalosaurus •
Parasaurolophus •
Pentaceratops •
Saltasaurus •

• This dinosaur had a long crest on top of its head that was about 5 feet long!
• This dinosaur had a very small head and a long neck.
• This dinosaur's tail ended in a big, bony club.
• This dinosaur had a hollow, rounded crest covering its head.
• This dinosaur had a long, thick tail, which added to its length of over 40 feet!
• This dinosaur had a horn above each eye and one on its nose.
• This dinosaur had a thick bone on top of its head with knobs and spikes sticking out of it.

168

The Cretaceous Period

Tyrannosaurus rex

Tyrannosaurus rex was a large carnivore that lived during the Cretaceous Period. It walked on two strong hind legs and had a massive head with large teeth that could easily tear apart food. Tyrannosaurus also had two tiny arms that may have been used to grab its prey. Studies of its skull revealed large sight and smell areas in its brain, which meant that Tyrannosaurus had an excellent sense of sight and smell. Tyrannosaurus's tail was straight, giving Tyrannosaurus the ability to keep its balance while running and turning fast. This dinosaur was about 40 feet long and weighed about 7 tons. Some paleontologists believe that Tyrannosaurus was a scavenger, eating animals that were already dead. Others believe that Tyrannosaurus was a predator that killed its own prey.

Answer the questions below in the blanks provided.

1. Tyrannosaurus lived during the **Cretaceous** Period.
2. It had **large** sight and smell areas in its brain.
3. Tyrannosaurus was about **40** feet long.
4. Do you think that Tyrannosaurus was a scavenger or a predator? Why?
   Answers will vary.

A Dinosaur Named Sue

The first Tyrannosaurus fossil was found in 1902 in Montana. There have only been about 30 different Tyrannosaurus finds since then, most of which were not even half complete. In August of 1990, Susan Hendrickson found an almost complete Tyrannosaurus rex fossil in South Dakota. The fossil was named Sue, after the fossil hunter who found it. Sue is the most complete and best-preserved Tyrannosaurus rex fossil ever found. There was a debate about who owned the fossil. In 1997, it was bought at auction for $8.4 million by the Field Museum in Chicago. This allowed Sue to be studied by scientists and seen by the public.

Answer the questions below in the blanks provided.

1. When and where was the first Tyrannosaurus rex fossil found?
   The first Tyrannosaurus fossil was found in 1902 in Montana.

2. **Susan Hendrickson** found the Tyrannosaurus, Sue.

3. Why is the fossil Sue so important?
   It is the most complete and best-preserved Tyrannosaurus rex fossil ever found.

4. Do you think that it was important for the Field Museum (or another museum) to get Sue? Why or why not?
   Answers will vary.

169

Velociraptor

Velociraptor was a meat-eating dinosaur. It was only about 6 feet tall. Velociraptor had sharp claws on its hands and feet. One claw on each foot was like a long, slashing knife. Velociraptor could run fast. Its name means "speedy thief."

Why do you think this dinosaur was called "speedy thief"?
Sample answer: Velociraptor liked to steal eggs from the nest of other dinosaurs and eat them.

How many different words can you make using the letters in the name Velociraptor?

VELOCIRAPTOR

Answers will vary.

170

Name That Dinosaur!

Complete the puzzle below by writing a dinosaur's name across each letter. Remember that the name you choose must contain that letter. The first one has been done for you. If you need help, use the Word Bank at the bottom of the page.

Word Bank	
Archaeoceratops	Brachiosaurus
Ankylosaurus	Triceratops
Giganotosaurus	Tyrannosaurus
Ornithomimus	

171

Dinosaur Diagram

A Venn diagram can be used to compare things. First, look at the picture to notice ways the two dinosaurs are the same. Then, look for how they are different.

Complete the Venn diagram below by writing ways Iguanodon and Triceratops are both alike and different.

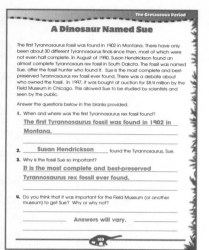

Iguanodon   Triceratops

Answers will vary.

Different   Same   Different

172

Get a Clue!

Read the 16 clues below about a certain dinosaur. Use a science book or other resource materials and your own logical thinking to guess the name of the dinosaur. When you are finished, write your own clues about another dinosaur. Give it to someone else to see if he or she can guess the answer.

I am a dinosaur.

1. My name means "three-horned face."
2. My skull was 7 or 8 feet long.
3. I had a beaked mouth like a parrot.
4. I ate plants.
5. I walked on all four legs.
6. I was 30 feet long.
7. I weighed up to 10 tons.
8. I was one of the last dinosaurs to live.
9. I had 3 claws on my front feet.
10. I lived in Canada and the U.S.
11. I had a thick neck frill.
12. I had 3 horns on my skull.
13. I am the best-known horned dinosaur.
14. I used my horns for protection.
15. I had a small hoof on each toe.
16. I was named by O.C. Marsh in 1889.

I am **Triceratops**

I am a dinosaur.

I am _____

173

Dino-Find

Find the hidden words in the puzzle below. The words may be written forward, backward, up, down, or diagonally. Circle the words. When you have located all the words, write the remaining letters at the bottom of the page to spell out a message.

ALLOSAURUS
APATOSAURUS
ARMORED
ARCHAEOPTERYX
BIRD HIP
COELURUS
DINOSAUR
DIPLODOCUS
FOSSIL
JURASSIC
MEAT-EATER
PALEONTOLOGIST
PLANT-EATER
PLATED
SAUROPOD
STEGOSAURUS

Hidden Message: During this period, shallow seas covered much of North America and Europe and rains came to the deserts.

174

Where's the Egg?

Color the correct set of tracks to help the dinosaur find the egg.

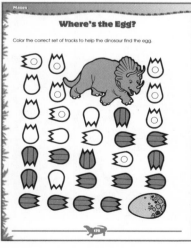

178

The Lost Dinosaur

Help the baby dinosaur find its mother. Color the path in order from A to M.

179

A Very Worried Dinosaur

Help the mother dinosaur find its baby.

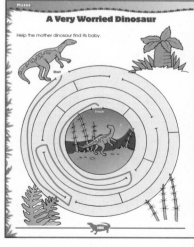

180

Parasaurolophus

Draw a line through the maze from the dinosaur's nose to its tail.

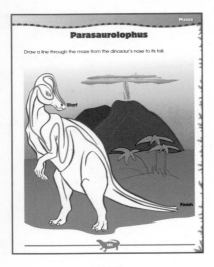

181

Volcano!

Follow the maze to help the dinosaur get away from the volcano!

182

Down at the Dig

Color to find the shapes in the picture. Use the key to help you.

△ = green   ○ = yellow   □ = red

183

More Dinosaur Dig

Find 7 shovels below and color them purple. Then, color the rest of the picture.

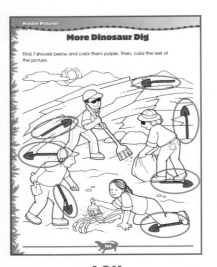

184

Claudia's Dinosaur!

Look at the Tyrannosaurus and Triceratops pictures below. One of them belongs to Claudia. Read the clues to find out which one. *Hint:* Columns go up and down. Rows go across.

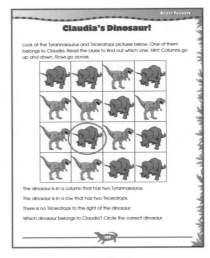

The dinosaur is in a column that has two Tyrannasaurus.

The dinosaur is in a row that has two Triceratops.

There is no Triceratops to the right of the dinosaur.

Which dinosaur belongs to Claudia? Circle the correct dinosaur.

185

From Shortest to Tallest

Look at the five different dinosaurs below. The dinosaurs are lined up from shortest to tallest. Read the clues to figure out the name of each dinosaur in the picture. Then, write their names in the blanks.

Apatosaurus is taller than Hadrosaurus.

Stegosaurus is taller than Saltopus.

Saltopus is taller than Compsognathus.

Hadrosaurus is taller than Stegosaurus.

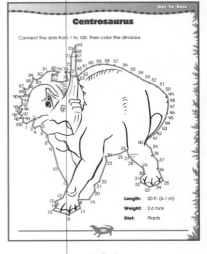

186

Making Moves

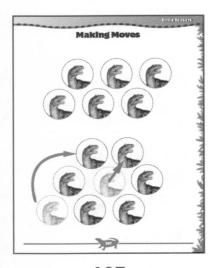

187

Flip, Flop

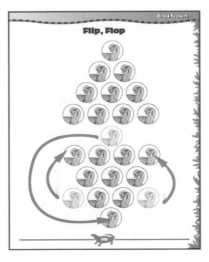

189

Centrosaurus

Connect the dots from 1 to 100. Then color the dinosaur.

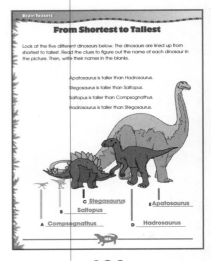

Length: 20 ft. (6.1 m)
Weight: 2.6 tons
Diet: Plants

191

Struthiomimus

Count by 2s to connect the dots. Then, color the dinosaur.

Length:	13 ft. (4 m)
Weight:	440 lb. (150 kg)
Diet:	Small animals, plants

192

Tyrannosaurus

Count by 5s to connect the dots. Then, color the dinosaur.

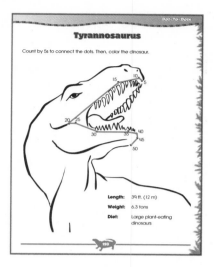

Length:	39 ft. (12 m)
Weight:	6.3 tons
Diet:	Large plant-eating dinosaurs

193

Apatosaurus

Count by 3s to connect the dots. Then, color the dinosaur.

Length:	69 ft. (21 m)
Weight:	24.6 tons
Diet:	Tree leaves, ferns

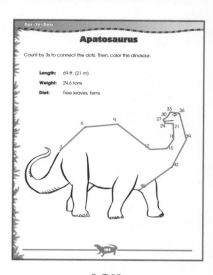

194

Paleontologist Tools

Connect the dots from A to Z. Then, color the picture.

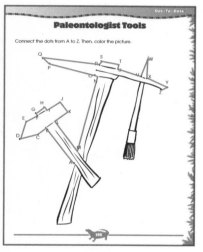

195

Deinonychus

Connect the dots to spell the dinosaur's name. Then, color it.

Length:	10 ft. (3 m)
Weight:	130 lb. (60 kg)
Diet:	Plant-eating dinosaurs

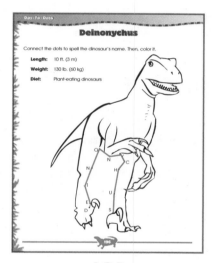

196

Troödon

Connect the dots to spell the dinosaur's name. Then, color it.

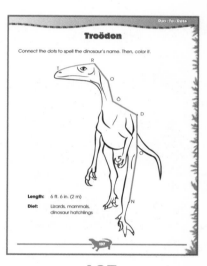

Length:	6 ft. 6 in. (2 m)
Diet:	Lizards, mammals, dinosaur hatchlings

197

Segnosaurus

Connect the dots to spell the dinosaur's name. Then, color it.

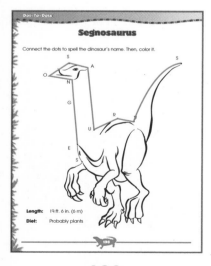

Length:	19 ft. 6 in. (6 m)
Diet:	Probably plants

198

A Nest of Dinosaur Eggs!

Count the dinosaurs eggs in each nest. Write the number of eggs on the lines.

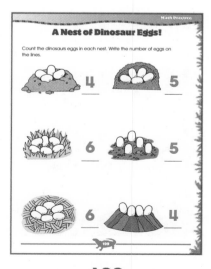

4

5

6

5

6

4

199

One Long Dinosaur!

Diplodocus was one of the longest dinosaurs. It was 90 feet long! Color the picture of Diplodocus below.

A school bus is 30 feet long. Color the number of school buses it would take to equal the length of one Diplodocus.

200

Answer Key

201

Dinosaur Tracks

An inch is a unit of length. Cut out the inch ruler at the bottom of the page. Use it to measure the impressions of dinosaur tracks below to the nearest inch.

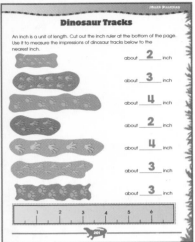

about __2__ inch

about __3__ inch

about __4__ inch

about __2__ inch

about __4__ inch

about __3__ inch

about __3__ inch

203

Sea Friends

Color the picture. Count the Shonisaurus. Then, answer the question below.

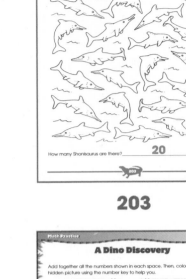

How many Shonisaurus are there? __20__

204

What's the Difference?

Circle the pairs that have a difference of 2.

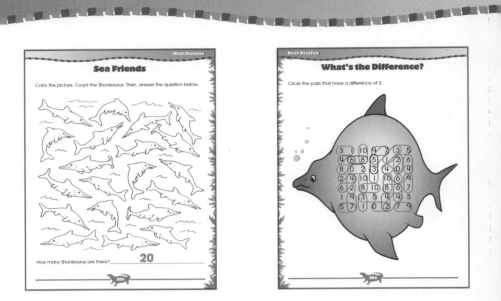

205

Building the Nest

Help the Maiasaura count the twigs needed to build its nest. Count by 5s. Write the numbers in the boxes.

5, **10**, **15**, **20**, **25**, 30, 35, **40**, **45**, **50**, **55**, **60**, **65**, **70**, 75, **80**, 85, **90**, **95**

206

A Dino Discovery

Add together all the numbers shown in each space. Then, color to find the hidden picture using the number key to help you.

even answers = **blue**   odd answers = **green**

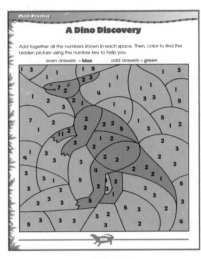

207

Adding Fun

Find a pair of dice. Roll one die and write the number of dots from the die in the top box. Repeat until all the top boxes are filled in. Then, complete the addition sentences.

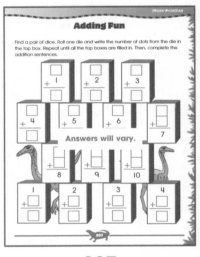

Answers will vary.

208

Add-a-saurus

Write the missing addend in each blank to help Add-a-saurus complete the addition sentences.

$3 + \underline{3} = 6$
$4 + \underline{1} = 5$
$7 + \underline{2} = 9$
$2 + \underline{2} = 4$
$3 + \underline{5} = 8$
$5 + \underline{0} = 5$
$8 + \underline{2} = 10$
$7 + \underline{1} = 8$
$6 + \underline{3} = 9$

$8 + \underline{1} = 9$
$4 + \underline{2} = 6$
$6 + \underline{0} = 6$
$5 + \underline{2} = 7$
$4 + \underline{3} = 7$
$9 + \underline{1} = 10$
$5 + \underline{3} = 8$
$7 + \underline{3} = 10$
$6 + \underline{2} = 8$

209

A Gentle Giant

Solve the equations in each space below. Then, color the spaces using the color key to help you find the hidden picture.

14 = **blue**   15 = **green**   16 = **yellow**

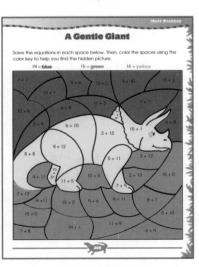

210

Dino-mite!

Add or subtract. Match the related facts.

$5 + 9 = \underline{14}$
$8 + 7 = \underline{15}$
$15 - 9 = \underline{6}$
$17 - 8 = \underline{9}$
$7 + 7 = \underline{14}$

$6 + 9 = \underline{15}$
$14 - 9 = \underline{5}$
$15 - 7 = \underline{8}$
$14 - 7 = \underline{7}$
$9 + 8 = \underline{17}$

Add or subtract to solve the problems below. Color spaces brown with answers greater than 12. Color the other spaces green.

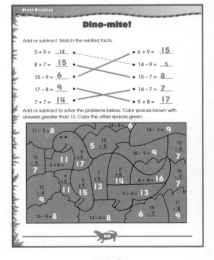

211 — Dan's Footprints

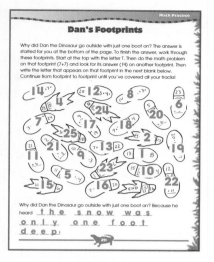

Dan's Footprints

Why did Dan the Dinosaur go outside with just one boot on? The answer is started for you at the bottom of the page. To finish the answer, work through these footprints. Start at the top with the letter T. Then do the math problem on that footprint (7+7) and look for its answer (14) on another footprint. Then write the letter that appears on that footprint in the next blank below. Continue from footprint to footprint until you've covered all your tracks!

Why did Dan the Dinosaur go outside with just one boot on? Because he heard __the snow was only one foot deep__.

212 — Prehistoric Problems

Prehistoric Problems

Solve the subtraction problems. Then use the code to color the picture.

Code:
25 — blue   57 — green
31 — yellow   14 — orange
21 — brown   11 — red

47 − 22 = 25
52 − 21 = 31
25 − 11 = 14
62 − 31 = 31
77 − 20 = 57
51 − 40 = 11
69 − 12 = 57
98 − 41 = 57
55 − 34 = 31

213 — Dino Code

Dino Code

How is a T-Rex like an explosion? To find out, solve the following problems and write the matching letter above each answer on the blanks.

He's **F U L L   O F   D I N O - M I G H T!**
195 185 92 92   171 195
265 74 183 171   93 181 191

Remember to regroup when the bottom number is larger than the top number in a column.

F = 348 − 153 = 195
L = 765 − 673 = 92
G = 427 − 382 = 45
T = 637 − 446 = 191
H = 878 − 697 = 181
U = 548 − 363 = 185
O = 824 − 653 = 171
N = 439 − 256 = 183
I = 447 − 373 = 74
M = 568 − 475 = 93
D = 748 − 483 = 265

214 — Racing to the Finish

Racing to the Finish

Solve the multiplication problems.

5 ×3 = 15   2 ×8 = 16   4 ×6 = 24   9 ×3 = 27   7 ×5 = 35   3 ×9 = 27
4 ×2 = 8   6 ×2 = 12   4 ×4 = 16   0 ×7 = 0   3 ×2 = 6   7 ×2 = 14
6 ×5 = 30   3 ×4 = 12   8 ×3 = 24   4 ×5 = 20   5 ×2 = 10   7 ×4 = 28
6 ×3 = 18   4 ×8 = 32   2 ×2 = 4   8 ×5 = 40   3 ×7 = 21   5 ×5 = 25
5 ×9 = 45   9 ×2 = 18   4 ×6 = 24   9 ×4 = 36

215 — Hunt For The Answer

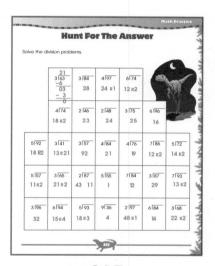

Hunt For The Answer

Solve the division problems.

3)63 = 21 (−6, 03, −3)   3)84 = 28   4)97 = 24 R1   6)74 = 12 R2
4)74 = 18 R2   2)46 = 23   2)48 = 24   3)75 = 25   6)96 = 16
5)92 = 18 R2   3)41 = 13 R21   3)57 = 92   4)84 = 21   4)76 = 19   7)86 = 12 R2   5)72 = 14 R2
5)57 = 11 R2   3)65 = 21 R2   2)87 = 43   5)55 = 11   7)84 = 12   3)87 = 29   7)93 = 13 R2
3)96 = 32   6)94 = 15 R4   5)93 = 18 R3   9)36 = 4   2)97 = 48 R1   6)84 = 14   3)68 = 22 R2

216 — Dino Divide!

Dino Divide!

Solve the division problems.

6)888 = 148 (−6, 28, −24, 48, −48, 0)   2)956 = 478   2)712 = 356   4)860 = 215   5)845 = 169
6)750 = 125   9)999 = 111   8)968 = 121   3)774 = 258   5)735 = 147   8)920 = 115
8)984 = 123   4)500 = 125   2)846 = 423   4)712 = 178

217 — Mr. Dinosaur Means Business

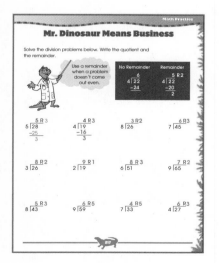

Mr. Dinosaur Means Business

Solve the division problems below. Write the quotient and the remainder.

Use a remainder when a problem doesn't come out even.

	No Remainder	Remainder
	6 / 4)24 (−24)	5 R2 / 4)22 (−20, 2)

5)28 = 5 R3 (−25, 3)   4)19 = 4 R3 (−16, 3)   8)26 = 3 R2   7)45 = 6 R3
3)26 = 8 R2   2)19 = 9 R1   8)51 = 6 R3   9)65 = 7 R2
8)43 = 5 R3   9)59 = 6 R5   7)33 = 4 R5   6)27 = 6 R3

218 — Dino Tic-Tac-Toe

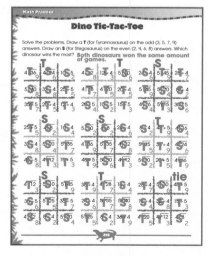

Dino Tic-Tac-Toe

Solve the problems. Draw a **T** (for Tyrannosaurus) on the odd (3, 5, 7, 9) answers. Draw an **S** (for Stegosaurus) on the even (2, 4, 6, 8) answers. Which dinosaur wins the most? Both dinosaurs won the same amount of games.

tie

219 — Reduce It!

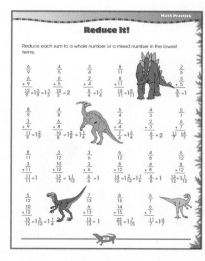

Reduce It!

Reduce each sum to a whole number or a mixed number in the lowest terms.

6/9 + 9 = 12/9 = 1 3/9 = 1 1/3
4/5 + 6/5 = 10/5 = 2
3/4 + 3/4 = 6/4 = 1 2/4 = 1 1/2
8/11 + 8/11 = 16/11 = 1 5/11
2/5 + 3/5 = 5/5 = 1

8/9 + 3/9 = 11/9 = 1 2/9
4/8 + 6/8 = 10/8 = 1 2/8 = 1 1/4
5/4 + 3/4 = 8/4 = 2
4/6 + 8/6 = 12/6 = 2
5/7 + 6/7 = 11/7 = 1 4/7

8/11 + 3/11 = 11/11 = 1
9/12 + 9/12 = 18/12 = 1 6/12 = 1 1/2
6/12 + 6/12 = 12/12 = 1
4/8 + 8/8 = 12/8 = 1 4/8 = 1 1/2
8/12 + 8/12 = 16/12 = 1 4/12 = 1 1/3

5/12 + 10/12 = 15/12 = 1 3/12 = 1 1/4
7/13 + 6/13 = 13/13 = 1
8/15 + 14/15 = 22/15 = 1 7/15
5/7 + 6/7 = 11/7 = 1 4/7

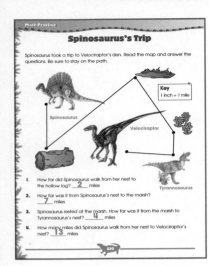

Spinosaurus's Trip

Spinosaurus took a trip to Velociraptor's den. Read the map and answer the questions. Be sure to stay on the path.

Key
1 inch = 1 mile

Spinosaurus

Velociraptor

Tyrannosaurus

1. How far did Spinosaurus walk from her nest to the hollow log? __2__ miles
2. How far was it from Spinosaurus's nest to the marsh? __7__ miles
3. Spinosaurus rested at the marsh. How far was it from the marsh to Tyrannosaurus's nest? __4__ miles
4. How many miles did Spinosaurus walk from her nest to Velociraptor's nest? __13__ miles

220

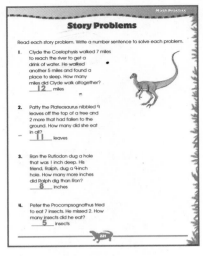

Story Problems

Read each story problem. Write a number sentence to solve each problem.

1. Clyde the Coelophysis walked 7 miles to reach the river to get a drink of water. He walked another 5 miles and found a place to sleep. How many miles did Clyde walk altogether? __12__ miles
2. Patty the Plateosaurus nibbled 9 leaves off the top of a tree and 2 more that had fallen to the ground. How many did she eat in all? __11__ leaves
3. Ron the Rutiodon dug a hole that was 1 inch deep. His friend, Ralph, dug a 9-inch hole. How many more inches did Ralph dig than Ron? __8__ inches
4. Peter the Procompsognathus tried to eat 7 insects. He missed 2. How many insects did he eat? __5__ insects

221

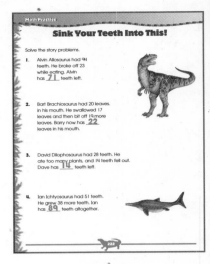

Sink Your Teeth Into This!

Solve the story problems.

1. Alvin Allosaurus had 94 teeth. He broke off 23 while eating. Alvin has __71__ teeth left.
2. Bart Brachiosaurus had 20 leaves in his mouth. He swallowed 17 leaves and then bit off 19 more leaves. Barry now has __22__ leaves in his mouth.
3. David Dilophosaurus had 28 teeth. He ate too many plants, and 14 teeth fell out. Dave has __14__ teeth left.
4. Ian Ichtyosaurus had 51 teeth. He grew 38 more teeth. Ian has __89__ teeth altogether.

222